WAITING IN JOYFUL HOPE

WAITING IN JOYFUL HOPE

Reflections on God-with-us In Everyday Life

HERBERT C. YOST, C.S.C.

All the best to you!

Fr. Herb

Corby Publications
Notre Dame, Indiana

Waiting In Joyful Hope

Copyright © 2009 Herbert C. Yost, C.S.C.

10 9 8 7 6 5 4 3 2 1

ISBN 978-000

Manufactured in the United States of America

Published by Corby Books
A Division of Corby Publishing
P.O. Box 93
Notre Dame, Indiana 46556
(574) 784-3482
www.corbypublishig.com

TABLE OF CONTENTS

INTRODUCTION

The road to this book began in 7th grade at St. Anthony's Grade School in Lancaster, Pennsylvania. Sr. Edward Marie, C.SC. gave the class an assignment to write a one-page essay on Christopher Columbus. When she passed out the graded papers a few days later, I received nothing back; instead, Sister told me to see her after class. That, of course, inspired some fear: "*Now* what did I do"? It's not like I was a perfect angel, you know! Turns out that I got an A on the essay, and Sister was highly complimentary of what I had written, saying: "Someday you will be a writer."

Fast forward to 1981, at St. Joseph Parish, South Bend, Indiana. The pastor, Fr. Paul Doyle C.S.C., received a request from Mr. Lou Jacquet, the editor of the diocesan newspaper, *The Harmonizer*. Lou had asked Paul to write a column on what it is like to prepare a homily. Paul demurred, telling Lou I was a far better homilist, and passed the request on to me. Lou liked what I had written, and then he floated the idea of a weekly column called *"Letters from God."* These reflections on the Sunday readings caused many folks to say that I should put them in a book. My response always was: "If God wants me to do this, a publisher will come knocking at the door."

In 1985, my Provincial Superior, Fr. Richard Warner, C.S.C., asked me to take over the work of the Holy Cross Association, a direct-mail fundraising operation for the Indiana Province. This ministry continues even now. In twenty-four years, there has yet to be a day when I've loathed the idea of coming to work. It's a wonderful synergy of personal talent, Province need, and being able to give good pastoral care to our benefactors. The fact that I have had wonderful co-workers over the years also helps. Carol Gromski has put up with me for all twenty-four years. The office and our benefactors have also been blessed by, in turn, Lori Gorny, Melissa Bates, and Kimberly Brunner.

In addition to the usual daily acknowledgment letters for gifts received, and letters to benefactors who need some pastoral care, or have questions about this, that, and the other thing, I write five appeals a year.

It took me about three years to settle on a good format for these appeals. They now consist of three parts: the first page is news about the Association and the Province, the last page is devoted to humor, and the middle two pages are a reflection on some aspect of spirituality, daily living, Church teaching, etc. It is these middle pages of *Cross Links* that are the content of this book.

Following in the footsteps of Sr. Edward Marie and the readers of "*Letters from God*," many benefactors asked: "When are you going to write a book"? "These reflections should be in a book"! My response was the usual: "If that's what God wants me to do...."

In early 2009, it wasn't a publisher who knocked at the door. It was a fellow C.S.C., Fr. Nicholas Ayo. Nicholas set the process in motion by reading through well over 100 *Cross Links* reflections, finding a publisher, selecting the best of the essays, as well as editing and organizing them. Since none of the essays had been preserved on electronic media, Carol and Kim retyped the ones chosen for publication. To these three people, dear reader, you and I owe a deep debt of gratitude. Were it not for them, I would still be saying, "If that's what God wants me to do...."

The title of the book expresses my hope for these reflections. That phrase, "waiting in joyful hope," comes from the prayer right after the *Our Father* at Mass: "as we wait in joyful hope for the coming of our Savior, Jesus Christ." In addition, the *Constitutions of the Congregation of Holy Cross* call us to be "men with hope to bring."

These reflections are the fruit of musing on my experience with life, as well as what I have learned while walking with others on their unique personal journeys. Year by passing year, I've grown in the conviction that "to be perfect as [our] heavenly Father is perfect" means acknowledging and accepting the reality that we are very imperfect human beings. Rejoicing in imperfection enables us to see how truly Abba, our Father, loves and cares for us. I've come to see how Jesus walks with us in daily life, though I'll be the first to confess that I'm all too often like the 100th sheep, wandering off on my own out of stubbornness, curiosity, or fear. I've also seen how the Spirit marks the canvas of each day with surprises great and small, with guidance, insight, strength when needed, as well as with opportunities for laughter, service, and love.

When it comes to deepening our awareness of God's presence in our lives, we try too hard. It's far less difficult than we were taught. Thomas Aquinas says that grace builds on nature. To fulfill our heart's desire of closeness to God, all we have to do is to be ourselves, to cherish our goodness and gently acknowledge our sinfulness. It's to believe that we do not have to earn our salvation, but that Jesus has already done all the work for us through his death and resurrection. It's to believe that no sin of ours is greater than God's love. It's to believe that we very ordinary human beings have a totally unique, irreplaceable, and extraordinary role to play in the history of the universe, past, present, and yet to come. Belief leads to hope, and the two together lead to a deeper love of God, others, and self. It is my hope that in these essays, you will come to see how everything works together for the good of those who love the Lord.

DEDICATION

If it takes a village to raise a child, it takes a community to help that person grow in wisdom, age, and grace. I dedicate this book to all who have given me life, beginning with my parents, Herb and Mary Yost, and my siblings James, John, and Joanne, and their families. Moving ever outwards, I include those who have loved me in special ways, my brothers and sisters in Holy Cross, and all who have accompanied and supported me on life's multi-dimensioned journey, whether for a brief moment or a long time. You know who you are. I am who I am because of your companionship.

PREFACE

The human story is the same for everyone. We are born unasked; we yearn for great love and happiness even if we do not know we do. We die, both sad to leave and glad to be gone. Only the details of each human life differ. The essays of Father Herb Yost, C.S.C., that follow this Preface are for the human being in every man and woman who lives here and now. We are part of a great band of pilgrims whirling through space on planet earth at breath-taking speeds, but all too often only going around in circles seemingly getting nowhere. Why did God make me? It is a question I remember from childhood catechism. And I recall the answer. "God made me to know him and to love him in this world, and to be happy with him forever in the next." Fr. Yost's essays are but commentary on that line, plain talk for simple folk, and earned wisdom for everyone about Christian living.

We are all wounded healers. Wisdom is learned by our mistakes and failures. Compassion is learned by our pains. Love is learned by our heartbreaks. The oyster turns the irritant of a grain of sand into a fine pearl. What was a wound becomes a jewel. The wounds of the crucified Jesus are not lost but glorified in the resurrection. We are all such wounded healers. Father Yost has been deaf since he was seven-years old. The inner life of silence in all its loneliness and inner contemplative richness has strung a string of pearls in these brief essays, crafted by a man who knows life is not easy, but yet beautiful and worth waiting for in joyful hope.

Mercy and compassion flowing from a universal forgiveness characterizes Father Yost's writing. He knows, as every pet-lover knows, a simple truth. It is hard to be a dog, and every dog, no matter its bother, is worth loving. It is hard to be a human being as well, and every one of us, no matter our misbehaviors, is worth loving. We are who we are. We are but creatures. We are given body, mind, and heart with pluses and minuses, and life is not easy on any one of us. We all, rich or poor, bright or dull, carry a cross, and we all carry a cross just beyond our ability to shoulder it. We fall. Father Yost knows what I say in his bones. He has been down, but not out. His words have lifted up others, just as Simon of Cyrene gave a helpful shoulder to an exhausted Jesus. We all walk the way of the cross – born as we are innocent and beautiful – and there remains no end-run around everyman's Calvary.

Jesus tells the parable of the wheat and weeds. A farmer has planted the field with good grain, and in the night the enemy sows weeds amid the grain. The servants wish to uproot the weeds, but the farmer warns them that the roots of both the good grain and the bad weeds are entwined. Only at the harvest can the weeds be taken away. In this life we do not always know wheat from weed. A rose in a wheat field is a weed, and good grain growing in a rose garden is a weed. In the providence of God what somehow enters our life belongs, and what truly belongs in our life will enter. How often we have been wrong about what we thought we must have and what must be good for us. Some friends turn out less so; some of our critics turn out to be blessings. Patient compassion for one's self as well as others characterize Father Yost's very realistic appraisals of ordinary life for ordinary folks.

We believe that "in the beginning" God created the heavens and the earth – the whole Creation story of the Bible – not in six days so literally, but surely created out of nothing. There was nothing prior to creation out of which to make anything, for God was infinite and God was everything. Because Creation was not a part of God, from nothing as it were, though not apart from God, we have a great mystery in Creation. We also believe that "in the ending" God is creating a new heaven and a new earth, the whole Creation story of the Redemption of the world in Jesus Christ. That ending will not be in time but in eternity, but surely created out of everything in time, good and bad, that happens to us and to our world. Nothing will be wasted. Even sin serves. God writes straight with crooked lines. Father Yost knows this truth so well, and if I had to pick a theme song for his "Waiting in Joyful Hope" meditations, it would be: "Send in the clowns." Our lives are a "Divine Comedy," a love story with a happy ending. No matter the foolishness along the way, God is not finished with us yet. Thank God!

Nicholas Ayo, C.S.C.

ACKNOWLEDGMENTS

I usually don't read the Acknowledgments in a book, so I have no idea how to write one! I feel like a winner at the Academy Awards: you want to be sure to thank everyone while omitting no one.

While I was staring at the monitor, wondering what to say next, my co-worker Carol texted me and asked if I was busy. I said I was trying to write this Acknowledgment, and she replied: "A book in itself." My response: "Not really, though it easily could be." Oh yes...very easily.

This, by the way, is a perfect example of how the Holy Spirit has always timed things so beautifully. Random remarks by someone, receiving a blessing or seeing a blessing being given, sudden insights, unexpected encounters with others, a sentence that touches my soul – time and time again the Third Person of the Trinity has come to my assistance. And that is why the very first acknowledgment must be to the Holy Spirit, who has gifted me with the ability to take the raw stuff of everyday life and place words on paper in some coherent, readable fashion.

I remember with gratitude my 7th grade teacher, Sr. Edward Marie, C.S.C., long deceased, who prophesied a future career. Mr. Lou Jacquet, former editor of *The Harmonizer* (newspaper of the Diocese of Fort Wayne-South Bend) and now editor of *The Catholic Exponent* (Diocese of Youngstown) was the first to encourage me to write for a wider readership.

Rev. Richard Warner, C.S.C., former Provincial of the Indiana Province, Priests and Brothers of Holy Cross, assigned me to a ministry which enabled me to use the gift of writing on a daily basis, thus enabling growth in writing proficiency, and growth in personal spirituality.

I give thanks for the guidance, wisdom, and healing skills of Robert Antonelli CSC, David Verhalen CSC, Maurice Amen CSC, Lem Joyner, PhD, Diane Prosser-Johnson, PhD, and Mark Sandock, MD. When life threw curve balls and bean balls, they were there for me as healers of mind, body, and soul.

It's a long way from thinking about writing a book to actually writing one. For that final push, I extend my gratitude to Nicholas Ayo, CSC, who edited and helped arrange the reflections in this work. My co-workers in the Holy Cross Association, Carol Gromski and Kimberly Brunner, spent hours re-typing these reflections, transferring them from paper to electronic media. This was done during working hours, so a special thanks to James Kramer, Director of Development, for enabling them to do this.

Chapter One

The Web of Life: Meditation on a Chair

Independence has always been an American trait. We place a high value on self-sufficiency, and resent other people telling us what to do and how to run our lives; we also resent having to ask for help. We lay claim to our possessions with the statement: "I worked hard for this." The poet John Donne said that "No man is an island," but all too often we think and act as though we *are* islands, sufficient unto ourselves.

In truth, we are utterly totally dependent not just on God, but on the earth and on our brothers and sisters. To show you this in a graphic way, let's reflect on a simple wooden chair. It's made of wood, glue, perhaps a few nails or screws.

First, the wood. Mother Earth gave us that wood (and without trees and other green plants, life itself would not exist as we know it). The original seed was either dropped from the tree above, carried to its location by a bird or animal, or planted by a human hand. Water, sunlight, soil conditions all had to work together just right to make that tree grow. Each species of wood has its own unique beauty and usefulness. In living and dying, each tree offers itself for the good of the whole.

In the fullness of time, along comes a logger. This individual comes from a family tree, stretching back to the first man and woman. Every single person in that chain of humanity had a role to play in the making of this individual. This logger also has an entire support system which enhances the quality of his life: grocers, bankers, stores, doctors and dentists, teachers, water and sewage departments, etc. Already, we have a web of hundreds, perhaps thousands of people supporting this one person.

The logger belongs to a lumber company. There may be ten employees, there may be a thousand (and each employee has his or her own life system). The lumber company needs chain-saws, trucks, machinery, petroleum products, and buildings to house all this. So we go to the chain-saw company, and the truck manufacturers, and the oil companies, and every other company, each with their workers, and each with their corporate and individual support system.

But the lumber company is not just tools and equipment. The company needs banks, it needs the U.S. mail, it needs telecommunications and computer systems and office equipment. It needs plumbers and electricians, scientists and engineers, janitors and security personnel. In short, the lumber company has a life support network of many smaller or larger companies, and each of those companies has its own system, and each employee of each company has his or her own needs that are met by still more companies.

And in addition, Mother Earth is still very much present, for from her come the ores and the petroleum and the fibers, the food and water, the air and energy. Some of those materials have recently been invented, and other materials, such as petroleum, were created millions upon millions of years ago by the living and dying of living plants and animals. Earth relinquishes these gifts to her human brothers and sisters, and again, each of the brothers and sisters has their own support system of still more people.

So the wood is harvested and milled. It must get from the mill to the furniture company. How many thousands of people have already been involved in the making of your chair? And we say we don't need anyone?

So now think of the transportation networks from the mill to the factory: the trucks and railroads that move the timber. By now you've entered into the spirit of the meditation, and you begin to think of the companies' networks, and the employees' networks. So now we include the highway departments that maintain the roads, and taxes that you and your brother and sister citizens pay to help maintain those roads. We include the train companies and the auto makers, the men and women who assemble the engines and cars, and the people who harvest the earth for the materials needed to make those pieces of equipment... all with their own life support system.

The entire cycle repeats itself in the furniture factory. You have the management, the secretaries, the crafts-men and crafts-women. They are who they are because of their parents, their teachers, their family and friends, all who have invested time and energy in their lives. The factory is the hub of a wide circle of activity, for remember: each chair is wood and glue and metal and cloth and fiber. All of those components have a life history of their own.

Now we are perhaps in the hundreds of thousands in terms of people who have made your little chair possible. Everyone had to fulfill their particular role, or the chair as a totally unique entity would not exist. Oh sure, you would have a chair... but it would not be *this particular* chair, because this particular chair has a history all its own.

So we move from the furniture manufacturer to a warehouse, and from the warehouse to your local furniture store... and remember that we are once again using transportation systems. Who provided the materials for the warehouse... who built it... who maintains it? Ditto for the furniture store.

And finally, weeks or months from the cutting down of that tree in the forest, the chair sits in your home or office. Can you even begin to comprehend how many people were necessary for that chair to exist? For sure, hundreds of thousands, perhaps even more than a million when you factor in the entire web of life. If you take this reflection to its conclusion, you could see that literally all creation, past and present, has gone into the making of this chair. And we still like to maintain that we're independent, that we don't need anyone?

And this is just one single chair. How about this piece of paper you're holding? Even the ink on this paper? Look around you. As I sit here typing this, I see a wastebasket, pictures on the wall, computer supplies, pencils and pens, a carpet, some knitted coasters, some CD's, mail, a lamp. I feel my clothing, and see some immaculate groundskeeping from the window. Every single thing you and I possess is the result of a vast web of life and creativity. These things just don't happen. They come into being courtesy of a gracious God who has given us the earth, and who has given each human being, past, present and future, skills and talents to be put at the service of everyone else.

The truth of the matter is that you and I are totally dependent upon our brothers and sisters, not just for our life itself, but also for all that sustains our life. We are the beneficiaries of a web of life whose strands stretch back to a time long before humans walked the earth. You could even say that we stretch back to the beginning of the universe, because some of the elemental and chemical building blocks of our bodies go back to the moment when God began the first act of creation.

Just by way of footnote, not even God is all alone. There is a Trinity of Persons, each belonging to the other. And God also needs us in this world to be the Trinity's hands and feet and mouth and eyes and ears.

All of this has repercussions on our present and our future. The things that I do or don't do today are weaving an infinitesimal strand in the web, and someone or something in the near or far-distant future will come into being because of what I am doing. We share responsibility for the future with God. We are co-creators.

So I hope and pray that all who are reading this reflection can be conscious of what they are doing, of their actions, words, gestures, and yes, even their thoughts. It does matter. It does make a difference.

I hope and pray that you can be conscious of the vast number of people who support your life. One very easy way to make this happen is to add one sentence to your blessing before meals: "Bless all those whose labor has brought this food to our table." It's amazing what this will do!

I hope and pray, finally, that you will remember with gratitude those who have died. They prepared the way for us, and from their place with God, they *still* prepare our way, for such is the nature of love. Remember them with gratitude. Remember too those yet to be born, for some day they will be remembering all that you and I have done to prepare *their* way.

Chapter Two

THE HOLINESS OF IMPERFECTION

How strange we can be sometimes! Some people will pay hundreds, if not thousands of dollars for an antique that is scratched and battered. Yet these same folks freak if they see one too many wrinkles on their faces. Pat is a generous soul who deals gently with misbehaving kids, yet treats himself harshly if he makes a small mistake. A teen tries to live up to the expectations of his or her parents, knowing that criticism and ridicule await any minute. The media tracks human imperfection 24/7, and when we see something good, we react cynically because we've been so overdosed by images of imperfection.

We have such a strange relationship with perfection and imperfection. People can literally kill themselves in their efforts to be perfect. Many Catholics over fifty have grown up in a church that put a great value on perfection. The Saturday confession lines were long. When we hear that sentence from the Gospels about being "perfect as your heavenly Father is perfect," we cringe and try to dismiss it, but it keeps haunting us.

Simply put, one of the greatest causes of human suffering is the desire to be perfect. Perfect job... hair... home... marriage... skin... children... meal... dress... grades... sex... car... vacation... body... and so on. In other words, we want a perfect life.

Now, you know as well as I do that there's no such thing. Into every human life, chaos is going to come, either from within or from without. You will experience great love in your life, and you will also experience great hurt. There is no avoiding it. Sometimes we will get hammered by one blow after another, and at other times there will be one uplifting experience after another. Throughout our life on earth there will always be a sense of being unfinished, of being incomplete. Even when you think you finally have perfection achieved in some area of your life, sooner or later you're going to want more, which proves that it wasn't so perfect after all.

So... what's the choice? Kill ourselves bodily, emotionally, spiritually, or mentally in our quest for perfection? Or acknowledge that we are imperfect, that others are imperfect, and that our world is fractured and broken. Does this mean giving way to deep pessimism and cynicism? No, not at all. In fact, it can be a solid foundation for a truly happy and deeply spiritual life.

Our imperfections are the single best way to God. For centuries, the opening words of the Church's morning and evening prayer in the Divine Office have been: "O God, come to our assistance. Lord, make haste to help us." My sins, my weakness, the inability to cope with the chaos that sometimes threatens to overwhelm me – all these things drive me right into the arms of God. In our darkness and emptiness there lurks a deep thirst for whatever may alleviate this pain of the human condition, this empty hole in our human be-ing. So we seek help... and as soon as we ask for help, there is an implicit admission that we are powerless. And in that acknowledgement that we are not in control, that we are powerless, a deep spirituality is born. We've finally realized two things: (1) that we have to quit playing God, (2) we're terribly weak, helpless human beings.

That's humbling, isn't it? Yet that very humility is a key component of holiness. If you happen to think you're pretty hot stuff, get some perspective. Remember those pictures of earth as seen from space? Where are you? Can you see yourself? You really are pretty insignificant. Yet, you're not a worm either. Humility involves letting go of an image of ourselves as the center of our world, yet also realizing that in the plan of God, our life does have extraordinary value, as long as we live it for God and others and not solely for ourselves. Humility means living with and rejoicing in and laughing at our mixed-up-ness and not fighting it. We are saint and sinner, beast and angel. Humility means to embrace ordinariness. I'm not saying we have to see being ordinary as "good enough," as settling for less. No, what I'm saying is that you and I are really good people, even in our ordinariness.

That leads to another important comment on the holiness of imperfection. I said "you and I are really good people." Let's think a minute about tolerance. When we accept ourselves in all our weakness and imperfection and chaos, then we can start learning how to accept the weaknesses and mixed-up-ness of those we love and respect. And then, with even more help from God, we can learn to accept the weaknesses and shortcomings of those we just cannot love. Tolerance is appreciation of the tremendous variety of human life upon the earth. But in the midst of this variety, we all struggle with the same demons. We have the same fears and sorrows. We all do the best we can with what we have. We're all grateful for those who can help us cope with life's chaos.

In human life, the greatest healing takes place among those who can accept their imperfections. It is our weaknesses that make us human beings most alike. That's why Jesus took on our weakness. When you look at another person and compassionately see their weakness and humanness, then your heart opens and you embrace the other and become one. Shared weakness is what creates real community.

In that real community of weak people, one gains a different perspective on individual strengths. From this perspective, you can then look at a strong person and realize two things. One: they are as weak and as mixed up as you are. Two: you hope that their strength will support you and help you in your weakness. The same thing is going on in reverse too, when someone looks at you. Jesus took on our humanity and therefore our weakness. He was a strong person in his own right, and we look to him for help, knowing that we will not be rejected. He knows what it's like to be powerless.

Put simply, tolerance is appreciation, which means that the third great gift of accepting our imperfection is a deepened sense of gratitude. Through gratitude, we recognize that everything is a gift. We do not work for it, we do not earn it, we do not merit it, it is not owed us by virtue of birth or status or wealth... no. Every single thing we have in life is God's gift to us. Everything we are is given to us. Everything we will be and will have is waiting in the wings, ready to be given to us at the right moment.

Gratitude is a vision of life. The truly grateful person and an egocentric person will look at the same thing with the same human eyes. But their reactions will be totally different. Gratitude says "Thank you." Greed says "Gimme." However, let me say this: greed and gratitude are always mixed up within us. Remember: we're imperfect. Time and again we have to make choices.

Greed leads to misery. Greed says we have to get more and more and more… to win more, to acquire more, to own more, to be more. Greed causes misery because it does not know the meaning of "enough." The greedy person thinks, "if only I can get enough then I will be truly free." It doesn't work that way, unfortunately. Only through gratitude can we see how truly gifted we are. People who are truly grateful will go through chaos just like everyone else, but somehow they are able to see the hand of God in it all and realize that life consists not in what you have, but in who you are and in whom you love and are loved by. When greedy people go through chaos, they are totally lost. The only thing they know how to do is to "buy" their way out of it, or to blame someone or something for causing the pain and hurt. Of course, neither way works.

Only those who can accept their brokenness and imperfection and the brokenness of other people are capable of really loving. That's why there are so many divorces. Time and again, I hear: "She or he is not the person I married." Well, duh… of course not. You married a chaotic human being. You are a couple affected by the brokenness of the world. All that changes a person molds and forms the individual and the couple. Only through acceptance of imperfection can love truly have a staying power. You can be perfect if you want, or look for the perfect marriage or relationship, but you're going to pay a terrible price in terms of human companionship.

The quest for perfection is ultimately doomed to futility. I wander through the self-help sections of Barnes & Noble or Borders bookstores, and am overwhelmed by the amount of verbiage that is being spent on this quest. It covers every area of life… how to be the perfect student, how to overcome childhood trauma, how to be the perfect parent, the perfect spouse or lover, the perfect employee or boss, how to make more money, and on and on. Diets, makeovers, spirituality, mental health, coping with disease – all these and more are included.

I'm not saying self-help is bad. Not at all. There are lots of good ideas there. I've read many books myself. But so many of those books have one major flaw: they are trying to do the impossible. They fail to recognize that we are fundamentally imperfect, flawed human beings, who interact daily with imperfect, flawed human beings, and we all together live in an imperfect, flawed world. Perfection is not possible this side of heaven, and even in heaven it's going to take an eternity to get it right! The more you accept your fundamental imperfection, the more you will come to realize with awe and gratitude how much God is doing for you in what you cannot do for yourself.

Holiness and imperfection are twins. I truly believe you cannot have one without the other. Through Jesus, God embraces our flawed human nature and thus sanctified imperfection. Through Jesus, God says: "You are flawed, sinful, broken people, but you are also the apple of my eye, the delight of my heart, my son, my daughter, my beloved."

It's not a case of either-or. God is not giving us a choice between perfection and imperfection. He can't give us a choice because he knows we are imperfect! He created us this way, for goodness sake! It would be utterly cruel of God to hold out the challenge of perfection knowing we cannot possibly meet it this side of heaven.

No… God encourages us to be ourselves – fully ourselves. So that means he accepts and understands our screwiness, our mixed-up-ness, our weakness, our fears. He encourages us to rely on the Spirit to bring to fruit within ourselves what we cannot do on our own. Perfect people say: "I'm gonna do this all by myself; I'm gonna lick this." And they're never at home on the earth, in their own skin. Imperfect holy people simply hold out their arms and say *"HEEELLLPPP"!* These are the people spoken of in the Beatitudes, who will inherit the earth, who will laugh, who will be consoled, who will have their fill, who will know mercy. Above all, they will see God. Who could ask for anything more!

Chapter Three

PUZZLE PIECES AND STONES

I'm writing this on January 24th. It's cold and snowy outside, and it is a perfect day for doing this kind of reflecting.

Yesterday afternoon I went over to Holy Cross Care and Rehab Center to preside at the Eucharist for the residents. Walking into the building, I noticed that little pieces of a puzzle were laying on the sidewalk, and thought to myself: "Oh-oh, someone's not gonna be too happy when they assemble the puzzle and find pieces missing."

The First Reading in the liturgy yesterday was the story of David and Goliath. In my homily, I mentioned that sometimes we're like David, a little person confronting a giant. For the residents of the Center, their giants might be things like medical or insurance bureaucracy, loneliness, fear of death, feelings of abandonment by family and friends, being tired of the slow pace of rehab, etc. It's scary. Yet we keep on trying.

David was just a little guy facing off with the big guy who had all the power. David had only himself, his past experience facing lions and wolves, his staff and five stones for the sling, and his trust that God was at his side. In other words, David had the necessary resources to fight his battle.

Going back to the car after Mass, I saw the same puzzle pieces and it immediately hit me that this really is like life. We move along the sidewalk of days, weeks, months and years. Every so often something happens that is like a piece of the puzzle that is our life. We pick it up, look at it, ponder it, turn it this way and that, trying to figure out where this piece fits into the whole. We might get hints from the color or pattern on the face. If it's blue, it goes somewhere in the sky, for example. But where exactly?

I started driving back home to Fatima. But those puzzle pieces were bugging me, and I kept saying to myself: "I think there were five of them." Well, halfway home I turned around, went back to the Center, and sure enough, there were five pieces! I picked them up and brought them home. Five puzzle pieces, five stones—coincidence, or the Spirit giving me some insights for my life, and to share with you via this reflection?

I'd like to connect the puzzle pieces and the stones. The puzzle pieces of our lives, like David's stones, become the weapons we can use to fight the giants that threaten our faith, hope, love, serenity, and stability. David carefully selected the stones. God carefully selects the puzzle pieces for us.

Let me give 2007 as a personal example. Last year turned out to be a pretty knee-dy year for me (pretty good play on words, eh?). In January I had arthroscopic knee surgery, and when that didn't work, it was a knee replacement in October. The latter recovery took far longer, so let's focus on that.

In October, my world became very small. In the hospital, it was my room and the physical therapy room. At Holy Cross House, it was my room, the PT room, the dining room, and the chapel. Time was not my own. In each place, there were schedules for eating, medications, exercising, etc.

The car sat idle, the woodworking was on hold. Those were things that broadened my world and provided variety. Ditto for the bank account, since I couldn't go shopping (didn't keep the bills from coming, though!). All the paraphernalia of daily life that seemed so important in normal circumstances either wasn't needed or couldn't be used.

I remember being in the recovery room after surgery. I had been given an epidural, and the nurse kept asking me to move my legs. It was the most God-awful sensation trying to will my legs to lift up, or my toes to move, and not being able to do it. For the first time, I realized the helplessness of victims of paralysis.

Impatience was a frequent visitor. "Let's get this stupid knee working"! Fear was an unexpected companion. I still vividly remember how I absolutely froze with terror when Mary Pat asked me to go down stairs using alternating steps. There was also a sense of shame, though I'm not sure that's exactly the right word. I had to ask for help with the simplest things such as carrying food to the table, putting my socks on – things I'm perfectly capable of doing for myself in normal circumstances. Frustration was there too: I remember getting really aggravated because the TV remote wouldn't work. Getting out of the chair to manually change the channel was a major hassle.

I don't want to make a big deal out of all this. The point I'd like to make is that any kind of illness or disability always brings with it a sense of powerlessness. It may be a passing sense, it might be a deeply abiding one – but it's always there. And if there is one thing we human beings hate, it's that helplessness, that dependency, the loss of freedom to do our own thing when, how, with whom, and where we want to.

Truly, this was a major puzzle piece of my life. It's the first time I had been hospitalized since I was badly burned in the 6th grade. It was hard to transition from being an active, self-starting individual to one who was somewhat confined in his choices. And that paralysis in the recovery room (inability to move my limbs) and going down those stairs (paralyzed by fear)… good Lord, that was powerlessness writ large! And the thing I think about every so often is that I'm almost sixty, and therefore these kinds of health issues might be more common in the future.

So how does this particular puzzle piece fit? For sure, I now can fully identify with all those who have had joint replacements, and that whole process of rehab. I can understand the fear experienced by those who are paralyzed. Ditto for the frustration of those who can only look out the window at life going by.

I also learned that personal attitude makes a huge difference in one's recovery. One can be bitter and complaining and give everyone a really hard time. But that not only hinders recovery, it also hinders care. Who wants to take care of or spend time with a cranky, bitter person? Having a positive outlook, a sense of humor, and faith in God goes a long way in reducing the feelings of powerlessness. Hey, I may not have been able to do simple things for myself, but I sure had the power to choose the way I dealt with it. I even decorated my cane! It had some flame decals on the bottom (like a racing car, y'know), a sticker that said "Are we there yet"?, and best of all, a bike horn. It seemed like *everyone* had to squeeze that horn when they saw it!

So this particular puzzle piece fit into my life in two ways. First, it helped pastoral ministry because I now know what such illness is like. Second, it brought home to me the power of personal attitude to bring healing, humor, and a faster recovery. As I said above, the puzzle pieces, like the stones, become a weapon to fight the giants that threaten different aspects of our lives. Having learned this, I'm better prepared for the future.

I can look back and see so many of those pieces. Falling in love six months after ordination, introduction to centering prayer, the year of study in Berkeley, California, Lou Jacquet asking me to write a Lenten column for the diocesan newspaper (first public use of the writing gift God has given me), taking over this work from Fr. McAuliffe in 1985, midlife in the early 90's, depression in 2001, change in work situation in 2006. I look back and shake my head. In almost every case the initial reactions were fear, anger, and confusion. But they all turned out to be deeply significant.

So, dear one, what are your stones? What are your puzzle pieces? This would make a good Lenten reflection, so that come Easter, you can more fully rejoice in the life that God has given you. As St. Peter said so beautifully: *You may for a time have to endure the grief of many trials, but this is so that your faith, which is more precious than fire-tried gold, may prove genuine and may result in praise, honor, and glory when Jesus Christ is revealed.* (1 Peter 1: 6-7). When you first experience the puzzle piece or the stone, you may not see Jesus, but you will. You will. And it will make all the difference in your life.

Chapter Four

THE WONDER OF IT ALL!!

While on a recent trip to Canada, I happened to watch a TV show which was on the equivalent of America's **The Learning Channel**. It was a story about movie-making and movie theaters, and how customers are demanding more and more special effects. These effects are not just in the film itself, but also in things such as seats that move in conjunction with what happens on the film and special 3-D goggles. One segment showed a film clip where a sea monster swam right up into the viewer's face (so to speak), and squirted a jet of water. At the same time, an actual jet of water came from the screen and wet the audience! It was strange. Consider:

The work of Michelangelo.
The shoe exhibit in the Holocaust Museum, Washington DC.
Photos and postcards in antique shops.

Why this demand for special effects, for the exotic, for more and more realism in games, etc.? Why the huge increase in those reality shows on TV, or the huge number of hits on NASA's website when a recent satellite probe made impact with a comet? Simply put, I think we are a people who have lost the sense of wonder, who need bigger and bigger spectacles to move us out of our boring lives. We're addicted to spectacle! Consider:

Prayerful moments, or even hours.
Watching people receive Communion and seeing the diversity of the Body of Christ.
Traveling from the city into the countryside and experiencing how my heart expands to fill the vista.

The dictionary defines "wonder" as a *"person, place, or thing that causes astonishment and admiration… the feeling aroused by something unexpected."* That's OK as far as it goes, but this kind of wonder comes and goes; it doesn't stick with us. So that's why we need more and more and more. It actually becomes an addiction, a temporary high, and like any drug is a way of briefly escaping the boring or painful reality of my life. Consider:

Wondering how she or he can love me despite awareness of all my insecurities and flaws.

The silence after Communion at Mass.

Holding and contemplating a baby.

I prefer to see wonder as something much more deeply spiritual, something which makes a lasting impression on our whole being, which touches us to our core. Spiritual wonder imparts an unmistakable feeling within. It's not the kind of feeling that makes us want to get up and go, but a feeling that roots us to the spot, filled with awe, wanting to thank God for what it is we are experiencing (even though sometimes we can't even find the words to express that thanks). Consider:

A long marriage.

Deep space photos from the Hubble telescope.

Doing woodworking and the parts actually fit!

How people sanctify adversity with their faith, hope for the future, and love of family and friends.

Wonder is a crucial element for a deep personal spirituality. Without a sense of wonder, we are doomed to move through each day with one underlying mantra: "New day, same old stuff." With wonder, there is always a new day with a multitude of new things and new experiences. Life can indeed have a tremendous amount of spice and variety with a well-developed sense of wonder. Consider:

A golf ball actually goes where I aim it.

Little flowers along the path that no one else will ever see.

A seed transformed into a plant.

The smell of a forest after a rain.

Spiritual wonder connects us to the web of life, to the divine energy and presence which fills the world and all its peoples. A person caught by wonder knows deep within that this is an unrepeatable event, a once-in-a-lifetime thing, and that is OK. Spiritual wonder does not demand that something repeat itself over and over again. In other words, the moment is sufficient unto itself. Besides, the next moment is going to bring another unrepeatable wonder!

Wonder is what happens to us when we are very near God, when we sense God's presence in an unmistakable way. This wonder can be evoked by people, places, things, and events; by the small and the gigantic; the complex and the simple; by joy and sorrow, health and illness. Since all creation is of God, you just never know how God is going to cause his wonder to touch your life at any given moment. The anticipation and the awareness makes for a pretty interesting life, to say the least! Consider:

> *The Saturn 5 moon rocket: thirty-six stories tall, three million parts, every one having to work perfectly. There was not one failure in thirteen launches.*

> *The human brain is a three dimensional maze of a million million nerve cells, each one drawn out like a wire to carry pulsed messages. If you laid all your brain cells end to end, they'd stretch round the world twenty-five times. There are about four million connections in the tiny brain of a goldfinch. Can you comprehend it?*

Spiritual wonder moves us from Rhett Butler's attitude of "Frankly, my dear, I don't give a damn"! to St. Paul's awe-filled realization that "in Him, we live and move and have our being." We realize that each day, God truly does show us a Father's love. We become passionate people, caring about life issues in a way we never did before. Wonder stirs within us a great desire for reconciliation and for justice. Whereas the addictive wonder leaves us isolated and withdrawn, fostering division and antagonism, spiritual wonder forms us into a community of like-minded souls, eager to gently bring God's life to our brothers and sisters. Consider:

> *A quiet calm lake in early morning.*
> *Growth in those who ask me to be their spiritual director.*
> *Aged-furrowed faces.*
> *The way my cat insisted on playing every evening at 7:30, without fail.*

Wonder involves all our senses, including imagination, and opens our heart to communion with the God who made it all. It breeds enthusiasm for life, because a wonder-full person knows that each day is new, each thing is new each day, that the world is always amazing, that there is always something to be learned. Such a person is rarely bored. One priest

I live with put it very nicely in a homily: "If you're bored, you're just not paying attention to life." Consider:

The difference in taste between fresh and dried herbs.

Significant retreat experiences making me aware of God's mercy.

Reading notes from folks on how their prayer has been answered.

Hearing from folks who tell me they still remember things I wrote about or preached about years ago.

I remember several years ago hearing Sr. Jose Hobday comparing faith to the regular lights and the bright lights on a car. I can use the same analogy for wonder. Addictive wonder is like moving through life with only the parking lights, or maybe the regular lights. You can see, but not very far ahead. Put on the brights, however, and the world appears with great intensity. The brights have a fierce power to penetrate the darkness. So too with wonder. Consider:

U.S. Route 12 through Idaho, and the Donner Pass in the Sierra Nevada: helping me appreciate what Lewis and Clark and the pioneers went through.

The generosity of Holy Cross's benefactors.

A tiny green shoot sprouting from a crack on a brick wall.

How can you deepen your sense of wonder? It seems to me there are several ways. First, spend time each day in prayer. There is something about prayer that enables the Holy Spirit to fine-tune our sensibilities so that we become more and more aware of just how much of our life is a word of God calling us to a deeper and deeper relationship. Consider:

Beethoven composing the 9th Symphony while entirely deaf.

Carol and I still working together after twenty-plus years!

Walking through old cemeteries, thinking of the general resurrection, wondering about the lives of the folks buried there.

My body in all its complexity: consciousness, organs, feelings, etc.

Second, cultivate your awareness. Instead of rushing from here to there, move slowly. Look around you. Look down, up, out, right and left. Smell, hear, feel, taste, touch. Within a three foot circle of where you are reading this, a whole universe of potential wonders awaits you. Paying attention to all that is around you expands your horizons instead of constricting them. Take time… time… and more time. Let go of anger and self-centeredness. Remove yourself from the center of the world. Trust me: you need never be bored or jaded!

Chapter Five

WAITING IN JOYFUL HOPE

I'm starting to write this on the first day of Autumn. I don't know what things will be like by the time you finally read this, but for sure, I would love to have stock in companies that make tranquilizers or anti-anxiety meds. Economic news especially has everyone on edge and quite rightfully worried. There's just a cascading series of events that no one seems to be able to control. It's all short-term reaction. It's hard to come up with long-term solutions when one is in panic mode! Faith, hope, and confidence seem to be as strong as a bowl of Jell-O.

In the last few years, one of my most heartfelt prayers has been the one that comes right after the *Our Father* at Mass. The celebrant asks God to deliver us from sin, evil, fear, and anxiety so that *"we may wait in joyful hope for the coming of our Savior Jesus Christ."*

Well, it sure would be nice to be delivered from my sins. Ditto for my fears and anxieties. But how come my sins persist? Why do I still lie awake at night worrying? Why am I afraid of what the next day, month, or year will bring? How does one wait in joyful hope anyway?

You can start off by asking a very basic, yet crucially important question: "How strong are my faith, hope, and love"?

Picture yourself standing on a solid floor. That solid floor represents the love in your life, past and present... from God and from others. It's the foundation of your life. Right in front of you is a wall, representing a problem, difficulty, obstacle, or trial. It's too high to look over, but by moving a few steps right or left, you can look around it. Hope is the inner push that keeps you looking around that wall for a solution or a resolution to the problem. Faith is the conviction that there *will* be a solution. It may be nearby, it may be off in the distance, but you know that if you keep looking you will find a way out. All too often our fixation is entirely on the wall. It need not be so. You have the gifts of faith, hope, and love present within you, ready to be used if you so desire.

Sadly, lots of people see only the wall, and so they complain. That brings us to the second way to strengthen our ability to wait in joyful hope: you can choose the direction of your thoughts. It's the half-full, half-empty glass analogy. It's choosing to rejoice in what you have, or bemoaning what you do not have. Buddhists quite rightly say that we cause a lot of our own suffering by the way we think. If something is happening that we wish *wasn't* happening, or if something is not happening that we wish *would* happen, then we get all bent out of shape. The way we think directly affects our sense of well-being -- mental, physical, and spiritual. I've long believed that the more one complains, the less one is able to see blessing.

That moves us into the third way: gratitude for blessings received. I like to joke with the guys at Fatima by saying, "Hey, *so-and-so*, I know it's gonna be a good day for you … your name wasn't in the obits this morning." Truly, what greater blessing can there be than the morning resurrection to new life, new possibilities, a blank slate, fresh beginnings? Jesus has promised us our daily bread; it is always there for the taking. God's blessings are mediated to us in prayer and silence, in companionship with others, through phone calls and e-mails and letters, through nature and pets, and yes even through our sins. God's love for us is limitless, and there is nothing that prevents God from bestowing his blessings on you and me. When you become aware of the cascade of blessings, then you have hope, for if God has been faithful in the past and is faithful now, who's to say that such fidelity won't continue in the future. This is God's covenant with us.

A fourth key to waiting in joyful hope is having a purpose in life. One with a compass rarely gets lost, for the needle always points north. Now this will vary a lot depending on individual circumstances. For some folks who are suffering from illness, addiction, hunger, or homelessness, it's enough to have the purpose of just making it through one day at a time. For now, that's all they can do. Tomorrow or next week or next month it will be different. The same can probably be said for parents of toddlers and caregivers, or folks in high-stress occupations.

When one can follow a definite direction, each day presents a new array of exciting challenges. For example, I have as my purpose really trying to help folks see their goodness, to see how God cares for them, and to find spiritual meaning in everyday life. I try to do this by using the gifts of writing and preaching which God has given me. When you have a purpose in life, your soul is engaged throughout the day, at work, in play, at prayer, in wrestling with the kids, in listening to your spouse or friend, and so on. Yes, we're tired at the end of each day, but it's a good tired.

Now let's make a distinction here. If my purpose in life is centered around my needs, wants, and desires, then waiting in joyful hope is probably going to turn into waiting with jaded cynicism. The most joy-full, faith-full, and hope-full people I know have two characteristics: they make service to others a priority in each day, and they also firmly believe that "less is more."

Jesus is right on target. If you want life for yourself, give life to others. So many times in the parish when I was having a bad day or starting to have a pity party for myself, it didn't take me long to realize that the best way to snap out of it was to go visit parishioners in the hospital. I love interacting with our caregivers here at Fatima -- the housekeepers, kitchen crew, office and maintenance staff. The same goes for the folks who staff the check-out lanes in stores, bank-tellers, and so on. So often they are made to feel invisible by those they serve.

Good Lord... you don't have to do great and wonderful things! It's stunning to think how many folks you encounter each day whose lives can be brightened by a kind word, a smile, a wink of the eye, etc. Giving life to others not only makes you an agent of hope, but it nourishes the faith and hope of those on the receiving end of your presence in their life. I guarantee you that if you do this often enough, you will be missed when you are absent.

Those who live in joyful hope usually subscribe to a philosophy of "less is more." In other words, the more you and I simplify our lives, the more time and energy we have for things that really matter. It takes a lot of time and energy to manage, maintain, and protect the material goods that are a part of your lifestyle. It takes a lot of energy to get through a day that is booked solid with things to do. If you have personal wealth, I can't begin to imagine the headaches you have over the market gyrations of the last few months. If I'm a controlling-type person, then my time is eaten up by obsessing over minutiae, and I go ballistic whenever anything or anyone seems to be getting away from my control.

Again, it's all a matter of choice. We can be poor in spirit and possess the Kingdom. Or I can be sated with excess, and live in a kingdom of my own making that can collapse without warning, and there will be no one around to help.

Of course, times are hard. Hard choices are having to be made. We live in a sick world, in the sense that our personal, national, and global world is ill and in need of better health. It's been my experience – personal and pastoral – that times of sickness are marvelous times to re-access one's priorities and determine what is really important in life. In other words, it's a time of conversion. May God grant all of us the grace to choose the way that enables us to live and wait in joyful hope, rather than stagnating in bitterness and disillusionment.

Chapter Six

CALLED AND CHOSEN

I'm typing these reflections while on retreat in a hermitage in the woods, sitting in the prayer room in the early evening. As I look out the window, the rays of the setting sun penetrate the forest. About thirty-feet away from me, a spot of sunlight illumines a branch, and on the branch sits a mourning dove. It's eerie to see how this gentle bird is highlighted, when all around it there are deepening shadows. Even as I type these few sentences, the spot of sunlight is disappearing as the sun moves down towards the horizon. The dove is fading into the leafy background.

How like us… a brief moment in the sun, and we fade away. All too often we look at our lives and wonder, "Have I made a difference"? In the long history of the universe, hundreds of billions of years old, has my tiny batch of fifty, seventy, ninety years really made any difference? In the vast size of the cosmos, with its billions of stars and galaxies, I am tinier than an atom. Are the things I've done of any consequence? Billions of people have populated Earth, and who knows how many more there will be in time to come. Am I really that significant?

There are so many variations on these questions. Does my vote really count? Is it worthwhile to express my opinion? Does my gift really make a difference to Holy Cross or to the other organizations who ask me for help? Am I just a number? Do medical personnel see me as a person, or am I just a set of unique symptoms ("the appendectomy in 431")? Do my bosses even know I exist, or my parish priest, for that matter?

Add to this the most important question of all: does God really care about me? Am I really real to God, or am I just lumped in with the rest of the human race whom God loves?

I don't know why, but for a couple of weeks now I've known that the topic of this essay had to be, "Called and Chosen." As I sat to write this, my prayer was definitely one to the Spirit: "This idea has to be from you, so you give me the words that are needed"! I know the questions above are important questions. We live in a deeply dissatisfied world. We know all is not right. There's a great anonymity, a fear of being left behind, a feeling that events are moving too fast to comprehend. It seems that more and more of our lives are being affected and controlled by institutions and people we cannot even speak to. When was the last time you got a real live person on the phone when you called to request help with something? Maybe after punching eighty-seven numbers you finally got to talk to a human being, but not before.

Called and chosen… called and chosen… yes, you are called and chosen by God. Despite what everything or everyone around you says, you are truly called and chosen. By the very fact that you are a living being, you are needed by the universe, you are needed in history. You are needed above all by God. Just as the potter with the slightest pressure of her fingers shapes a bowl, so too you are the finger of God, shaping the cosmos, forming the Church, the nation, your parish, neighborhood, family, workplace, and home. You don't have to do anything special or extraordinary. All you have to do is to be you.

Called and chosen. Over and over again in Holy Scriptures, God tells you and me through the sacred writers how crucial we are to history. Jesus time and time again assures us that we are not anonymous cogs on a vast cosmic wheel, but we're known and loved and needed by God. Oh, how we're needed! If you could only comprehend how much you're needed, how much God values your presence on earth all these years. If you could only understand how deeply God grieves when someone dies tragically as a result of war, violence, crime, abortion, execution, human carelessness and indifference. God had hopes and dreams for these people. The shape of God's world and the happiness and growth of countless people depended on these people being alive and exercising their gifts and talents. But now that they are gone before their time, God must adapt, and we must adapt.

What is the nature of this call? Is it like the call of the apostles or the prophets, like St. Paul being knocked off his horse? Is it like suddenly coming to the realization that one is to be a priest or religious, or that one has to enter marriage, or in some cases, leave an unhealthy marriage? It's none of these, really. Most ideas of being called and chosen have to do with *doing* something. I am called to do this, chosen to go there and do that. That's not what I'm thinking of.

God calls us simply to be who we are, with all our skills, talents, potential, failures, and limits. We cannot love every single person we meet. We cannot do everything that has to be done. We cannot fix our family's problems. All God asks of us is that we do what we're capable of doing (and those capabilities are God's gifts to us) and to stay out of his way by not doing more than we're asked to do. After all, God has called other people also!

We were sent into the world because God has a dream, and we are part of that dream. What is that dream? Ah… there's the rub! Our understanding has to unfold; our life has to unfold. For example, never would I have seen myself in this position of being Director of the Holy Cross Association. But looking back, everything that happened prior to 1985 (when I started this ministry) was like a preparation for this work. Everything that has happened since 1985 only confirms that this is where I need to be to fulfill God's dream for me. And not just for me, but also for all the folks with whom I am in contact. Somehow, what God wants for you and for me and for our Church and world is happening because we're together in the Association. This newsletter goes to 6,800 homes. I would imagine that maybe 3,000 folks are reading this (hey, one can dream, y'know!). Think of that specialness right there! In the entire history of the world, past, present, and yet to come, there are only 3,000 people sharing this moment. Something is happening to each one of us and to our world as a result of this encounter. And all we're doing is simply being ourselves, loving and caring for each other in our strength and our weakness. And what does the future hold? Who knows? It has to unfold. Our future is hidden from our eyes. All we have to rely on is the conviction that God is faithful and that we have each other.

Is the call always clear? Will you and I always feel chosen? No. There are times when I feel very much confused about life. I feel pain over my suffering or the suffering of others. I question whether God cares, if God is listening. I look at the chaos that visits me because of someone's anger or vindictiveness or carelessness. I doubt the future, and doubt my ability to forgive those who have hurt me, and God's ability to forgive me. In some situations I thrive; in others I die.

Cloudiness or darkness does not have to obscure the sense that you are called and chosen. In fact, those times may actually deepen your sense of being someone truly special. Let me use some examples from nature to show you what I mean.

In Texas right now, there is extreme drought. On the evening news of the day as I'm typing this, the reporter said there has been no rain for fifty-nine days. Without clouds, life lacks a vital element: water. The earth cannot be replenished or nourished, and living creatures die. Without the cloudy days of our lives, the days without sunshine, our life cannot flourish and grow. We need the drizzle of yucky days, the thunderstorm of an angry fight at home, the torrential downpour of those times in our lives when it seems like one damn thing after another is happening. In these times, we can experience a new sense of our belief in God, a new awareness of how other people help us, a stronger faith. It is possible to come through the clouds with a much deeper sense of who we truly are and of our place in God's dream.

Or take fog. Fog causes us to slow down while driving, to take extra time and caution, to look more carefully ahead of us. It's sometimes scary too, and we find ourselves praying for safety and protection. The same thing can happen through the foggy patches of our lives. We slow down, look ahead, proceed cautiously. And then somehow, someway, through the cloud and the fog we hear the voice that Jesus heard on the mountain of transfiguration: "You are my beloved child."

Our vocation of being called and chosen, of being God's beloved child, is risky. It means a lot of trust, a lot of letting go. Hardly a day goes by when we don't wonder: "Am I getting this right? Isn't there something else I'm supposed to be doing"? Most of us have to get rid of a notion that we must be doing something good, something significant and worthwhile, in order to merit God's love and care. Not so. All we have to do is to be ourselves, to claim our place on the branch like the mourning dove and let the sun shine upon us. It just calls for a deep trust in the God who proclaims in so many ways how special we are.

Can a mother forget her infant,
be without tenderness for the child of her womb?
Even should she forget
I will never forget you.
See, upon the palms of my hands
I have written your name.
(Isaiah 49.15-16)

Chapter Seven

FURRY THEOLOGY: WHAT OUR PETS TEACH US

One of the great movements in spirituality since the year 2000 has been an increasing awareness of how connected we are to Mother Earth: to the water, land, atmosphere, to all the animals and plants. Each and every piece – including us humans – has its place in the whole. Harm one piece, and the effects ripple throughout creation. The old Industrial Age attitude of "The earth is mine to dominate and use" is giving way to something new: "We are stewards of creation. To the extent that Mother Earth prospers, to that extent do we." We are fashioning a deeper understanding of the fact that every living thing reflects and shows forth some aspect of God.

For many folks, our primary concern with the flora of the earth is our yard, or the potted indoor plants. Local parks and national parks offer us wider vistas. So too do the shows on the *Discovery Channel,* or the *Travel Channel.* I am just so fascinated by the great variety of plant life on earth and how it has adapted to life over the centuries. Ditto for animal life. *Animal Planet* is hugely popular, as are the above-mentioned shows. Zoos rival national parks in popularity. Eco-tourism and photographic safaris are growing in popularity for those who can afford them.

But for most of us, animal contact comes through our pets. That's what I'd like to reflect on with you. After all, spring is the season of birth; the little ones are all over the place. With all the heaviness of war and economic distress that weighs us down, it's good to do something a bit more light-hearted. Looking at our pets, what can they reveal to us about God?

That's not a silly question. Though animal spirituality – whether or not they have souls – has long been debated, more and more recognition is paid to the spiritual and mental-health role animals play in our lives.

The attention shouldn't come as a surprise. Almost six in ten American households have a relationship of mutuality and reciprocity with a family pet. Animals have long been revered in religion. Every major world religion recognizes the divine origin of animals and humans. Buddhism regards animals as beings in different stages of reincarnation. Hinduism and Jainism embrace vegetarianism out of respect for all life. Islam teaches respect for animals as part of God's creation. Some theologians say that a common respect for animals as spiritual beings could serve as a bridge between religions, because it rises above doctrine, rituals, and practices. Churches and synagogues are bringing animals to the front of religious consciousness, and in some cases, right up to the altar. Consider the Blessing of the Animals on the Feast of Francis of Assisi.

Let me start with my own pet history. When I was a toddler, we had a Collie named Laddie, but I don't remember him at all. I do remember growing up with a Beagle named Poochie, and in my teen years there was an Irish Setter named Patsy. We had a rabbit named Hoppy, a parakeet named Sam. There was a horned toad in there somewhere, a turtle, and, of course, the goldfish won at parish festivals. My brother John had a hamster. One of the great family stories is how that beastie got out of the cage and into my brother Jim's bed late at night! But I didn't really have any relationship with those pets, either because I was too young, or because I was away from home (in the seminary) most of the year.

As an adult, I enjoyed the company of an Akita named Frodo while serving at our novitiate in Colorado. In the parish, I had an aquarium. That was OK, but it's hard to develop a relationship with fish! But it sure kept the kids occupied while I talked with parents. While at the Solitude, I had a cat named Grady (who has since died), and now, here at Fatima, a cockatiel named Gus.

My personal spiritual development was not advanced enough to really appreciate Frodo's role as "religion teacher." Sure, he had a dog's unconditional love. He was a wonderful companion on walks, while sitting in the yard, at playtime. To my amazement, he quickly picked up that I was deaf, and would jump on the bed if something happened at night, or if a car came up the driveway or someone came into the house by the back door. It was a great consolation knowing he would do this. But I was in a very different place spiritually when Grady entered my life, and that has extended to Gus. What have those creatures taught me about myself, God, and about care for others?

What leaps first to mind is the respect and patience Grady and Gus have taught me to have towards other human beings. You deal with a cat and a bird on their terms, period. I have no choice but to let them be themselves, to do things in their own way, and their own time. If I don't, they bite or claw. This has helped me be far more patient with the foibles and idiosyncrasies of others than I used to be.

The one time I did get really angry with Grady brought a startling revelation about God. I had tried to coax her up on my lap, but she just would not come. I yelled: "All I do for you, the least you could do is come sit on my lap"! Then it hit me like a two-by-four. God would certainly be justified in saying this to me! But God never does. He waits till I'm ready, and in the meantime continues to bless me with all I need for everyday life. God's "lap" is always there for me.

When our pets are in the kitten and puppy stage, they absolutely enthrall us (not quite so with non-mammalian babies!). We love their antics, their playfulness, the way they have of falling all over their feet. Though it's exasperating, we tend to excuse the trouble they get into -- soiling the carpet, chewing the slippers, clawing the furniture. After all, they're too little to know better. The lessons to be learned? First, see how easily we put aside our seriousness and concerns and play with them. They bring out a neglected dimension of our humanity, and we are to-tally un-self-conscious about showing it. Second, see how we are patient with their accidents. Does that extend to our family, friends, co-workers? Third, before God, aren't we like puppies and kittens, falling all over our-selves, goofing up? Does God love us any less? Does he condemn us for our mistakes?

I'm not prepared to say that animals have souls like us, but I know they have feelings and consciousness. When Gus looks in the mirror, he may not be aware that he's looking at himself, but he knows he sees an-other bird like himself and responds accordingly. He also reacts in differ-ent ways to different people. Grady would fall asleep in my lap, and before long I'd know she was dreaming because of her leg movements and snapping teeth (I'm afraid to know what she was dreaming about!). Dogs do the same. This makes a difference in how I relate to other animals, and how I react to cruelty towards animals.

I definitely believe animals have intelligence and a reasoning ability. They figure things out, learn quickly, and know how to push our buttons. I could never figure out how Grady got from the living room floor to the top of a bookcase eight feet up. She knew how to guilt me when travel meant boarding her at the vets. Gus has a penchant for de-leafing green houseplants. Usually a loud noise will get him off the plant. He takes a few steps, looks at me, takes a few steps, looks back. He knows he's not supposed to be near the plant, but he's gonna try anyway!

We are so alert in our pets to any signs of illness or an out-of-the-ordinary behavior, and we immediately respond to that. With other human beings…?

Grady taught me the value of a good deep stretch, as well as the value of quietly sitting in the sun and watching the world go by. Gus and Grady both told me about the value of a good nap. Gus loves to welcome the morning with song and to sing a Vespers medley as the sun goes down. Both pets taught me the value of persistence, especially when it comes to feeding time or waking up time or "Get out of my chair, please." If I sooner or later give in, so will God.

Both beasties taught me spontaneity, especially when it comes time to play. Gus drops things over the edge of the table, and fully expects me to pick them up so he can drop them again. When I'm trying to work on the laptop, he'll trot from one shoulder to the other, under my chin, across the chair top, and back around again… over and over till I stop and either rub his head (boy, does he like his head rubs!) or talk to him. So often I would be reading, or watching a favorite TV show, or just be plain tired from the day, when here came Grady. She would flop down on the floor and look at me with an eye that said, "Get down here and play with me! Now"! Not infrequently the thought ran through my mind that this is what parents go through every day with their little children. It's a sacrifice of what I want to do for the sake of another.

Grady taught me what it was to fully trust another and become vulnerable; Gus continues the teaching in his own way. They fall asleep on my lap or shoulder, trusting that I will not harm them. Both allow me to stroke the most vulnerable parts of their bodies: Gus his back, and Grady her tummy. So how do I trust God or a loved one or a counselor with my vulnerabilities?

There's a lot more I could say, but the point is that our pets are not just wonderful companions, but they are also great teachers. In their own unique way, they can help us become more fully human, more fully attuned to the ways of God and the needs of other people.

And to answer a question I frequently get asked: yes, I do believe our pets will be in heaven with us. We never lose those whom we love, and that includes our pets. When we get to heaven, every good thing and every good person that has passed through our lives will be ours to enjoy more fully than we have ever been free to enjoy in this life. Every happy experience we have had will again be ours.

I think the Church recognizes this too. In the Fourth Eucharistic Prayer, we read this conclusion: "Then in your kingdom, freed from the corruption of sin and death, we shall sing your glory *with every creature* [italics mine] through Christ our Lord, through whom you have given us everything that is good."

And to that I can say only, "Thanks be to God."

Chapter Eight

"A BROKEN, HUMBLED HEART, OH GOD, YOU WILL NOT SPURN"

(Psalm 51)

I'm starting the first draft of this reflection the day after Valentine's Day. It may seem strange to be talking about broken hearts – and I assure you that my heart has not been broken recently. But I'm sure there were quite a few broken hearts yesterday, when hoped-for Valentine gifts or cards did not materialize, when people who have recently lost loved ones pondered their loss, and so on.

In addition, the Winter Olympics are currently going on. Broken hearts abound, as athletes who have trained for years leave the playing fields because of injury or dumb mistakes, or simply because someone else was 1/100th of a second better.

I've no doubt that your heart has been broken in the course of your lifetime, or at the very least, cracked. Why can I say this? Because you're a human being who loves, who cares, who feels, who hopes for some return on your emotional and physical investments.

The only people whose hearts cannot be broken are those who have walled themselves off from human life and human love. Those folks do know what it is to love. It's just that they've been shattered so many times that there comes a point when they cannot bear the thought of any more hurt and disappointment. Erecting a fortress around their heart and not allowing anyone to come close seems to them to be the safest way to go through life.

Loss, change, and unfulfilled hopes and dreams are a part of your life and mine. We experience the death of loved ones, or the death of a relationship, or the death of a beloved pet. Children choose a different life path or a different spiritual path than the one you hoped they would take. Perhaps there is outright alienation within a family, and nothing you do seems able to pull things back together and bring reconciliation.

Advancing age or circumstances beyond our control force us to move from a beloved home. Natural disasters wipe away a lifetime of equity and memories.

We loyally spend our lives working for a corporation or supporting a church, only to have the rug unexpectedly pulled from under us with no warning or consultation. Or worse yet, we are fed a steady stream of lies – think of those corporations, for example, who tell stockholders and employees that everything is fine, only to declare bankruptcy or come under criminal investigation a week later.

If you've managed to avoid a broken heart, perhaps there have been times when your heart has been cracked, so to speak… or perhaps a better word is "wounded." You get stood up by a date, a promised ride or call or note doesn't arrive. You find out that someone you trust has been deceiving you.

A long-awaited trip is cancelled because of weather or security, or not enough people have signed up. You receive news from a beloved friend that someone in her family is suffering from a major illness. It probably won't break your heart, but it will wound it because you love the friend so much. Or maybe you are the victim of malicious gossip, spread by those who don't know all the facts or who have an axe to grind.

The list goes on and on. You could add many of your own experiences, as could I. But the point of this reflection is this: given that we have experienced a broken or wounded heart, what to do about it? As mentioned on the previous page, you could choose to wall yourself off from life, but that would be like living in a limbo of gloomy grayness. Sure, you can try to ignore the wound or the brokenness. That'll work for awhile, but sooner or later your psyche or your body is going to react.

There's plenty of stuff on the Internet and in bookstore self-help sections about healing broken or wounded hearts. In some situations, the help of a wise and gentle counselor is needed, and should not be avoided. Those folks are gifts of God to you and to the human race.

What more I would like to suggest is this: the shards and cracks of your heart are the pathway through which divine life flows into you, and from you out to the world. Your model is Jesus' heart, pierced on the cross, from which blood and water flowed, which we call the fountain of sacramental life in the Church.

Over and over again in Scripture, we hear the desire of Yahweh and of Jesus to heal our broken hearts. But the healing they promise is not something that will instantaneously fix everything up, and make it as though it never happened. What Jesus will do, if we let him, is to take the raw material of our grief, sorrow, or deep disappointment and fashion something new from it. He is always willing to create for us a new heart, one much better suited to love deeply and passionately. But we have to let the raw material flow into his hands, instead of bottling it up or giving it to "potters" who promise an easy fix.

It's always been my contention that the wisest, most beautiful people on earth are those who have been through much suffering, and have not let it embitter them. Instead, they are a source of life to others. You've known people like this. What's their secret? They've gathered up the broken pieces, given them to God, and received in return a heart that truly, deeply cares for others. Oh sure, they still have bad days, and cranky days, and times when they wonder where God is. Good Lord, we're all human, after all! But those times pass, and it's not long till the inner light shines again through the cracks and shards.

Might I a suggest a simple meditation? You can do it daily or as needed. If you are experiencing brokenness or "crackedness" right now, close your eyes. In your imagination lay all the broken pieces on a table in front of you, or visualize the cracks. Or you can actually break something – say a clay flower pot – and lay the pieces before you.

Then imagine the waters of God's grace flowing through and around and within... washing away the hurt and pain, the ugliness, the despair. Keep the water flowing as long as you can. Come back to it day after day if you need to. See it, hear it, maybe even reach out and touch it. Tears may flow, you might feel sick, there will surely be anger, but let it come. That's all part of the healing process. Don't hinder it. The poison can and will be washed away. The shards won't come back together. Once broken, they're broken. But... but... but something new will be created. We have the promise of God on that. That's what Easter and resurrection are all about.

Chapter Nine

WORDS, ACTIONS, AND TOLERANCE

From the AP wires: *"Long before he killed 32 people in the worst mass shooting in U.S. history, Seung-Hui Cho was bullied by fellow high school students who mocked his shyness and the strange way he talked, former classmates said… As soon as he started reading, the whole class started laughing and pointing and saying, 'Go back to China,'"* Davids said.

We all have the capability of inflicting injury, with what we say, do, or permit. It's not limited to the political, entertainment, or religious worlds. Even Pope Benedict is not immune to this (i.e., his comments in Germany about Islam and violence). The scary thing for me is that it is so widespread, and so tolerated and "acceptable." It starts from the top and filters down.

I Googled "political credibility" and source after source talked about the importance of credibility in every aspect of human life: economics, foreign policy, domestic leadership, media, religious life, and family life. It's a worldwide problem. You name it, it's there.

The world, and more critically the United States, is suffering from a bankruptcy of credibility. Deception seems to be the accepted standard. If someone gets caught out, it's spin, spin, spin. Didn't we used to call that "lying" in the old days? Obviously, this behavior breeds deep suspicion and cynicism towards those who exercise political leadership, business management, and ecclesiastical authority.

The media aids and abets. Reporters have falsified stories. Sex sells. Does it ever! Pope John Paul makes a historic visit to Cuba, but the media focuses on Clinton and Lewinski, and all the stars and starlets. Reality shows – it amazes me what people will do for a buck. And what of those who allow themselves to be debased on shows like Montel, or some of the "Judge" shows. Supermarket and TV tabloids, Washington's shouting experts on weekend television, talk-radio know-it-alls, gossip-mongers, and blogs on the Internet, paparazzi: not exactly life-giving and inspirational, is it?

As one benefactor from Canada reflected: *"I love to listen to radio and the bunch that make their living out of biting, hurtful, and sometimes vicious words. They say them but I wonder how responsible we are for listening, tolerating their actions, and doing nothing. For me that is acceptance and makes us someway responsible."*

You and I do it too, through gossip, Freudian slips of the tongue, or outright spite and malice. Sometimes we cloak our words and actions under the guise of "caring for the other," or "teasing," but no matter… the hurt is still inflicted. No doubt you yourself have been the victim many a time.

Now on the positive side, maybe things might start to happen because of the "Imus factor." On the day I'm typing this, the morning news said that Rosie O'Donnell was being removed from *The View.* Supposedly it was a contract dispute, but I wonder. Music executives who have hip-hop artists under contract are struggling with the line between artistic expression and the hurt inflicted by three particularly noxious words. No resolution yet, but at least they're looking at it seriously.

I truly believe that we as a people are forgetting that words and actions have consequences. Equally consequential are our personal levels of tolerance. I wonder – are our words, actions, and tolerance levels more influenced by our personal comfort levels, our pocketbooks, and the short term? Or are they more influenced by the common good, the long term, and the Gospel (and by extension, the Bible, Talmud and Midrash of the Jews, the Koran of the Muslims, the Shruti of the Hindus, and the Theravada (Writings) of the Buddhists).

By no means am I sinless myself. My life is filled with words and actions that have hurt people. Sometimes I accepted the consequences, and at other times I ignored them, secure in my self-righteousness ("They're wrong. I'm right"!). Of course, sometimes those unaccepted consequences do come full circle and bite me back badly. Oftentimes my tolerance level is too high, in that I'm too ready to make excuses for others instead of confronting them. At other times I think, "Well, it doesn't affect me, so why bother"?

And quite frankly, oftentimes I just want it all to go away. Right now. You and I are exhausted by the never-ending suffering, horror, and tragedy that assaults us daily. So we immerse ourselves in our computers, our cell phones, our I-pods, our books, addictions, and anything else that helps us shut out the world.

At every age of our life, with every person we meet, our words and actions have consequences, ranging from the serious to the mundane. Moreover, the effects of words and actions can be cumulative. It's highly doubtful that any one person said something or did something that sent Seung-Hui Cho over the brink and out onto the campus of Virginia Tech armed with two pistols. He took too much time to plan it. But that does not negate the prior abuse that went on. The wounds were too deep.

Or take someone like a child or spouse who is subjected to endless verbal abuse. Eventually there may be one word or one assault too many and the abused individual snaps and strikes back without pre-meditation. The volcano of rage, capped for so long, erupts.

My words and actions might be the tipping point. Am I prepared for that responsibility? If not, then why speak or act that way in the first place? What *possible* good is it doing, other than giving me a chance to vent my own insecurities and animosities?

In short, if you and I speak kindly and do good to one person, we are affirming not only that one person, but all others with whom she or he comes into contact that day. We may literally be saving a life. If I speak cruelly, negatively, and with hostility towards another, then I need to be prepared for the consequences. I *am* (emphasis deliberate) suffocating that person's self-image and spirit. It makes no difference whether you are talking about that person's race, gender, sexual inclination, appearance, weight, intelligence, job, or work performance. Negativity stifles growth and happiness.

What of tolerance? Where do we draw our personal line? What will finally make us say "Enough"! My good, or the common good? My family, or the human family? Now this is not easy to deal with. That's part of living in a democracy. Maybe I'm wrong… maybe I'm cynical… but it seems to me that so much of public policy nowadays is dictated by those who have the loudest voice, the most money, the most connections, or the electoral power. In other areas, policy is dictated by those who hold the institutional power that traditionally comes with a given position.

Freedom of speech, a great and wonderful part of our country, can be life-giving, or it can be destructive. It is invoked by those who want peace and those who support the war ... by pro-life and pro-choice groups... by ministers like Topeka's Fred Phelps and the Conference of Catholic Bishops... by country singers and hip-hop rap singers... by painters and sculptors, et al. Try to put limits on destructive speech and behavior and boom: up goes the flag of "First Amendment"! We need that amendment – it's part of what makes our country tick. But man, when does the tick become a "ticking time bomb"?

Somehow the middle ground gets lost. Instead of win-win, it becomes a matter of win-lose, for me or against me. The collective wisdom of those who live day-to-day *real* life is never tapped. The self-righteousness of those in power is a turn-off to most people with common sense and good will. Is that an acceptable state of affairs? Do you tolerate it? I tolerate it if I shrug my shoulders and do nothing. Ditto if all I do is complain.

I confess to feelings of powerlessness. I don't have money, connections, status; I'm not a member of any group that vociferously advocates for this or that. But darn it, I gotta do something! To do nothing is to give my approval to the status quo.

So what are my options – our options? Write, phone, join, give financial support, shop intelligently, and vote. Those are the Big 6. Those are the ways in which you lend your voice to those who value the things you do. Will your lone effort count? Absolutely. That's where you have to have faith and conviction. Yours may be the voice, letter, contribution, or vote to start to bring definitively cultural transformation.

For example, we used to serve Orange Roughy at Moreau Seminary. One day I casually mentioned to our cook that it was an endangered species because of overfishing. This was news to him. One month later, out comes a memo from the ND Food Service that Orange Roughy and several other species would no longer be on the university food menu. Did my comment bring that about? I have no idea. But at least I said something.

Change is not going to come from above. God will not do for us what we can do for ourselves. It will come from those of us who believe that the Spirit has given everyone a piece of truth, and that everyone's voice needs to be heard in order to build consensus and effect lasting change. *"Whatever you do for* (or say to or permit to be done to) *the least of my brothers and sisters, that you do unto me* (or say to or permit to be done to me), *says the Lord"* (Mt 25:40).

I pray that you and I can stand before the Lord and say that we refused to participate in the social sinfulness that permeates our society and diminishes the quality of life for so many of our brothers and sisters.

It's gotta start somewhere. Why not with us? All it takes is awareness of what we say, do, and tolerate.

Chapter Ten

"I PRAISE YOU FOR I AM FEARFULLY AND WONDERFULLY MADE"

(Psalm 139:14)

arol and Kim, my two co-workers, have been lovingly hassling me for the last two weeks to get this newsletter done and get it to the printers. My problem was that the muse was not stirring, and when the muse isn't stirring, it's useless to even think about writing something. At one point I threatened to make the newsletter topic "How It Feels When I'm Nagged," and mentioned how that topic would strike a blow of freedom for nagged men! Just cuz I'm a priest, guys, doesn't mean I'm free from it. 'Course, having a pair of hearing aids I can turn off is a definite advantage, but... I wonder if Mary nagged Joseph and Jesus?

Seriously, I have been thinking of a topic, but just wasn't sure how to address it. This being the Christmas newsletter, and Christmas celebrating the Incarnation of Jesus into a human body, I was thinking about writing some reflections on our bodies. Now this may seem like a rather unusual topic, but that's precisely the point. I do believe it's one that is not talked about much in this day and age, and this leads to a very unhealthy stance towards the human body. The late John Paul II gave well over one-hundred Wednesday conferences on the theology of the body, so there is precedent in talking about it.

— I Praise You for I am Fearfully and Wonderfully Made

Admittedly, I'm not John Paul. Nor am I some kind of Adonis, with rippled abs, bulging biceps, etc. I'm a sixty-one year-old balding, frumpy, arthritic, overweight, saggy-armed male with eyeglasses, hearing aids, four crowned teeth (soon to be six), a big overbite, a bum that's too wide for the allotted space in the ND football stadium, and a brand new fake knee. And yet, this body is all I have. It's me. It's my way of being in the world for the years that are allotted to me.

Christianity has a real love/hate relationship with the human body. When I was growing up, I was taught that religion and spirituality are really about the soul and the things of the soul. The body and its needs did not matter. The body was the soul's prison, and salvation happened when the soul was liberated from the demands of the body through prayer, fasting, confession, and self-discipline (especially a lot of cold showers). In short, physical desires were to be resisted, even extinguished, if possible. Does all that sound familiar to you?

All through the centuries, different religious movements have promoted this negative view of the human body. Gnosticism was an utterly pessimistic tradition, with a nearly feverish desire to be freed from the body. Gnostics sought a special wisdom or mysticism that would somehow undo the cursed spell of human existence. In Manichaeanism, there was a perpetual battle between the good part of the human being (the soul, composed of light) and the bad part (the body, composed of dark earth). The Albigensians taught that the human being is living contradiction, a battlefield between a good principle (who created the soul) and a bad principle (who created the human body). The liberation of the soul from its captivity in the body is the true end of our being. To attain this, even suicide is commendable.

All these teachings have one thing in common – they've been condemned by the Catholic Church as dangerous heresies. Despite this, they somehow persist in modern thinking, especially amongst fundamentalist Christians. I'd also like to suggest that the modern preoccupation with the body can in some instances be interpreted as a rejection of the body that has been given to me. If you look at things like plastic surgery, bulimia and anorexia, obsession with weight and appearance, extreme devotion to personal fitness, botox treatments, etc. – don't they in some way constitute a rejection of the body and a loathing of the way we look?

41

Ironically, the New Testament itself has indirectly fostered a contempt of the human body. The Gospel of John, the letters of John, and many letters of St. Paul speak of the sinfulness of the flesh. Now when we hear that word "flesh," we automatically equate it with the human body. But what many folks (including preachers!) don't know is that for John and Paul, "flesh" had nothing to do with the human body. Simply put (since volumes have been written on this topic), "flesh" refers to the sinful tendencies that we humans have because of original sin. It's the dark, unredeemed side of our human nature, and manifests itself in sinful, selfish, and self-centered behavior.

In contrast to these heresies mentioned above, the Catholic Church (including John and Paul) follows Genesis One to teach that the material world and the human body are masterpieces of God's loving creativity. Five times in the Genesis story of creation we hear the words "God saw that it was good." And when human beings were created, God saw that it was "*very* good."

In sum, the body is integral to who we are. We are enfleshed spirits. Jesus did not come to save souls but to save human beings. He fed the bodies of the hungry and healed the bodies of the sick even as he forgave their sins and taught them how to live well and love deeply. And because the human body is very good, the desires of the body for such things as food, drink, sleep, and sexual union, are fundamentally good and not bad. Furthermore, we believe not just in the immortality of the soul but in the resurrection of the body. We proclaim that every time we pray the Creed. If the body is bad, why make it a part of eternal life?

Pope John Paul II, as mentioned above, spoke eloquently about the human body. He insisted that the body is not simply a container for the soul. Instead, the body manifests and expresses the soul. In other words, the soul and body act as one. They encompass every dimension of human existence, from animal instinct to abstract reason, sensation and intellect, passion and reflection, imagination and curiosity, sorrow and delight, natural talents and supernatural longing, flesh and spirit. We are one unity. Our bodily life is also the life of the soul, possessed of a supernatural dignity and a vocation to union with God.

Even today, I keep hearing things such as "Tell me what I must do to save my soul." Well, you can't save the soul without at the same time saving the body! That should be clear by now. This is why Jesus placed such insistence on eating and drinking as signs of the Kingdom. It's why he healed physical illness and drove out demons. It's why, in Matthew 25, he spoke of eternal reward to those who did "bodily things", such as visiting the sick and prisoners, sheltering the homeless, feeding the hungry and thirsty.

Your hands and mine are the hands of God touching a sick world. Your voice is the voice of God speaking words of gentle love and recognition. Your feet, your heart, your mind – every part of your being – was formed and created by God, with the help of your parents, in a very specific, non-repeatable way. You and I were custom-designed, if you will, for the very specific purpose of reflecting God in a very specific way to the specific part of the world in which we live and move and have our being. Your body (i.e., the entirety of your humanness) is good because it was created as such by God. It is through my body that God connects himself with our world, and I too am connected to the world and all its peoples.

When I say that we are connected to all peoples, I mean that in a literal sense. One of the great scientific breakthroughs of your lifetime and mine has been DNA research. Researchers are engaged right now in mapping what we could call a DNA genealogy. I participated a couple years ago in research sponsored by the National Geographic Society. Using the Y-chromosome, passed from father to son generation after generation, research is showing that all humanity originated in Africa. Over thousands of years, various groups left the African homeland and migrated throughout the world. These migrations are tracked by specific gene mutations. My group was identified as M-170, which goes back 60,000 years to the first non-African male. My ancestors migrated to southeastern and central Europe, and also further north into Scandinavia. The exact region that nourished my ancestors will be discovered as more people are added to the database, thus increasing the possibilities for genetic matches.

On the maternal side, things get even more fascinating. This research focuses on mitochondrial DNA, which is inherited from my mother, who inherited it from her mother, et al. It's passed only from mother to child with very little change from one's remote female ancestors. And who might they be? Research has indentified 36 women, who lived thousands of years ago, and from whom almost everyone on earth is descended through the maternal line. For classification purposes, these women were given names, and my deep maternal descendent is named Helena. She lived about 20,000 years ago, on the strip of land that joins France and Spain. Her descendents are the most widespread of the 36 women... they can be found in the Alps, the Scottish highlands, in Norway, and as far east as the Urals and the Russian steppes. Where did my specific maternal ancestors come from? Again further research is needed.

I find all this tremendously exciting, and I hope it hasn't bored you to death. Scattered throughout this world, right here and now, I have thousands – perhaps hundreds of thousands – of relatives, all sharing a common ancestry dating back to the dawn of the human race. There are today relatives of Mary and Joseph and Jesus out there, as well as the Apostles and saints. The connection is real, it is living. I literally bear in my body the life of God alone knows how many people. So yes, the human body is very good, in so many ways.

I could go on and on, but space is limited. I just want to make the point that God thought the human body was the best thing God ever created. He was so enamored of human beings that he wanted a body all his own, just like ours. That's the beauty of the Incarnation; God became one of us. God honors us. And in assuming a human body and soul, God shows us the way to happiness, peace, and ultimately, eternal life. We don't gain happiness and peace by neglecting our bodies. Nor do we gain them by a narcissic over-emphasis on our bodies. We gain happiness and peace by being happy with the body the Lord has given us, and letting God use us a means of showing his love and care for the world.

Chapter Eleven

HOW TO AVOID SUFFERING

I showed that headline to Carol, my co-worker, and after she read it, I said, "You're fired"! She gave me "The Look"!

Seriously... I have a strong suspicion that you looked at that title and wondered: "Has Fr. Herb lost it"? I can assure you that I have not. No life is devoid of suffering; it comes because we are human beings. It is part and parcel of our humanity. The kind of suffering I have in mind in writing this reflection is the kind of suffering that we inflict on ourselves by the way we think.

Let me start off with four stories.

1. In 1991, I made a Buddhist retreat. For ten days, for twelve hours a day, we simply sat and observed what was going on in our bodies and minds. It was a profound experience, and the lessons I learned remain with me to this day. The first lesson was that "This too will pass." After awhile, sitting without moving a muscle can become quite painful! So we were taught to simply observe that pain, to focus on it and let it be. Every single time, it quickly passed (to be just as quickly replaced by another pain somewhere else!). There were also those all-too-rare moments when I actually felt good... but they too quickly passed.

The second lesson was that much of our suffering is self-imposed. We get upset and angry and off-center because something is happening to us that we wish were *not* happening, or because something is *not* happening that we wish *would* happen. So we retreatants were taught that the only way to maintain our equilibrium and inner peace was to quietly accept whatever was happening right now, realizing that it would pass.

2. One Holy Saturday morning, I had to make a quick run into South Bend to get some wood for a project I was working on. Coming back, I decided to take the back roads. I passed a little country church, and I was really affected by the message they had on their little signboard out front. It said: "We spend our lives crucified between two thieves: the past and the future."

3. About twenty-two years ago, a routine physical revealed a lesion on my lung. At the time, I smoked one to two packs of cigarettes a day. The doctor told me (with a marvelous bedside manner), "You stop or you die." Well, as any ex-smoker knows, quitting was not a pleasant experience. Very quickly, I found that there was one thought I had to avoid at all costs. If I found myself starting to think about a whole lifetime without cigarettes, I quickly got off that subject, because I instinctively knew that particular thought would defeat my efforts to quit. I made the focus more immediate: "Well, I can get through this next minute without a ciggie." One minute I could handle… a lifetime I couldn't.

4. A spiritual directee gave me a wonderful book. *Simple Abundance* by Sarah Ban Breathnach is a book that contains reflections for each day of the year. While written primarily for women, I find it enormously nourishing to my spirit. The reflection for July 4th really grabbed me. Here's part of what she said: *Personal happiness hinges on a practicality: if your reality lives up to your expectations, you're happy. If it doesn't, you're depressed…. Many of us mistakenly think that lowering our expectations means we must surrender our dreams. Absolutely not. Dreams and expectations are two very different things. Dreams call for a leap of faith, trusting that the Spirit is holding the net, so that you can continue in the re-creation of the world with your energy, soul gifts, and vision. Expectations are the emotional investment in a particular outcome: what needs to happen to make that dream come true. The passionate pursuit of dreams sets your soul soaring; expectations that measure the dream's success tie stones around your soul. I don't think we should just lower our expectations; I believe if we truly want to live a joyous and adventurous life, we should relinquish the expectations.*

Now I suspect that I could stop this newsletter right here. Chances are pretty good that you saw yourself in at least one of those stories. I've been through all these things... I know you have too. It's part and parcel of what it means to be a human being. I can't begin to count how often I've gotten upset because things didn't work out the way I wanted them to, or because I had to change my plans. I get angry, I pout, I take it out on a co-worker or a fellow CSC or the cat, and I get very very silent. Anyone who's struggled with an addiction knows exactly what I was thinking, as do those of you who have lost someone dear to you through divorce or death. Some things from my past haunt me, and God alone knows what else may be buried so deep I don't see it, but which nevertheless affects my present actions. And the future: sure I worry about it just as you do. And Ms. Breathnacht was right on target. When my expectations aren't met, do I throw a hissy fit!

Life can often be brutal in the suffering it inflicts on us. Illness, death, personal or family crises, life transitions, natural disasters -- all these tear us apart inside and stretch our emotional and physical resources to the limit. But it's been my experience that most of us can cope with these major crises. We expect them to happen, they're a part of life, and we know that we can draw on God's help, our inner resources, and the help of family and friends to get through it all. Once the initial shock and grief are past, we can consciously and deliberately make our choices. We can choose to slowly and gradually pick up the pieces and continue our life's journey, or we can choose to sit still and stagnate into bitterness and blaming and finger-pointing because life didn't work out the way we had planned it.

I really believe that it's the mental choices we make that cause by far and away the most suffering in our lives ... and by extension in the lives of others. We think too much! We don't trust God or other people or ourselves. We're afraid of anything or anyone that threatens to upset our daily, yearly, or lifetime plans. Our minds go round and round and round, making Plan A, Plan B, Plan C, and we end up never using any of them! We do to the doctor and cannot help but think about all the bad things that she or he could find. The kids (or parents) leave on a trip, and we worry. A few snowflakes fall and I break into a cold sweat: "Will I be able to get home"? Chris doesn't get into Notre Dame (or the football team loses a few games) and the world comes to an end. Surgery doesn't bother me, but the recovery period petrifies me. You hear a rumor that a person you loathe is going to become the new supervisor, and you start to think about working elsewhere. Your child doesn't bring home straight A's, so you either blame yourself for being a lousy parent or make an appointment to see if he or she has a learning disability. And on and on it goes.

So how do we avoid all this self-inflicted suffering? I can only share with you two ways that I've tried to help myself.

First, I have to catch myself when I become aware that I'm thinking and reacting in these destructive ways. Once I catch myself, I bring myself back to the present moment. It's just a matter of awareness, of observing our minds and the pattern of our thoughts. It takes an awful lot of practice to develop this awareness, but once you have it, it makes a profound difference in your life. It will not reduce all the self-inflicted suffering, but it certainly helps to control it and prevent it from taking over your life.

Second, let the destructive thought patterns trigger some prayer... I find these to be a marvelous invitation to prayer and to the subsequent healing that will come. This prayer has three parts. First, you call upon God. Second, you name what you're feeling and why. Third, you beg for God's help.

So let's say I'm upset at "Sam," because he put a whoopee cushion under my chair and I ushered a benefactor into the office and sat down (I know this is a ridiculous example, but face it, folks ... a lot of the things we get upset about *are* ridiculous!) Now I can let my mind run its normal course and get angry and plot revenge and all those others things that we do when we're upset. Or I can simply use it as a moment for prayer: "Beloved, I'm angry at Sam because he embarrassed me. Help me, please." If I have to repeat this little prayer 500 times in 5 minutes, at least I'm doing something that is life-giving, and not inflicting suffering on myself or on the other person.

Jesus came to free us from this kind of self-inflicted suffering. Look at the lilies of the field, he said, and the birds of the air. Your heavenly father takes care of them, and he will take care of you, so stop worrying. "Enough then, of worrying about tomorrow. Let tomorrow take care of itself" (Mt 7.26). Jesus promised to be with us. But that promise only holds for the present moment... not for future moments. Right here and now at 9:35 AM, there isn't anything that you and God can't handle together. You don't yet have grace for 9:36 AM, because it's not here yet, and when it gets here, it may be entirely different than you anticipated.

So stay in the present as much as you can. If you live in the future, you are there alone. No one else – including God – is with you. You're left to your own resources, you know they're inadequate, and so there is crippling fear. If you live in the past, with all of its heavy burdens, you will be there alone. No one will be around to help you carry the burden, not even God, so there is despair and depression. Only in the present will you find God, yourself, helping hands, and peace and strength.

Chapter Twelve

"RESURRECTION IS FOR US A DAILY EVENT"

As I prepared to write the 2007 Easter newsletter for the members of Holy Cross Association, I asked our Director of Development, Jim Kramer, if he had any ideas. Almost immediately he mentioned the above excerpt from the *Constitutions of Holy Cross* as a personal favorite. I liked his suggestion... and it was an obvious choice given the approaching feast.

Let me just add a footnote here. You may not be familiar with the term "Constitutions" as it applies to religious life. The Constitutions – and in some religious communities, the Rule – describe the way we wish to live our life as a religious community. Holy Cross's Constitutions cover such things as our mission, our call by God, the vows, authority, prayer, community life, etc. They are an ideal which is held out before us. Sometimes we succeed in living it well, sometimes not.

Now as I reflect on the resurrection, there is one way in which it is truly a daily event. That's when we wake up from sleep. It's truly a matter of faith when we lie down to go to sleep, since we have no guarantee we'll wake up. Sleep is literally unconsciousness. As one scientist put it, sleep comes when *"the tuberoinfundibular region projects rostrally to the intralaminar nuclei of the thalamus and to the cerebral cortex."* Wowser... that's good stuff to know, eh?!

In REM sleep, which is the deepest kind of sleep, your body is literally paralyzed. Breathing slows down, as does heart rate. Body temperature drops. Awareness of external stimuli is greatly reduced.

A close relative to sleep is the unconsciousness that comes from anesthesia. I had that experience with a recent knee surgery. At 3:30 PM, the nurse gave me a shot and said, "This will help you relax." I remember going through the set of doors leading to the operating rooms, and then next thing I knew it was 5:30 PM.

It takes a lot of faith to submit to sleep or to general anesthesia. It literally is a resurrection when we waken. In regard to sleep, there is presented to us an entirely new day; in anesthesia, something is different and new with our bodies. This new awakening brings challenges and graces that were not present to us before.

Ah, those daily challenges and graces. Ya gotta love 'em. That's where the daily event of resurrection takes place, not once, not twice, but many times a day.

It's important to note that resurrection is not something we do on our own. Jesus did not do his own resurrection. It was the work of the Father. Resurrection is a gift of God. It is the fruit of our response to a grace from God. God gives us the grace to meet a particular challenge. If we say yes to that grace, there is resurrection to a new life, however miniscule that new life might seem to you. If we say no, then life continues as before, and we're left with the realization that we missed out on a chance for growth.

Furthermore, the daily resurrections not only benefit our personal growth, they also affect the growth of other people. Jesus' resurrection was not for him alone. It was for us also. Absent the resurrection of Jesus, we'd have no reason to love, no reason to hope, no reason to have faith.

What are some examples of these daily resurrections?

• Getting an e-mail, letter, or phone call from a friend just at a time when you really need the boost.

• Ignoring something that needs to be done because "it's not my job," then changing your mind and doing it.

• Going to an event you really don't want to attend, and something unexpectedly good happens.

• Having a "Wow"! experience that fills your being with deep gratitude or awe.

• Having days, or weeks, or months of discernment or searching or struggle coming to fulfillment with a job offer, an insight, an approval, etc.

• Realizing that you need to keep silent instead of saying "I told you so"!

- A sudden feeling within that you need to pray.
- Recuperating from an illness, or from rehab, and suddenly realizing that you *do* feel better.
- Deciding to go for counseling in an attempt to resolve personal or relational issues.
- Deciding to leave the past to God's mercy, and the future to God's discretion. Remember that living in the past and future can kill present joy. The present moment is the only time in which God can bring forth new life.
- You can bring new life to someone by really seeing them, calling them by name, acknowledging their presence in your life at this moment. Adding this small portion of joy to that person's life brings him or her new life.
- Resurrection comes when you practice gratitude, and thereby slay the forces of boredom, taking-for-granted, and despair.
- Resurrection comes when you have confidence that ALL things work together for the good of those who love God. Therefore, God can make something good happen from your selfishness, anger, greed, hatred, etc.
- Laughter, play, spontaneous silliness – these are resurrection moments.
- Welcoming change into your life signals your openness to all the new possibilities that this change will bring.

I can go on and on. Perhaps you can add some examples of your own. If you look at all the examples, you can see what I said on the previous page: resurrection affects not just my life, but the lives of others.

What I always find interesting about the resurrection moments is how unexpected they can be. They always seem to catch me by surprise. The pace of resurrection is interesting too. Sometimes it comes suddenly, sometimes it comes slowly, like an unfolding plant.

It's also important to remember that the Resurrection of Jesus brought about a new world too. In this day and age, we might have a hard time seeing this. But there are unmistakable signs that something life-giving is going on.

- A deepening awareness of the necessity to do something about global climate change.

• A deeper questioning of war and capital punishment.

• The disillusionment with political partisanship, and a greater desire to work for the common good.

• The growth of the European Union.

• The tremendous increase in vocations to the priesthood and religious life in Africa and Asia.

• Moderate leaders of the world's religions trying to mitigate extremist excesses, and voters rejecting extremist candidates.

• The willingness of laity to speak up and confront religious leadership.

• The number of young people devoting time to community service.

• The response of ordinary people to disaster victims.

• A deep hunger for spiritual meaning which is arising throughout the world.

Again, I'm sure there are many more examples, but space is running short.

We don't always want to rise. All too often we're comfortable with our tried and true ways of living, thinking, feeling. Fear of change overcomes desire for life. Fear of others stifles our desire not to be lonely. The desire to live more fully and humanly gets smothered by TV, stress, creature comforts, addiction, resentment, bitterness, blaming others.

We practice the daily event of resurrection by gratefully seeing beauty all around us in the world and the world's peoples; when we swallow our pride; when we ask forgiveness or forgive someone who has hurt us. We practice resurrection when we start over with living after a loss; when we take the risk of loving deeply and passionately. Resurrection comes when we say NO to the forces of evil and suffering in our world, and actually do something that says YES to the forces of life.

Above all, we know we are in the joyful, exultant throes of daily resurrection when we find ourselves – with the Spirit's help – growing our souls and living a larger life.

What more could we want?

Chapter Thirteen

REFLECTIONS ON LEISURE

I'm writing this while on retreat. About an hour ago, I was walking along the beach (of Lake Erie), enjoying the wind and waves and looking for odd and unusual stones. Suddenly I found a particularly misshapen piece of driftwood, and immediately saw in my mind's eye how I could use it in a vase I have. At least I think it's a vase! It's one of those pottery creations where I suspect the potter made something just for the heck of making it. I tried some Lucky Bamboo, but the bamboo shoots were too "stumpy." Most recently I had a small peace lily plant in it. That was very close to being right for the vase, but the poor thing died. It did tell me that whatever goes into the vase has to be vertical, kinda tall-ish, and have gentle curves. So when I saw that piece of skinny driftwood, I knew it would fit, and so I started to look for other pieces. They will be taken home, arranged, and put in my prayer corner. The vase will remind me of the earth; the wood will be like my upraised arms to God, dancing in gentle praise.

Now you may be thinking; "What does all this have to do with leisure"? I guess it all depends on how you define leisure. Some would say I was simply taking a break from work so as to recharge my emotional and physical batteries for another week of work. Some would say, "Well, you're doing this newsletter while on retreat, so that's work, not leisure." Others would say that I was not being productive. Walking along the beach and collecting driftwood is nice, but it's not really ministry. Another school of thought holds that leisure is the time when we do all the things we can't do at work, while others hold that having time for leisure means you're too rich, or you're sponging off taxpayers, or that you don't have enough to keep you occupied (i.e., there's a flaw in your character somewhere).

As I read letters from benefactors, as I look at my own family and friends, as I walk with spiritual directees, when I hear seminarians tell me how they wish they could make some time for hobbies, I am constantly astounded at how busy everyone is. Working long hours, coming home to the demands of family and household upkeep, social and familial obligations, parish and civic activities, it all adds up. Twenty-four hours a day, seven days a week, it is go-go-go, do this do that, be here be there, pick up this drop off that, meet this deadline, do my exercises, take the dog for a walk, cut the grass, weed the garden, get dinner ready, feed the family and then put it all out again when Pat comes home from sports practice, get my prayer time in, call my folks. Gets you all worn out just reading it, doesn't it?

Some days it seems as though we go through life zooming by the store windows, catching glimpses of all the leisure goodies we think we cannot have. Yes, work is a necessity. But so is leisure. We cannot blame anything or anyone else for the choices we make as to how we spend our time. Those are our choices, period.

Perhaps you think I'm crazy for talking this way, that I don't have any sense of what it's like to work for a living, raise a family, maintain a home. As a religious, I know I have opportunities not available to most folks. I know a week-long retreat or a month-long sabbatical is not possible for most of you. Leaving the office at 2:30 PM to do woodworking would be wonderful leisure, but again, it's not an option for many of you. It's nice to have two or three hours of prayer time each day, whereas you're lucky to have 15 minutes. In fact, oftentimes I feel religious life is not "real" life, and if I really want to learn to trust God for the daily necessities of life, then I have to live the same kind of life you do. So that's why I try to use my leisure not just for my own wellness and wholeness, but for yours as well. I minister to myself so that I can better minister to you.

So yes, you have every justification to say to me, "Get real, Fr. Herb… where do you expect me to fit leisure in"? But my response would be to point out that this is the wrong question. The right way to be thinking about this is wondering where God expects you to fit it in, for leisure is extremely important from God's point of view. Leisure is not just "taking time off," it is not a vacation. Leisure is a gift of God to us, which we can freely accept or reject. This acceptance or rejection will have a direct impact on our growth as human beings.

The Church has never really developed a good theology of leisure. Much has been written on the theology of work, but very little on leisure. That's sad, for leisure is part and parcel of life with God. It's something that God values deeply. Thomas Aquinas said that we cannot live without pleasure and beauty. He's not saying we're made for pleasure (that's too hedonistic). He is saying we need leisure to be fulfilled human beings because joy and delight are gifts of the Holy Spirit. Both beauty and pleasure have their source in God. God wants us to seek those gifts as much as he wants us to use our talents and abilities. It is not God who makes us feel guilty when we're not being "productive." It's our society, our cultural values, the expectations we've bought into.

We're all familiar with how God rested on the seventh day. But there are many other places where leisure is mentioned. God walked with Adam and Eve in the cool of the evening. God spent time conversing with his friends. In the *Book of Wisdom*, Wisdom plays day by day before the Lord. David loved to sing and dance. The *Song of Songs* is a tremendous tribute to marital leisure. Many psalms speak of playing, relaxing, sitting by a stream, stargazing. The prophets often speak of how Jerusalem will become so safe that all can play in the streets like children.

Jesus liked leisure. He would often take time alone. He loved looking at lilies and birds and discovering how God spoke through them. He thoroughly enjoyed parties… and was known to provide the drinks! He jumped all over those who tried to hem in Sabbath activity by shoulds, oughts, and musts. Jesus affirmed Mary's desire to sit at his feet and quietly converse with him.

Paul's first letter to Timothy has some more good words on leisure (see Chapter 4 of that letter). God richly supplies us with things to enjoy. Food and marriage are meant to be enjoyed. They provide moments of leisure. It is wrong to say that the enjoyment of these blessings is sinful.

Before going further, let me affirm that work is good. There is plenty of Biblical affirmation of work, and tons of Church teaching about the value of work for human life and creativity. Work is necessary for what is *essential* in life. You do need food on the table, clothing, a roof over your head. You need insurance protection from the accidents of life. Your children need a good education. You need transportation, medical care, and you also need to set aside something for retirement. In work, you exercise stewardship for your world. In leisure, you exercise stewardship of yourself.

The key word is "essential." Look around you. How much of what you have – of what you do – is really *essential* to your life? I could give some examples, but hesitate to do so, because if I get started I'll become critical and judgmental. Everything you deem "essential" exacts a price measured in time, energy, money, and anxiety. The more "essentials" you have, the less time, energy, and treasure you will have for leisure.

Leisure is crucial to full human growth. Through leisure we *develop* our talents, *deepen* our relationships, *learn* to appreciate our world and all its creatures. We *discover* how God is present as gift in our lives. It is *refreshment* for our bodies and minds. It is a time to *worship* God and *celebrate* his greatness and goodness. Leisure develops our *awareness* of times and peoples and seasons and history. It is a time for *play*, whether it be on a golf course, wrassling with the kids or the dog, whatever. Leisure time enables us to pause for *reflection and prayer*, to *discern* our place in the world, to *see* how God is walking with us, to *hear* the love in his voice and the voices of others, to *taste* good wines and good foods, to *touch* the smooth skin of the beloved or the rough bark of an old maple tree.

Note all the italicized words. Those are the "leisure words," so-to-speak. For most of us, our work does not include time to engage in those activities. Even if you want to develop new skills for work, for example, you often must do it on your own time, not company time.

Time is, of course, the big thing when it comes to leisure, followed closely by money. Yet these do not have to constrain you. You can be ingenious and think "outside the box." Two years ago, I took a woodworking class on "Design and Craftsmanship." In the first class, the instructor had us draw a square made up of nine dots -- three parallel lines, three dots in each line. He told us to connect all the dots using only four straight lines, without lifting pencil from paper, without re-crossing a line. None of us could do it, but then on the blackboard he connected the dots by making sweeping straight lines way outside the box. We assumed we had to stay within the circumscribed area. So too with leisure. Our fears and uncertainties, what others say or think – these limit options, strangle creativity, and restrict our vision of what is possible.

If you have the opportunity to make time in your day for some leisure, then go for it. It's going to take discipline. Generally speaking, if we have extra time in our day, we're going to use it not for a leisure activity, but to do some work. In my experience, most folks will first of all have to do some prioritizing. What is really essential for my life? Unless you do that, you're wasting your time. Even with prioritizing, however, time and money can still be precious.

But tell me: how long does it take to touch the bark of a tree, to hear a blackbird sing? Is it worth it to get up fifteen minutes early to watch the sunrise? Or, to sit in the backyard for a few moments as the day wanes? A contemplative walk around the block will reveal a whole world to you. Ditto for watching the Discovery or History Channels as opposed to some of those reality shows. Cutting the grass yourself instead of hiring it out, eating lunch outside with a friend instead of sitting at your desk surfing the Web, eating your meal with a good biography instead of with the TV on, taking a long hot bath instead of a quick shower, taking off your watch when you go to Sunday Mass as a sign that you're on God's time now, reading the Sunday paper in bed, taking that art course you've always wanted to take—the list goes on and on.

Leisure can last a day, a moment, an hour, a week. But the important thing to remember, folks, is this. In leisure, you really learn a different dimension of what it is to love God, self, and neighbor!

Chapter Fourteen

WHAT IS "SOCIAL JUSTICE"?

On Sunday of this past Labor Day weekend, I went to a friend's house for a picnic. Joe, Mary's husband, had to go to the 5:00 PM Mass, and when he came back nothing seemed amiss. After dinner, sitting around a fire in the backyard, Joe asked me with some exasperation, "Would you tell me what 'social justice' means"? It turns out that the homily at Mass dealt with that topic, but the homilist never really explained what it was. He basically said that everyone should practice social justice.

Like politics, that topic can ruin a delightful evening! So I was kinda vague in my answer: "It can range all the way from 'Do unto others' to being a voice for those who have no voice." I said something else, but can't remember what it was; I was just grateful that the topic quickly changed.

For the rest of that weekend and quite a few times since then, I've thought of Joe's question. Really, what *is* social justice? It *does* seem as though all those talking about it expect you to know what they're talking about!

For sure, it's a very charged topic. On the one hand, official Church teaching is quite clear that social justice is as important to the life of a Christian as prayer and sacrament. On the other hand, it's one of those topics we wish would go away... but it never does.

Throughout my years of pastoral ministry, as well as throughout my years of living with myself, it's become increasingly clear to me that those who are most threatened by any kind of social justice talk are invariably male and usually white – and that's to be expected. We males (including the one who's writing this) are, after all, the ones who control most of the access to power, wealth, opportunity, etc. Our red flags go up whenever we feel threatened in those areas, and the words, "social justice," are a guaranteed flag waver! I hate them too!

I feel threatened when I hear the words "social justice" for several reasons. First and foremost, as mentioned above, there's a sense of "my turf" being threatened. Second, they make me feel guilty about my comfortable lifestyle. Then I get to thinking that I'm not doing the works of social justice unless I'm marching in anti-abortion protests, or spending hours down at the homeless center, or joining in the campaign against land mines. I'm really a quiet, shy person, and "social justice" has connotations of being in the public eye, on the front lines… and that's not me. So again, I feel threatened, and want to rebel.

My big problem with many people who speak of social justice is the guilt trip they lay upon the rest of us. Admittedly, some of that guilt is deserved. I do tend to look out for #1 and put my own wants before others' needs. But I've often felt that the best thing a social justice activist could do is to follow the example of Jesus: to go quietly, with determination and passion, about his or her work, and then when asked about their work, to explain and challenge. Nothing is accomplished by guilt trips or by making people feel threatened. That is not the way of Jesus. But having said this, I must ask myself: is this my way of wishing that social justice speakers would go away?

Despite all the fears, I'm coming to see that social justice doesn't have to be a threat to anyone. It's something that most of us already participate in according to our gifts and talents.

So what is "social justice"? Its most basic expression is found in the Bible. In the Old Testament, the prophets constantly call the people to care for widows, orphans, and strangers in the land. In the New Testament, a perfect description is found in the judgment scene of Matthew's Gospel (Chapter 25): "I was hungry, thirsty, sick, naked, in prison… and you took care of me."

In the *Catechism of the Catholic Church* (§1928-1933), we read that "respect for the human person entails respect for the rights that flow from his or her dignity as a creature. These rights are prior to society and must be recognized by it." The article goes on to say that we have a duty to make ourselves neighbor to others, and to actively serve them, with emphasis on the disadvantaged and those who think and act differently than ourselves.

On a more personal level, the definition I've been working with is this: social justice is wanting others to have what I have, and taking steps to insure that they have the opportunity to obtain these gifts of God (because really, everything I have is gift of God). This includes values such as food, clothing, housing, safe and clean neighborhoods, economic security, employment, recreation, medical security, non-discrimination, education, and religious expression. It is not enough to just *want* these things for others; I have to *take active steps* to help others receive these gifts.

Now, it is vitally important to realize that God does not ask us to do things that would do violence to our selves. The works we are called to do are totally compatible with our strengths, personalities, gifts, and also our weaknesses. Take me, for example. Because of my hearing I cannot man a phone bank. I do however have the gift of being able to write, be it newsletters, letters to Congress, or checks… and by using this gift I try to help others find for themselves the gifts I have received from God. Daily solitude also lends itself to extended prayer for the needs of the world.

The works of social justice begin first of all with you as an individual. Jesus did, after all, say, "Love your neighbor *as yourself*." What is it that you are hungry for? What are the things which imprison you? Where do you feel naked and vulnerable? My friend (Joe's wife), for example, was hungry for more quiet time and less stress, so she has finally learned to delegate and prioritize. This is doing justice to herself; it is meeting a legitimate need she has. I am more and more frequently saying "No" to attending large parties or gatherings. With my hearing handicap, those things are no fun for me at all. They are 100% pure unremitting work. Another person I know has started assertively to challenge other people when they put her down. A benefactor told me of her daughter who took a year off from her work as a lawyer to spend it with her growing children. If someone in your parish or at work asks you to do one more thing or serve on one more committee, the most just thing you can do sometimes is to say "No." You practice social justice if you are a single Mom nailing the children's father for non-support, and you also practice justice to yourself if you refuse to be emotionally, verbally, or physically battered by another person. Doing justice to yourself enables you to be a servant of justice to others.

As I said above, the works of justice are intricately connected with your personality, your gifts, your life situation. If you are chronically ill and homebound, you can't be on the front lines. So... maybe you can write letters to government or church officials, and for sure you can pray. Perhaps you can also send gifts to charitable organizations who can then feed the hungry, clothe the naked, care for the sick, etc. Parents of an active growing family are intimately involved with the work of justice, because they face sickness and hunger and thirst every day in the demands of their children, and many are also having to care for aging parents.

You and I engage in social justice when we bite our tongues and refrain from gossip or criticism, because we know that other people often have reasons for what they say or do, and we do not know what those reasons are. Joe Smith prides himself on a pretty lawn, and so he refuses to throw his ciggie butts out the window to litter someone else's lawn. Pat's nephew has told the family he is gay, and Pat is re-examining her stereotypes because she knows that her nephew has much integrity and goodness. Leslie knows that Tom is suffering from alcoholism, and so she will practice tough love, yet also give Tom another chance to rebuild a shattered life. Chris refuses to laugh at racist jokes, because refusal to laugh tells others that such behavior and the attitudes which underlie them are unacceptable. Father O'Brien allowed altar girls and allowed women to have their feet washed on Holy Thursday (even though both actions were then against Church law) because he took seriously Paul's statement that "in Christ, there is no male or female... but all are one."

Simply, social justice is being a warm, gentle, compassionate, human being, one who wants for others what he or she has received from God. Such a person has developed, through prayer and reflection, an attitude of surrender to God, of dependence on God for all good things of life. Prayer also helps us to see with God's eyes, and the point will come when we can no longer remain blind or silent! Injustice invariably arises because we humans have a deep desire to control our destiny and make sure things turn out the way we want them to. Through prayer, the attitude of "I worked for this and you can't have it" eventually gives way to the attitude of Jesus: "The gift you have received, give as a gift."

The circumstances of everyday life at home and at work and in the parish and neighborhood give us ample opportunity to practice social justice. We don't have to do anything extraordinary. I guarantee you that if God wants you to do something above and beyond your ordinary everyday life, you'll know. If you think this is too good to be true, if you think that your quiet everyday attempts to act justly aren't really worth too much, just remember what Jesus was able to do with the little boy's gift of five loaves and two fish!

And finally, we'll always need homilies on social justice. This is just God's way of making sure that we're being honest with ourselves! It's a good reality check!

Chapter Fifteen

"BE FAITHFUL IN
THE LITTLE THINGS"

Several years ago, while living alone out at the Solitude of the Savior, I had one of those periods when doubts started creeping in. "Is this solitary life worth it? Does anyone care? Is anyone thinking of me now"? It was late Fall, days were getting shorter and colder. I think you know how it goes. It's a very common human experience. I was just having a "pity party."

One afternoon in late Fall, work at the office was light. So I decided to leave early and head for home to do some yard work around the house. At one point, I carried some pots of flowers over to the compost pile, emptied them, and then started walking to the garage, carrying these four empty plastic pots. Suddenly right out of nowhere, came the insight that my carrying those four pots was absolutely crucial to the salvation of the world. I knew beyond doubt that this is what God needed me to be doing at that moment, and my doing it was somehow, someway helping God's kingdom come. Don't ask me how it was helping. I only knew that it was. God was using that simple labor to bring about some good in our broken world.

I share my own experience to highlight something that we need to hear time and time again: everything we do – everything – has an effect in our world. I don't know how familiar you are with something called "chaos theory," but this scientific theory has been receiving a lot of attention not only from scientists, but from theologians as well. At first it started out with meteorology ("The flapping of a butterfly's wings in Mexico is one of the contributing causes to a typhoon in Australia.") But now it has spread to touch on nearly every aspect of human life.

Put simply, chaos theory has nothing to do with what we normally understand as "chaos" (i.e., state of confusion, lacking order, etc.). There are two main components of chaos theory: (1) systems – no matter how complex they may be – rely upon an underlying order, and (2) very simple or small systems and events can cause very complex behaviors or events.

Edward Lorenz is generally credited as the first experimenter in the area of chaos theory in the early 1960's. Lorenz, a meteorologist, was running computerized equations to model and predict weather conditions. He ran a particular sequence, and then decided to replicate it. Lorenz re-entered the number from his printout and left it to run. To his enormous surprise, the results of the second run were radically different from his first outcome. What happened? Well, for the second run, Lorenz entered a rounded figure of .506 instead of the precise number, .506127. According to all scientific expectations at that time, the results of the second run should have differed only very slightly from the original trial. Because the two figures were considered to be almost the same, the results should have likewise been similar. But they weren't, and repeated experimentation caused Lorenz to conclude that the slightest difference in initial conditions – beyond human ability to measure – made prediction of past or future outcomes impossible. This was an idea that violated the basic conventions of physics.

Maybe I can make this a bit more real for you. If you've ever been in an auto accident, you've no doubt wondered, "What if I had left a minute earlier... or even ten seconds later"? Who knows how things would have been different? This is chaos theory at work.

So there perhaps are many who might pooh-pooh my insight about the four flower pots. Maybe they're right. Who knows? All I can say is that I am certain of what I experienced, and I am equally certain that it applies to your life also.

Look at it this way. How much of your day is made up of those minute little common ordinary actions that you would never give a second thought to? Putting dishes in the dishwasher, signing letters, saying a cheery good morning to a co-worker, dusting and vacuuming, pushing the grocery cart, chauffeuring kids or elderly parents, taking a shower or bath, stuffing envelopes, feeding the pet and taking out the garbage. The list goes on and on. Most of our day is composed of these kinds of little things. Most of our lifetime is spent in these little things that go absolutely unnoticed by anyone else (unless of course you screw up somehow! Then everyone seems to notice!).

But if you look at chaos theory, those little actions do have an effect. Those little actions are of great significance. Even Jesus applied the principle when he spoke about giving a cup of cold water to a disciple: "Your reward in heaven will be great." Mathematically speaking (look at the number Lorenz used), maybe all your action was worth was .000127. But that infinitesimal number made a huge difference in the outcome. And if it makes a difference mathematically, can you imagine what a difference it will make in the hands of God!

So many folks wonder if they really are making a difference in the world. Sure, they can see it perhaps in their family, their parish and workplace and neighborhood. But outside those places? "Ah, I can't do too much. My contribution won't make a difference. My letter to my Congressman won't matter, and neither will my vote... My prayers aren't worth that much." It gets particularly hard for those who are elderly or disabled in some way. Our society places a great premium on being able to produce and work; anyone who can't is somehow seen as second-class, a freeloader, a sponge. How utterly false that is! *Everything* you do, no matter how small, affects our world for better or worse. As many of the saints have said, do the little things and do them well. Know beyond doubt that you **are** having an effect on our world. God is using every single one of your deeds and prayers to bring his Kingdom to completion.

Mr. Butterfly ... Madam Butterfly ... move your legs, flap your jaw, hold out your arms, carry or set down something or someone ... whatever it is that you do, do it with the full knowledge that God is joyfully and happily using your little efforts to do great things for his people.

Chapter Sixteen

SPIRITUALITY AND THE WORKPLACE

We have been brought up to believe that spirituality is something that is confined to special times of day in special places such as a church or a prayer room or retreat house. But how much of our life is actually spent in those places? Heck, most people can't even find a special *time* during the day, let alone a special place! If someone were to tell you that your workplace can be a source of personal spiritual growth, you'd look at that individual with skepticism. The workplace (whether it's an office building or at home) is noisy, crowded, demanding, stressful, awash in rivalry and gossip, oftentimes cutthroat. How can it be a source of growth?

Remember, first of all, that even though we think we're confined to special times and certain places, God isn't. Look at Scripture. Moses was tending sheep when he saw the burning bush. The prophet Amos was pruning his trees. Ruth was gleaning grain when she met Boaz. Peter and Andrew were mending fishing nets. Mary was probably busy with household chores when Gabriel visited her. God can touch our lives, and we can speak to God no matter where we're at, what we're doing, what time of day it is, who we're with. God is not absent from us when we're working, nor do we need to be absent from God.

Before continuing, maybe it would help if I defined "spirituality" to make sure we're on the same wavelength. I define spirituality as *being aware of God's presence in your life and responding to that presence with love for God, other people, yourself, and the world.* This is not an awareness that occupies you every second of every hour of the day. That's humanly impossible. It's like a background noise if you will -- always there, but sometimes it breaks into awareness, and your response is going to be some act of love. Spirituality is not limited to praying or to saying prayers. There are plenty of times when I've been praying and have not been at all aware of God's presence! With that in mind, what are some ways you can deepen your spirituality while laboring at work or at home?

First, God is present in your work, and your work can be a way of responding to God in love. Your job is God's gift to you, as are the abilities you possess (physical, mental, and emotional) to do the job. So just as God walked with Adam and Eve in the Garden, so too God walks with you as you move through your various tasks. Just occasionally being aware of this fact can do wonders for your growth in holiness. Sometimes you can do it on your own. You can think of God as naturally as you think of your child or spouse or friend. But most of the time we need reminders because the task occupies so much of our energy and attention.

It helps to have something on the desk or wall that you can look at to remind you of God's presence. Many folks have photos of family or pets. Well, why not something to remind you of God? For example, on my desk I have a little marble sculpture of a young shepherd carrying a sheep around his shoulders. I have for a long time now thought of myself as the 100th sheep (remember how Jesus left the ninety-nine to go in search of the one who was lost?). This is my reminder that God is with me, bearing me through the day. It's on loan to a friend right now, but I also have hanging on the wall a carving of the single word: "Whatever"! This is my reminder to keep perspective and balance, to realize that it's OK not to have answers, to remind me that most of the stuff I get all worked up about really isn't worth getting worked up over!

A little crucifix or statue, a pocket bible or scripture verse, a printed sentence, such as "Good morning. This is God! I will be handling all your problems today and will not need your help. So have a good day," a picture of a place where you experienced God in a profound way, a rock or a seashell—there are a hundred and one ways you can remind yourself of God's presence with you. One person I know takes off his wristwatch and places it next to a little picture of a broadly-smiling Jesus. This is his way of acknowledging that all time belongs to a God who takes enormous delight in him.

Your work enables you to respond to people with love (go back to the definition of spirituality above and you'll see the pattern I'm following). Admittedly that's sometimes hard to do. This past Labor Day the newscasts told of a survey where sixteen percent of those surveyed were often angry enough to strike or kill a coworker. No doubt about it, people can really be jerks! But look at Jesus with the apostles! I also look at myself, for I know there have been plenty of times when my behavior and speech have been destructive.

You can sanctify your workplace and encounter God by making an effort to acknowledge the goodness of others, to say "Thank you," to not join in gossip or pass it on to others. You can listen to others respectfully, even if their values be different than your own. Remember, the Spirit gives each person a piece of the truth!

Humor is a tremendous way to make your workplace holy and whole. The growing popularity of e-mail enables folks to pass jokes and humorous material all around the world. In the Provincial Accounting Office next door, there is a big paper shredder, and someone posted a sign next to it: "Please make two copies of everything you shred."

Above all, I can learn to live with and make allowances for mistakes and imperfections. This really brings me close to God, who lives with all my imperfections. Instead of reacting negatively when someone is less than perfect or does a less than perfect job, what an ideal opportunity to turn to God in prayer, asking for strength, patience, understanding and compassion. What a great chance to experience the Spirit's gift of wisdom, as you quietly try to discern why the other person acted as she or he did (remember, you can never make a fully informed judgment until you have the answer to one question: why?). Imperfections are a part of life. When I build a cabinet or table for someone, for example, I want it to be perfect. Yet there will always be flaws. I once read about an old master cabinetmaker who deliberately built a flaw in every piece of his work, because "only God can make a perfect object."

Awareness of God's presence in your work enables you to respond to yourself with love. Yes, you have imperfections, and your work will never be fully one-hundred percent perfect. But that's no excuse to simply shrug your shoulders and say, "Well, what else can they expect"? Just because I know there will be flaws in the china cabinet I'm making doesn't give me the excuse to get sloppy. Our work must be the best we are capable of doing *at that moment.* Keep it in perspective. That's why I italicized "at that moment." If I have a cold, then that's going to affect my work. If my parent is sick in a hospital, if my child is struggling at school, if my supervisor is having a bad hair day, these are all going to affect the quality of my work. I won't be able to put my whole heart and soul into it right then and there. I still am called to do the best I can. Maybe tomorrow it will be different. I also show love and care for myself by following the guidelines and procedures that are in place to ensure good quality, as well as taking advantage of any opportunities for professional development and increase in my skills.

As you grow in your awareness of God-with-you at work, you may find yourself wanting to make time to be with the One who loves you so much. So you go for a brief walk at lunch, or close your office door for some silence. You learn how to say "No" to requests for additional work or service. So much of the pressure and unhappiness at work comes because folks have a hard time deciding what is enough. So they take on more and more and more and become frazzled and unhappy. No wonder God feels absent! Balance is so badly needed between work, family, community, church, and personal needs. God does not want your work to be your life. Your job is not the sum total of who you are. A perfectly clean house really is of no importance to One who was born in a stable. Instead of spending hours poring over the minutiae of the Law, Jesus chose to spend his time with his people.

And finally, your work has significance for the world, whether it be making decisions that affect the well-being of hundreds or thousands of people, or practicing recycling of paper products. You may think of yourself as an anonymous cog, but that's not reality. You are needed by God right where you are. Now this does not mean you have to stay in a dead-end job. Not at all. As I said above, one of the ways you can love yourself is by taking advantage of new opportunities, because as you grow you will become more the person God calls you to be, and therefore you will be able to be even more creative in the ways you help God bring the Kingdom to its fulfillment. Ultimately, that's what it's all about. You are working hand-in-hand with God to bring creation to fulfillment. May God prosper the work of your hands, your mind, and your heart.

Chapter Seventeen

FORGIVING: WHAT IT IS AND WHAT IT IS NOT

Coach Vivian Stringer: *"We, the Rutgers University Scarlet Knights basketball team, accept – accept – Mr. Imus's apology, and we are now in the process of forgiving."*

Once the words are spoken, the damage is done. The words cannot be recalled, nor can the actions or gestures. Apologies can and must be offered; hopefully they will be accepted. But that will not be the end of it. Wounds – sometimes deep wounds – were inflicted and must heal. Trust must be restored. Respect has to be earned all over again. Coach Stringer had it exactly right: *"we are now in the process of forgiving."*

Forgiveness is a process. It takes time. Our emotions will go back and forth from wanting revenge to telling ourselves to let it go. *Real* forgiveness is not easily arrived at. Sometimes it won't come until long after the offender has died.

Perhaps it would help to make some distinctions. Forgiveness is reserved for serious betrayals and wrongs. It is different than excusing; that's reserved for less serious irritations or injuries. Excusing is willing – however grudgingly – to make allowances for human failings. Pardoning releases the wrong-doer from punishment, such as governors or Presidents will do. But the one pardoned still bears responsibility for the damage caused by his or her actions.

Forgiving is *not* the same as accepting or understanding. Forgiving is reserved for acts, which in the view of the one injured, are *not* acceptable and *not* justifiable. They affect the core of who I am as an individual. They key words here are "the one injured." Don Imus saw nothing wrong with his words, and he offered excuses. But the basketball team did not excuse his words. They're the victims. Calling those women "nappy-headed ho's" struck right at the heart of their identity as women.

Forgiveness does *not* mean you forget the injury. You can't; it's nearly impossible to forget. As healing progresses, the time between moments of remembering may lengthen considerably, but even if the wound is healed, the scar remains. Nor does forgiveness mean letting the offender off the hook. Legal action may be required. Furthermore, there is no obligation on your part to restore the offender to his or her previous position in your life. You can never make things the same way they were before the hurt was inflicted. One's trust has been shattered.

So what is forgiveness? How about this for a definition: Forgiveness is the elimination of all desire for revenge, and the elimination of personal ill will towards those who deeply wrong or betray us.

Whoa Nellie! That's hard! Now you can perhaps see why it is a long process. I can certainly look back over events in my own life, some long ago, some recent. In terms of long ago, I have forgiven the ones who hurt me. I still remember clearly what happened, but the emotional impact is long gone. I bear no animosity. However, I have also learned some lessons and applied those lessons in my life. It's somewhat like the saying, "Fool me once, shame on you … fool me twice, shame on me."

Events of recent years find me still fighting the interior battle. In quiet moments, a memory arises, and with the memory, feelings like anger, guilt, rage, enmity, shame, and resentment. I confess to being smugly delighted when bad things happen to "those people," or I wish bad things would happen. On the other hand, I know this is wrong. So when those feelings of delight or revenge arise, I simply pray, "Jesus, please heal me." The healing is taking place, but it's slow. As mentioned above, I've learned some lessons. For sure, I'm being very, very careful whom I trust. I've erected walls. And that's hard, because by nature I'm a trusting, open person. Remember: the work of forgiveness is hardest when what happened affects the core of who you are as a unique human being.

It's important to remember that forgiveness does not necessarily lead to reconciliation with the injurer. Those are two separate acts. Forgiveness is my personal responsibility; it does not depend on what the other does. I do it for the sake of my own well-being.

Reconciliation is the responsibility of the one injured and the one(s) who inflicted the injury. Sometimes both parties are injured, and both have to work towards forgiveness and reconciliation. In an ideal world, the situation would play out as recorded in the parable of the Prodigal Son. Here, there was forgiveness and reunion (notice that the father did not divide his estate a second time. The younger son wasted his share, so he takes the consequences). But our world is less than ideal. Some folks are incapable of seeing or understanding or ceasing the hurt they've inflicted. If the one who hurt you is like that, then you have to accept the fact that reconciliation will probably be impossible. You'll need to keep your distance and have firm boundaries. Again, it's for your own well-being.

Now all of this being said, is forgiving worth all the hard work? Absolutely. A couple paragraphs ago, I mentioned how the angry, vengeful feelings arise in quiet moments. I think for most people, that's true. Do you want to spend every quiet moment of your life waiting for the demons of anger and bitterness to arise? Do you want to give the offender rent-free living in your mind for the rest of your life? Do you want your prayer to be constantly asking for healing – or maybe you even avoid prayer altogether because it's a quiet moment and you know what happens then!

But it's not just quiet moments. Do you want your conversations to turn again and again to all the awful things that happened to you because so-and-so did this to you? Are you willing to endure painful backaches, headaches, ulcers or intestinal problems, or diseases like cancer, stroke, depression, or heart attacks? How about sleeplessness?

This is why both Jesus and St. Paul insisted so strongly on the need to forgive. They knew that an unforgiving heart means disruption in our relationship with God and with other people. Jesus is deeply concerned about your well-being and mine. He's concerned about how the residual bitterness and anger will affect the life he needs you to give to others. I mean, who wants to be around angry people? If you and I obsess over life's hurts, how can we be Christ-bearers to others?

I'm not diminishing the hurts. They are real. They cut deep. They must be healed by whatever means possible, from prayer through counseling. But I just feel so sorry for people who use past hurts as a cop-out for living life to the max in the here and now. It's not what God wants.

Jesus also wanted us to learn how to forgive others because then we come to more deeply appreciate how God forgives us! I've done plenty of things in my life that would deeply hurt God, were God a human being. But he is always there with forgiveness and reconciliation. Always.

As we mature in wisdom and age and grace, as we experience more and more of God's mercy and compassion, perhaps we'll come to the point where we can once again see the humanity of the person(s) who hurt us, instead of demonizing them.

Speaking of grace, how do we know when the process of forgiving is near an end? I believe two things will happen. One, our lives will not be negatively defined by the injuries we've suffered. We won't dwell on the past as though it were a curse. We may even come to see past injuries as a positive blessing. An example would be how a deep hurt drives us to counseling and we discover and tap inner resources we never knew were there.

The second thing will be our experience of a deep inner peace. This is the work of the Holy Spirit. If forgiving is the elimination of all desire for revenge or ill will towards those who hurt us, then *only* the grace of the Holy Spirit will make it possible. You cannot will it or fake it. Since grace builds on nature, it may take years for full peace of heart to arrive. A lot depends on whether or not we *want* to forgive in the first place. Not infrequently, instead of praying, "Jesus, help me to forgive," I have to be honest and pray instead, "Jesus, help me to *want* to forgive."

By the way… let's not forget our own acts of betrayal and hurtful words and behavior. Although the focus of this reflection has been on the hurts done to "me," it helps to read this while standing in the shoes of those *we've* hurt. Doing this might help us take the scary steps needed for forgiveness to become reconciliation, if indeed the latter is possible.

Chapter Eighteen

YOO-HOOOO!
WHERE ARE YOU, GOD?

Do you remember question #15 in the old Baltimore Catechism (this presumes you're at least in your 50's or maybe late 40's)? Give up? Well, that question is very simple: "Where is God"? The answer: "God is everywhere."

Carol came wandering in as I typed the above, so I asked, "Where is God"? She made her typical "hmmmm" pause, and then said rather flightily, "He's in you and me." A second later, and in a much more wistful tone of voice, she said, "... we just have to find him."

Melissa had already left for the day, so I asked her the same question the next day. She said, "He's everywhere." "Any place specific where you can really find him"? I asked. "When you're quiet," she replied.

My own answer to the question has undergone an evolution over the years. A couple of years ago, while on retreat, I felt that the best answer I could come up with was "God is all that is/All that is is God." There's two distinct thoughts there. First, God is literally in everything that exists, seen and unseen. All creation, past, present, and future, is of God and shares some aspect of God's life. If it didn't, it would simply not exist. The second way I understood this statement was that only in God will we find everything our heart desires. Teresa of Avila said it better: "God alone suffices."

That was a few years ago. Now the only thing I can say to the question of "Where is God?" is simply that "God is." That's all. God is. God just "is." Human language cannot capture the location of God. Who is God, where is God, what is God ... it's all one and the same question with only one answer: "God is."

We human beings have a deep need to "localize" God. That's been true since the dawn of humanity. Mountains, caves, valleys, bodies of water, oceans, trees, rocks, temples, the sun, moon and stars – every age of humankind has set aside sacred spaces and said, "Here you will find God." The ancients had their own perceptions of what God was like, and that perception determined where they would find God.

Now there are two very interesting things about the "Where is God"? question. First, that question assumes a belief in God's existence. We're not questioning God's existence at all. We're simply wondering where God is in our lives right now. The second interesting thing is that this question almost invariably arises when I'm hurting, when I'm having a tough time in my life, when things seem to be falling apart.

When faced with difficulties in our life, we know deep within that most of them can be surmounted only with God's help. But where do we go to find that help? Where is God? In a more innocent time, the instinctive reaction was to go to church, and there pray quietly before the Blessed Sacrament in the tabernacle. We knew that God was there in the person of Jesus. Yet where do we find an open church nowadays? Outside of liturgical times, they're locked up.

If there is no recourse to the Blessed Sacrament, then perhaps we close our eyes, or gaze heavenwards, or look "out there" in the distance, or go to the hospital chapel, or perhaps a local shrine or grotto, or a favorite place in nature. As I mentioned before, we gravitate to a place where we intuit that God is present. Even if we can't actually feel that presence, there is "something" that draws us there. We trust and hope it is God's presence.

I might add by way of footnote, that one of the reasons we have such difficulty finding God nowadays is that we, as a nation and as individuals, have quietly asked him to disappear. We've asked God to absent himself from our schools, places of business, the marketplace, our governments, our national rituals, and our sports. Our human need to locate God in a specific place has forced us to say: "You stay over there, God, and don't interfere with my life. I'll come to you when I need you. And when I do come to see you, I don't want to hear any talk about politics, economics, social justice, business values, and all that stuff." Weird, isn't it?

So that's our question: "Where are you, God"? I believe that God's answer would be very simple and direct: "I am where you are." The key to understanding this response is to realize that you are the Body of Christ. It's not just the Church that is the Body of Christ, nor just the Eucharist, but you, as a unique individual. Where you are is where God is, in your person.

If you are hospitalized, God is present in the love of each person who visits you. God is present in the skills and the care of your doctors and nurses. You are God when you try to help your roommate, or strike up a conversation with the orderly wheeling you to the operating room. You are God to others in your sense of humor, helping others to laugh at those crazy hospital robes, at the hospital food, the waking you up from a sound sleep to give you a sleeping pill.

If you are grieving the loss of a loved one, you are God grieving the loss of his beloved son or daughter. God knows what it is like to see a loved one die a horrific death. He was there in Mary, in the Beloved Disciple, in the faithful women, weeping and mourning, who felt like their world had come to an end. These are all things that you feel. God is feeling them because you are feeling them. God is there before the casket because you are there.

If you are struggling through each day because of unemployment, too many bills, too much illness, a special-needs child, care of an aging parent, being a single parent, know that God struggles with you because you are the Body of Christ, you are his son, his daughter. Just as you try to do all you can to meet your daily obligations, so God does all he can to give you your daily bread. Where is God? Right there in the middle of your effort to just get through the day in one piece. It might help to recall the words of Paul: "We are hard pressed on every side, but not crushed; perplexed, but not in despair; persecuted, but not abandoned; struck down, but not destroyed" (2 Cor 4: 8-9). These words are true. They are validated by your existence at this moment. If you were destroyed, crushed, abandoned, you would not be reading this.

We know that we'll experience problems in life. Life is brutal and unfair at times. However, if we face those difficulties, large and small alike, while knowing that God is present with us and in us and through us, we can react to them with a different perspective and with a strength that is not our own. No problem has the capacity to be insurmountable to God. He is bigger than all the problems that can hit us, and we are not left alone to deal with them.

Sometimes it really does help to change the perspective. Just by stepping to one side a tad we see things differently, and in the seeing, receive strength, wisdom, peace, encouragement – all signs of God's presence with us. I have a huge heating bill. Yes, but that means I have a home. Many don't. I have a huge pile of laundry to get done. Yes, but that means I have clothing. Many don't. I asked my teenage son to help clean house. He's doing it but he is driving me nuts with his muttering. Yes... but that means he's not on the streets. I complain about taxes. Yes, they're heavy, but it means I have a job. It's a pain to find a parking spot close to the store entrance. Yes, I have to park further away, but it means I am capable of walking and have been blessed with transportation. All my clothes are too snug, but that just means I have enough to eat. Yeah, that alarm goes off in the morning and signals me to get up and start another yucky day. But it also means I'm alive.

To find out where God is in my daily life, sometimes it helps to take a step or two to one side and look at things from a different perspective. The heating bill, the whiney teenager, the pile of laundry, everything – are they problems? Or are they signs of God's presence? God is where you are.

Look in the mirror. God is where you are. Look around you... sideways, up down, in back... look within too. God is there. The ground that supports you, the air you breathe, the water you drink, the food you eat, the laughter and joy, tears and pain, frustration and success, silence and noise, peace and chaos: God is there. Every person you encounter today, whether in person or on TV or in the print media: God is there. In every single room of your home, you will find God, as though that room were a tabernacle.

God is present to you; you are the presence of God to others. Through you, God holds a hand, gives a hug, offers an encouraging word when someone is struggling. The twinkle in your eye is God's, and so is the playfulness. Making love with your spouse, wrassling on the floor with your children, playing fetch with the pup or birdie with the cat... God is there. Calling the plumber or electrician, noticing a co-worker's sad eyes and asking if everything is OK, chauffeuring the kids to yet another soccer practice – God is there.

Where is God? *"A little while now and the world will see me no more. But you see me as one who has life, and you will have life. On that day, you will know that I am in my Father, and you in me, and I in you"* (John 14.19-20). Where you are is where God is.

P.S. A friend sent me this quotation from the Internet. I think it's a wonderful quote, especially apropos for Lent: *"Life is not a journey to the grave with the intention of arriving safely in a pretty and well preserved body, but rather to skid in broadside, thoroughly used up, totally worn out, and loudly proclaiming – WOW – What a Ride"*! (Anonymous)

Chapter Nineteen

MAKE A JOYFUL NOISE UNTO THE LORD

This is a reflection I've wanted to write for a long time! We need a good healthy dose of levity, and what better time than now, when so much is going awry in our country and world, forcing us into new and different ways of living.

I am absolutely convinced that the one sound which Satan hates most is laughter. Now I need to be specific here. Laughter that is mocking, that excludes, that takes delight in someone's infirmity or embarrassment: this is of Satan. The whole purpose of Satan's existence is to squash us, to prevent us from ever knowing the delight of being a child of God. Satan wants us to be bitter, cynical, disillusioned, weighed down by a sense of our sinfulness and inadequacy. He wants us to be judgmental of others, to help him weigh down the spirits of other people by our lack of care and compassion. So we have all these political figures, as well as celebrities, clergy, and just plain ordinary folks who are the butt of cruel and vicious humor. Yes, they mess up royally and I do not condone their actions... but still, no human being should ever be treated the way they are. Any kind of laughter that comes from these attitudes of mind and soul is not life-giving; it is definitely not a joyful noise unto the Lord.

Satan hates the laughter that comes in the midst of suffering. He hates it when people gather at the death of a loved one, start sharing their favorite memories, and pretty soon everyone is laughing. He loathes people who joke about their infirmity and illness. I remember, for example, when I entered into a bit of a depression and wasn't a pleasant person to be around. The anti-depressant medication was starting to take effect, and life seemed to be worth living again. My co-workers were beginning to be more relaxed. A big bottle of the pills arrived in the mail. I walked into the office holding the thing high, and said, "Behold, ladies, your salvation"! They knew what it was, and started salaaming to the bottle, and we were all able to laugh about it. My hearing handicap brings much delight. A couple of weeks ago I went in for a blood test. The medical technician asked me all the usual questions: name, address, social security number, etc. And then she said, "You edible"? I said, "Huh"? "You edible"? "I'm sorry. I'm missing something here. Are you asking me if I'm edible"? "No... no... your *date of birth*"! Many letters arrive in my office from folks who have chronic and painful illness, and I am humbled by their good spirits, sense of humor, and the joy they take in living life. Satan doesn't like practical jokers, the people who will do odd things to lighten up the mood in a gathering that is taking itself too seriously. He can't stand people like Bob Hope and all those who traveled with him to visit our military people overseas, serving in situations that were anything but laughable.

When I was growing up, I don't ever remember laughing in church. Being a Catholic was serious business. Our sole concern was the salvation of our souls, and there was to be constant vigilance against any occasion of sin. That was pretty darn hard, given that nearly everything seemed to be an occasion of sin! If I started laughing in church, Sister would come up behind me and knuckle my head. St. Augustine praised weeping; John Chrysostom said that Jesus never laughed. There was a sense that laughter leads one away from God because it's too worldly.

Well... does God laugh? Did Jesus laugh? My answer is "yes." How can God not laugh when he looks at the messes we humans, in all innocence and goodness, get ourselves into? Now this isn't a vicious laughter. It's the kind of laughter that I tried hard to stifle when a little 6-year-old girl told me that she committed adultery. Now that's impossible, right? Sadly, my first instinct was child abuse, so I gently tried to see what had happened. "Father, I behaved like an adult." Well, that got me wondering. I'm still thinking abuse. "OK, how did you do that"?... "I tried on my mother's bra."

Yes, God laughs! How can you doubt it when you see the zany creatures that are on the earth. Scientists say the universe is expanding. Sure it is. God can't stop playfully creating stars and universes and worlds. The

Psalms are filled with references to God's delight and joy in us. In a beautiful passage in the Old Testament, Wisdom describes how she played day by day at the feet of God, and God utterly delighted in that play.

Jesus laughs too. Do you think he sat at the wedding of Cana like a bump on a log? He had quite a good time eating with sinners and tax collectors. I think he enjoyed those times when the leadership tried to bait him, and he got them all tied up in a knot with his responses. I mean… don't *you* enjoy a little bit of one-ups-man-ship once in awhile? Or take the fishermen who had caught nothing all night. Jesus appears and tells them to cast the net on the other side of the boat. "Oh yeah sure… we're professional fishermen and you're a carpenter… yeah, like you know all about it." Did he not laugh at their bug-eyed response to the catch they made? Jesus came that we may have life abundantly; he wanted our joy to be full and his joy to be in us. Does this joy exclude laughter, celebration, or fun? I think not.

Play and fun are not incompatible with Christianity. They're an essential part of our belief. Seeking enjoyment, fun, and play is our duty as children made in the image of a joyful Creator. So if I make a conscious choice to be unhappy or to make life miserable for someone today, I am short-changing God's hopes and dreams for the world.

The Jewish people have a great word for someone who is always choosing to be unhappy or grumpy. They call such a person a *nebbish*. These folks are not tragic figures… they're just bland, enervating. They don't have enough energy for real despair, nor do they acquire wisdom from suffering. They just simply wallow in hopelessness. They're the kind of people who would say, "Don't go to the movies. If it's any good they won't let you in. If they let you in, it's a flop." Or… "Don't learn too much. The less you know about what you're missing, the better off you'll be. But probably not. You'll be wondering anyway." We all have a little bit of *nebbish* in us. But it doesn't have to become a permanent affliction.

Belly laughs are moments of grace. We are transformed. Our perspective shifts completely off our problems and the problems of the world. We are lost in our mirth, and of course, laughing is contagious. It quickly wraps others in its embrace. This is what religion is all about: transformation, embracing others, shifting perspective from death to life.

There are also physical changes which take place when we laugh. Laughter *is* the best medicine, and there is plenty of research documenting its effectiveness as an agent of healing. Laughing releases two brain chemicals. One group is called catacholemines, which reduce inflammation, and the other is called endorphins, which are the body's natural pain killers. So laughter provides almost immediate pain relief.

I recall reading somewhere about a man who was diagnosed with terminal cancer. Instead of submitting to chemo and radiation, the guy went out and bought tapes of every Three Stooges episode, tapes of the classic comedians like Bob Hope, Red Skelton, Carol Burnett, Tim Conway, Harvey Korman, as well as comedy books, and he proceeded to laugh the cancer right into remission. The movie *Patch Adams* is right on target: humor heals.

Erma Bombeck, herself a victim of cancer, wrote a book called, *I Want To Grow Up, I Want To Grow Hair, I Want To Go To Boise*. She described her experience at a camp for children who were suffering from terminal illness. The kids were never at a loss for humor. One child, without hair because of her chemo, said, "My daddy is Kojak." A teenager with throat cancer described what happened when he went to the bank and pushed a note through the teller's window. Another teen described how he went for a car ride and in the crowded back seat he had to hold his artificial leg on his shoulder. A passing motorist stared at him. He lifted his wig in mock salute.

Laughter performs a deeply religious function at times of human pain and suffering. We humans find it so hard to speak of pain, death, disfiguration, suffering. We often react with fear, confusion, embarrassment, shame – we don't know what to say. Laughter and humor give us a way to speak the unspeakable and to accept reality. Laughter is the visible outward expression of faith and hope in God. It's an acknowledgement of how clumsy we are and how much we need God and each other.

Let me return to something I mentioned early on. Laughter is not only healing and restorative, but it is also bound by some moral and ethical norms. Laughter can be used to wound and abuse people, to humiliate them in public, to deny their dignity as a child of God. The derisive laughter of the scribes and Pharisees was one of the worse pains inflicted on Jesus while he hung on the cross. Laughter at another person is a mark of cowardice. Have you ever noticed how we laugh at others when they are not present, or when they cannot defend themselves? Laughter which occurs at the expense of human dignity serves no religious, healing function whatever. It is barbaric.

Now there is a fine line here. Sometimes we can laugh at people and it is perfectly acceptable. President Ford always seemed to be bumping his head on something, and both of the Presidents Bush mangled their syntax at times. We laugh at them, but it's a laughter of companionship. We've been there, done that. *Candid Camera* was a wonderful show because we see human beings in all their good-hearted naiveté. Ditto for some of the blooper shows. Again we've been there, done that. The laughter is directed not so much at the person, but at the situation they're in. It's the delighted laughter of God as God sees the goofy knots we tie ourselves into sometimes.

Does all this mean we should laugh our way through life? No… not at all. There is a time to mourn, a time to be serious, a time to be silent. What I have been trying to say is that laughter and humor are a vital, essential part of any spirituality that seeks union with God and with other people. Laughter is the language that crosses all national and tribal boundaries. Laughter unites divergent theologies and ways of life. Too often we see humor and fun and playfulness as not professional or as indicative of an empty mind, or as a sign that someone is not serious enough about the task of living life. Laughter and humor are a sign of Easter. All heaven and earth laughed with delight when the stone rolled back from Jesus' tomb. And now we know that laughter is one of the precious freedoms which belong to us as children of God. So enjoy! And if today or in the coming week you see or hear something that delights you, enjoy to the max! It's not a sin! In fact, it may lead you directly to God.

Chapter Twenty

"THOUGH I WALK IN THE VALLEY OF DARKNESS"

Valleys get a bad press in the history of spirituality! It seems as though mountaintops are God's favorite place to contact human beings! Even the plateaus and level places of life, rocky patches and all, receive a better press than valleys. Valleys are bad... dark... evil... associated with the absence of God.

I used to buy into that scenario, but no more! God is extraordinarily present in the valleys. The dark moments of our lives are times of great intimacy with God, special periods of graced growth. It may feel like God is absent. The sadness and emptiness in your soul may be total, but in reality God is so close to you that he can't be seen! The gray days are as important to your growth as a human being and as a child of God as the days on the mountaintops.

Now let's be careful. What I'm talking about are the normal "blues": the gray, yucky days that everyone goes through now and again. During these times, you can do what you gotta do, but there's no spark of vitality. It is just a grind-em-out, muck-your-way-through time. There may be tears, anger, loneliness, a need for solitude or withdrawal, a lack of desire to talk, sadness, and feelings of "I'm no good." This state of affairs can last for a day, a week, a month; then somehow you "wake up" and find yourself OK again.

However, if your days are black, if you have a complete lack of interest in everything that's going on in your life, if you're not getting enough sleep or sleeping more than usual, if you keep wondering "What's the use"?, if you're thinking that death is better than life, get thee to your family doctor, parish priest, or spiritual director. Here we're talking about something a little more serious, namely clinical or chemical depression. It's still a valley, and God is still there with you, but it's a valley that you need help getting out of. You can usually find your own way out of the "gray" valley mentioned in the paragraph above, but this creature is different. If you don't have help or guidance, you could really get lost!

I hope you understand that distinction. It's really important. Even if the plain ole' gray days continue for a little too long, you may want to seek out some advice and help. Perhaps something is out of whack with your diet, medication, metabolism, stress levels, etc. If you're not sure what kind of valley you're in, err on the side of caution -- talk with someone!

With those cautions behind us, let's move on. God is totally present to you and is continuously loving you, and that love continues in the gray or black times of life. It may feel like God has abandoned you, or that he doesn't care, but I assure you the contrary is true. God does care, God is with you. He walks and sits with you, cries with you, listens to your stories of sorrow. He keeps vigil over you, just as you keep vigil over a loved one who is sick.

Gray, dreary days are part of nature's cycle. They are part of the human cycle also. We need those gray days in order to grow in wholeness and holiness. I would almost suspect that God builds in cycles of "the blahs," because he knows this is the only way we'll grapple with the important questions. Blah times and depressions are truly a blessing. Here I'm defining a blessing as anything that gets right to the center of your life and expands your capacity to love God, others and yourself. A blessing may not always be painless, but it will always bring growth!

One of the greatest blessings of the sad days is that it forces us to look squarely at the question: Who am I? What is the meaning of my life? We're so used to defining ourselves by what we do. The valley days force us out of the normal routine of doing things. They take away our being-in-control, to remind us who we really are -- creatures who are poor in spirit, totally dependent on our Creator for everything. We are given a chance to confront death, loneliness, change, and to let go of the illusion of self-sufficiency. Because of this letting go, we can turn toward God in expectation and trust, and experience his blessing. Remember

Jesus' promise: "Blessed are the poor in spirit, for theirs is the kingdom of heaven."

The gray days make us aware of time's passage and our aging. But the good news is that aging brings experience and wisdom. We mourn the passing of youth, but we can also rejoice in the new powers that come with growing in wisdom and age. Scattered ideals and values begin to come together, and we clearly see what it is that guides our lives. We can then affirm those values, or discard them for something newer, something that more truly reflects who we have become. Our lives begin to have substance, firmness, wholeness. I'm sure you will agree with me that your best growth as a person and as a Christian has taken place when you've passed through the fire and darkness of the valleys.

The blah days are marvelous tools for self-knowledge, which is a prerequisite for fully loving God and neighbor. Psychologically speaking, depression is anger turned inward. So when you are aware of being depressed, ask yourself: What am I angry at? Who am I angry at? Is evil really touching my life, or am I just upset because things aren't going according to my plans and desires? Depression is one of the ways that your mind and body tell you that they're tired of running away from this or that, tired of your refusal or reluctance to resolve this issue or that unfinished business from the past.

It's so exhausting to be cheerful all the time! Melancholy actually gives us time to recharge our batteries. One of the greatest mistakes we can make with people who are going through melancholy is to tell them to cheer up! They don't need that. They need the space, the solitude. They need to have their melancholy respected as a sacred time. Coldness, darkness, and emptiness are as necessary to human growth as warmth, brightness, and fullness.

The poet Ranier Maria Rilke, in his work *Letters to a Young Poet*, devotes an entire letter to the times of sadness: *"Were it possible for us to see further than our knowledge reaches,"* he says, *"perhaps we would endure our sadnesses with greater confidence than our joys. For they are moments when something new has entered into us, something unknown."* That *"something new"* is like a guest entering your house; the guest's presence transforms the house in small, subtle ways. *"So do not be frightened if a sadness rises up before you… if a restiveness passes over your hands and over all you do.*

You must believe that something [good] is happening to you, that life has not forgotten you, that it holds you in its hand; it will not let you fall."

Where is God in all this? Well, remember that new life burst forth from a tomb on Easter. You can't have the new life without the period in the tomb! Our faith assures us that the stone has forever been rolled away, and no power in heaven or earth can ever roll that stone back. No matter how black or cold the tomb of melancholy may feel, there is always a way out… always!

God is present when you pray your pain. Let your feelings shape your prayer. Cry if you want to, rage if you need to. Beat up your bed with a tennis racket. Throw out your hands in utter weariness and say: "My God, where are you"? If you can't pray, tell God that, and then go for a walk, listen to music, or get out and play with dirt! That's what I do. I get out and get my hands dirty. There's something about contact with Mother Earth that is tremendously curative.

If depression breaks us out of the familiar routine, then it stands to reason that we're not going to be able to see God responding to us in the familiar ways. So we have to look in different places; God's answers come in unexpected ways. For example, shortly after I was ordained I was in a blue funk, ready to give it all up. Prayer didn't help at all, neither did my spiritual director. I was ready to chuck it all. Then over four days, I received a number of comments about my confessional and preaching style. On the fifth day it dawned on me: this was the way God was answering my prayer! Another blue period ended when I became totally wrapped up in playing with a couple of kittens at the farm where I lived at the time. You just never know where God's gonna show up! And the beauty is that you don't lose your old ways of seeing God; you've added some new ones.

Be gentle, be patient. The worst thing you can do is rush things. The soul and heart have to work things out on their own, with a little bit of help from your intellect (for example, trying to figure out what I'm angry at) and from other people. Try not to run away from the sadness and emptiness. In other words, don't rush out and buy things, or don't rush out to movies or have the TV constantly going. Watch your eating and drinking, for these too can be ways to escape the dreariness.

I guarantee you that the payoff will be great if you can ride with the melancholy, however blue or gray or black it may be. You will have a deeper sense of who you are, you'll be less fearful, more gentle and compassionate towards others. The only thing I can't guarantee is *when* this new life will come. It's like the common cold: we know when it starts but we can't pinpoint its end. All we know is that one day we wake up and the cold's gone. See the dreary, melancholy days as the common cold of the spirit. It's no fun, but neither is it fatal!

Chapter Twenty-One

MAKING MORAL DECISIONS - WHAT'S A PERSON SUPPOSED TO DO?

In recent years, many Catholic bishops have spoken about politicians and the Eucharist. Some bishops made a policy to refuse Communion to any politician who did not actively work against abortion. One even said that Catholics who *voted* for a pro-abortion politician should refrain from receiving the Eucharist. Other bishops did not want to use the Eucharist as a weapon or a political club. There was no clear-cut unanimity.

In their pastoral letter "Faithful Citizenship – A Catholic Call to Political Responsibility" (2003), the bishops state: "*We seek to form the consciences of our people. We do not wish to instruct persons on how they should vote by endorsing or opposing candidates. We hope that voters will examine the position of candidates on the full range of issues, as well as on their personal integrity, philosophy, and performance. We are convinced that a consistent ethic of life should be the moral framework from which to address issues in the political arena.*" Note the reference to the "full range of issues" and the "consistent ethic of life." Very much the same thing was said in the 2007 Pastoral Letter just before elections, only a bit more focus was paid to abortion.

Well, of course, that raises the question of what we're supposed to do. If bishops cannot agree among themselves, then how do we ordinary Catholics react? How do we decide what's right and wrong? And it's not just morality. So many people ask, "What does God want me to do with my life? Should I go right or left, say yes or no, act or refrain from acting, speak up or stay quiet, stop or continue"? In the hearts of many there is an unspoken plea: "All I want is for someone to just tell me what to do so I can get to heaven."

Folks, we *have* been told what to do. On the most basic level there are the Ten Commandments. Over and over again in the Old Testament the prophets tell us what to do: care for the widow, the poor, the orphan, the stranger. Trust God to meet your needs; care for the land; repent of your sins and make restitution; be fair and honest in your business dealings. Do these things, say the prophets, and there will be life. Neglect them, and there will be alienation, enmity, and exile. Jesus takes it to the next level: love your enemies, do good to those who hurt you. Visit the sick and those in prison, feed the hungry and shelter the homeless. Do not judge others. Forgive those who have sinned or wandered away and make them a full part of the community again. Pray often. Love your Father with your whole mind, heart, body, and soul, and your neighbor as yourself.

That's a complete blueprint for a happy, fulfilling life. It won't protect you from life's disasters or curve balls. It won't protect you from evil people, or prevent you from making mistakes or sinning. No one is immune to those things – not even Jesus was exempt. But I am convinced from my own life experience that even in the midst of suffering and pain, this blueprint enables us to maintain a strong center or core of life which will keep us solidly connected to God, to others, to our own best qualities and instincts, and to our earth.

But what of all the large decisions that mark a human life? Using the guidelines above, sometimes the decision is obvious. It's just a matter of having the desire to do it! It's like exercise – we all know we gotta do it, but we don't *want* to do it. Some decisions require no discernment; we just need to make an act of the will, get off our physical or spiritual derrieres, and get to it!

There are, however, times when the choice isn't as clear-cut. What if all the available options seem like good ones? What if I have to make a decision that involves a total leap of faith because I can't see anything out there that will catch me after I leap? What if the Teachers of the Church say one thing, but every instinct in me says the opposite?

The first key to sincere discernment is to ask two questions of yourself: "Who am I? When I stand before God, what kind of person do I want to be"? At this present moment, you are the sum total of all the decisions you've made in this life. The world around you has also been affected by your decisions. If you have made mistakes in the past, God has forgiven you. You now have a blank slate. What choices will best help you be the person God wants you to be? If you do this exercise first, the "What do I do"? answer might become quite evident and no further discernment would be needed. All you have to do is follow through on what you discovered.

The second key is to ask the right question. The Pharisees and Sadducees constantly tried to trip up Jesus by asking him loaded questions. Ask the wrong question, you get the wrong answer. So much of discernment hinges on asking the right question, and it's so easy to ask the wrong one. That's why Ignatius of Loyola recommends that we spend some time clarifying the question before we start discerning the answer. Say you've had minor back problems for years. Doctors can't find anything wrong, no matter how many tests they run. Instead of asking "Why can't the doctors fix me," maybe it's time to ask a different question: "Is my pain indicative of some deeper problem"? The body never lies. There are times when "It's all in your head" really is an accurate diagnosis! Or you might ask: "How can I get Pat to leave me alone"? That fuels anger and resentment. A better way would be to ask yourself why Pat bugs you, or why she acts this way. Understanding brings compassion, and compassion brings change in behavior for the better.

Or say you're trying to figure out if you should take this path or that one. Might the actual question be whether you should move at all. What's the motivation for moving? Are you running toward something or just away from something? Ignore those questions and persist in trying to discern which path to take, and you probably won't feel a clear sense of call in any direction. "Try to love the questions themselves," says German poet Rainer Maria Rilke. Don't be in a hurry to get an answer.

The third key to sincere discernment is to avoid the two extremes. There are those who basically say: "It feels good, it's not hurting anyone else, so there's nothing wrong. Besides, the hierarchy are old white men who are out of touch with the modern world." There are others who insist that every pronouncement from the Vatican or the Diocesan Chancery must be obeyed without hesitation or question. Both extremes abdicate our God-given reasoning and thinking powers.

92

And by way of footnote, let me add that invariably those folks on either extreme focus on the "Big Three": sexuality, liturgy, authority. When it comes to social justice issues, there's a reversal. The absolutists say: "Social justice teachings don't count." The "anything goes" group says: "Social justice teachings must be heeded." Odd, isn't it?

A fourth key to discernment is to recognize that we human beings are a mass of conflicting feelings, emotions, backgrounds, agendas, etc. Not only that, but the particular issue we're trying to discern also has many complexities. Reality is all too often not as black and white as we would like it to be.

For this very reason you and I need some kind of objective outside help to sort things out. For Catholics, this help is found first in the Gospels and second in Tradition or Church teaching. These aids focus our attention on what really matters: will my decision be governed by love? Will it center me on Jesus? Will it build up the Church and the human community? Will it create in me a deeper spiritual maturity, and help me to be the person God has called me to be? And above all, will I be able to stand before God, look God in the eye, and be accountable for the course of action I decided to take (or not to take)? Our choices either build up or tear down our personal humanity as well as humanity in general. Note how this goes back to what I said above: the very first question has to do with the person you are becoming.

As far as consulting the teachings of the Church, do not let your sole source of information be the news media. I cannot emphasize that enough. They are looking for the controversial stuff. Every statement, encyclical, or teaching made by the Vatican or the National Conference of Bishops can be found on the Internet. There you can also find discussions of these teachings by theologians and experts. This is all part of the process of discernment.

Don't discount your life experience, either. It has an important part to play. For example, if there have been instances of muscular dystrophy or Huntington's Disease in your family, do you want to have a child? If not, then that might mean using some form of contraception, or foregoing sexual relations altogether. But at the same time remember that most human beings prefer a life experience that is peaceful and risk-free, i.e., somewhat selfish.

True discernment is always open to learning new things, to listening, to talking with others. We continue to grow; society continues to grow. Remember: at one time many people could make a "good conscience" case for slavery. God speaks to us in many and various ways. In addition to Scripture and Church teaching, God also speaks to us in the physical and human sciences. He speaks through competent professional advice from counselors, lawyers, doctors, spiritual directors, and so on. God may also speak through family and friends, but there you have to be careful, since family and friends have their own vested interests. If you change, they're going to have to change too, and no one likes change.

The Spirit moves us in many different ways. A chance encounter with the right person, a persistent and growing thought or conviction, a Scripture verse that comes to mind and just won't go away, something said in conversation that just sticks with you, an opportunity which suddenly opens up – these are all things to look for.

I like to use what I call the "Rule of Three." If someone says something to you about a course of action, it may just be coincidence. If a second person, in an entirely different situation, place, and time says the same thing, then it might be coincidence, but it might be God. But if a third person, in a completely different situation and place, says the same thing, then chances are pretty good it's God speaking and trying to guide you in a way that will help you move closer to God, the world, the human race, and to yourself.

Another element of discernment is that God will not ask us to do something we're incapable of doing. Note the choice of words. I said "incapable." I didn't say "don't want to do." There's a huge difference. Grace builds on nature. God will not ask me to be a mathematics teacher or an opera singer, for I have absolutely no talent in those areas. What about becoming pastor of an inner city parish? I have the talent and the capability, but the desire is lacking. While desire is an important consideration (because if there's a lack of desire then my pastoring might be ineffective), it could also point to an inner laziness or selfishness. Discernment sometimes calls for obedience to a way that we'd rather not walk – just like Jesus on the way to his suffering and death.

And of course, the most vital component of discernment is prayer, prayer, and more prayer. And when you think you've prayed enough, pray some more. Generally speaking, the folks who make the best moral decisions and life decisions are those who regularly spend time with the Lord, allowing Jesus and his Spirit to form their lives. If you only seek a solution during times of crisis, then the discernment task is a lot harder. The best decisions flow from long term and faith-filled Christian lifestyles that embody the values found in the Gospels.

Only if you do all your homework, and then bring it all to God in prayer, and then make your decision, can you say that you have made a decision in conscience. Even then there's still a possibility that it may be a wrong decision. But given that you have really tried to discover the truth, and done all you can to find it, all you can do is place your trust in God and move on.

There are a couple of signs that could indicate you've made the right decision. The first is a feeling of deep peace. It's very hard to describe this feeling in words; all I can say is that you will know it when you experience it. Even if there still are feelings of nervousness and anxiety, as well as questions floating around your head, underneath it all is this peace. Since God is not a God of confusion, he wants us to have some sense of security about what we do. Doors will start to open for you. Things will fall into place in unexpected ways, you will find surprising sources of support and help. Through the Spirit, we will have peace.

Another sign, oddly enough, might be persecution. People will be angry and upset at you because you've upset the applecart, you've opted to not do what "everyone else" is doing, you've forced change. "Blessed are those who are persecuted for my Name's sake."

You may experience a great increase in energy because you've finally stopped fighting God. Patience, kindness, compassion, and union with others are also fruits of good discernment and moral decision-making. The truly beautiful thing about discernment is that we're acting not from instinct or knee-jerk reactions or laziness, but from the depths of our God-given humanity. It doesn't get any better than that!

Chapter Twenty-Two

MAKING TIME FOR GOD

There's hardly a day goes by that I don't get at least one letter in which the writer wonders where time went! Many a Friday has come when I look back and wonder where the week went. Parents never seem to have enough time: they go bonkers trying to balance the demands of marriage, their children's activities, work, and home maintenance. Active retirees tell me they never have enough time to do all they want!

Yet on the other hand, time can drag tremendously. Ask anyone who has sat in a waiting room at the hospital while a loved one undergoes surgery, or anyone who's sat by the deathbed of a child, parent, spouse, friend. Evenings drag for widows and widowers, especially in winter. I've sat many a time in morning prayer and kept looking at the clock. Isn't my prayer time up *yet*?

In the midst of all the hurly-burly of everyday life, we try to make time for God. We want to do this. Deep down we know our spirits and hearts desperately need this daily bread. It doesn't matter if the yearning is impelled by need or by guilt. We know that time with God is something that needs to be woven into the fabric of our life.

Then, when by some miracle we do make time for prayer, it seems that not much happens! We sit down to pray, and immediately our minds scurry hither and yon, and we think about everything ranging from tonight's meal, to sex, to how angry I am with Pat. We find ourselves doing anything but praying, and when time runs out, we look back and think, "What a waste of time that was"! I can guarantee you that if we knew with 100% certainty we were going to have an ecstatic vision of God every single time we prayed, we would definitely have no problem making time each day! But it seems that the only vision we have is of things to do, or of ourselves. How utterly boring! It's not much inducement to spend more time in prayer tomorrow or the next day.

Precisely because time is so precious, what better gift can we make to God? It is a real sacrifice because it hits at the core of our personality. Time given to God is time not available for other activities. That means that if I am an achiever, I will achieve less today. If I need to be around people, it means I will have to spend a few minutes in solitude. Time given to God is time not available for my own personal pursuits or the incessant demands of others. It's an act of faith that God is perfectly capable of running the world for the 5-10-20-30 minutes that I've set aside for prayer.

There are times when prayer comes automatically. You are drawn to it like a child to the Good-Humor wagon! When you face a personal crisis of some kind, prayer arises unbidden. Consider worries about employment, having a child or grandchild in the hospital, sitting by the deathbed of someone you love, sitting through a terrible storm or driving in a sudden blizzard. Prayer just comes, regardless of the time or place, and you can pray for hours on end if need be. You don't worry about what to say or do; it just happens.

At other times, you may feel a sudden inward urge, a yearning to pray, a reaching out of the heart to the divine, a fullness of the heart with peace or joy. These urgings come without warning or prompting (sometimes at very inconvenient places or times). They can come at a pause between tasks, when you're engaged in work or play, in the office, kitchen, bathroom, backyard, church, wherever!

These yearnings are extraordinary gifts of God. Because you and I are God's sons and daughters, we are in continuous relationship with God. For the most part, we aren't aware of this until those moments when we get those stirrings to pray. It's exactly like God is knocking on the door of our life saying:"Here I am… pause with me for a moment."

In those moments, your whole self is being drawn to God and you cannot control it. All you can do is respond, either by ignoring it or by responding with a deeply whispered word of recognition and thanksgiving. It may last only seconds, but it is truly a moment of graced communion, a glimpse of heaven. Believe me when I say that those stirrings cannot be made up or manufactured or faked. They are either there or not there, and when they are there, it is the surest sign you have of God's presence with you this side of heaven.

But we don't have stirrings every day. We don't face crises every day. Most of our days are the same old, same old. So how does one build in a time for God?

First, you have to *want* to do this. It's like anything else. If you and I don't want to do it, we either won't do it or find every excuse possible to get out of it. So a certain honesty is needed. Do you really want this relationship with God? Do you want to deal with the changes that are going to come if you develop this relationship? Now note: "changes" is not necessarily a bad word. Yes, you will, in God's good time, have to change certain attitudes and patterns of behavior as you increasingly come to realize how inconsistent they are with this relationship. But prayer will also bring a fullness and a wholeness and a groundedness that are in stark contrast to the empty, fruitless wanderings that so many folks feel today.

So how does one begin? Obviously, the best way is to block out one or two fifteen-minute periods of time each day. Maybe that's too daunting. After all, when you start a program of bodily exercise, the professionals tell you to start small and work up to a certain level. How about this? The oldest prayer suggestion we Christians have comes from the *Didache*, which is a book of Christian teachings that appeared around 150 A.D. The author recommends stopping what you're doing three times a day, and very consciously and deliberately praying the *Our Father*. It takes about thirty seconds to do this. That's a minute and a half out of your day. There are lots of thirty-second time chunks in a day! Many stop-lights take at least thirty seconds. What a great time to pray! Waiting for the elevator. What a great time to say a quiet *Our Father*!

Another prayer that I have recently become attached to is the *Divine Praises* we use at Benediction. This too is a prayer marked by brevity and simplicity, and each individual praise has the potential to move your spirit into a deeper communion with the Lord.

Now you're saying, God wants more than this. Sure God does, but maybe all you can give is that thirty seconds, that minute and a half. Any gift of time, no matter how meager it looks to you, is precious to God. This thirty-second prayer expresses our desire to give something precious to God and also expresses our poverty (that we can't right now give any more than that). Remember the widow's mite? What's important is that prayer is prayer. This minute and a half, if done every day, will be like a wedge opening your heart to more and more experiences of God's presence and to a deeper desire to spend more time with God.

I'm convinced that it is possible to block out time periods for God. Face it... if Publisher's Clearinghouse called and said they were gonna be at my house one morning this week at 4 AM with a check, I'd be awake and ready to go every morning this week at 4 AM! If I had to do thirty minutes of exercises each day to protect myself from a fatal heart attack, I'd do them faithfully. Like I say, it's a matter of priorities and desires. So why not a brief time when you rise, and another before you call it a day? Lunch breaks are a possibility for another block of time. Prayer before and after meals can be meaningful.

Your prayer can use words. Speak from your heart. Speak your feelings to God, whatever they may be. Reflect on the scripture readings for the day. There are several little booklets published monthly which give a daily reflection on Scripture. Pray a psalm each day. There are some utterly beautiful translations out now. Sometimes you feel a need to simply be silent and listen to the laughter of children in the distance or hear the rustle of the leaves in the breeze... fine... that's prayer.

What's important is to find the time. Once you make a commitment to a special time (realizing of course, that everyday life sometimes demands some flexibility) it won't be too long before you instinctively know how vital this time is to your well-being. The current of prayer will run throughout your day, and you will come to more and more easily sense God's presence, which will result in a desire to be even more faithful to your time alone with God. You will find yourself growing more gentle, more compassionate and understanding, and more accepting of your own personal faults and limitations.

There will always be resistance. There will always be a thousand and one excuses not to make that time. Prayer time itself will more often than not seem like a total waste because "nothing happened." Crises will continue to come and go in your life, and so will problems. You will still experience suffering and regret. Yet because of your fidelity to prayer, there will be a difference in how you handle these things.

You may have noticed by now that I gave very little space to the "how to" of actual praying. That was deliberate. First, it could be the subject of a whole other consideration. Second, the actual things you do in prayer are very personal and individual. It's best to talk with a good spiritual director on that, or write me if you want. But the big reason for the absence of the "how to's" is because I feel so strongly that setting the time is paramount. Once you have the time, once you've disciplined yourself to use it, and once you're started to look forward to that time with God, it's simply a matter of starting your prayer as painlessly as possible and then getting your ego out of the way and letting God take over. Your time is your ultimate act of surrender to God, your ultimate act of faith, hope, and love.

Chapter Twenty-Three

DARK NIGHTS

Like most folks, I was profoundly surprised by the revelations of Mother Teresa's spiritual crisis in the years before she died. I cannot fathom what it must be like to live through fifty plus years of literally praying in emptiness.

The words "praying in emptiness" are as good a description of the Dark Night of the Soul as any. John of the Cross went through this "night" for several years when he was imprisoned by his fellow Carmelites. His writings describe a journey of a soul through several stages. The starting point is the Dark Night of the Senses, and the arrival point is the Dark Night of the Soul.

A Dark Night is not an uncommon experience for those who are deeply devoted to God. Theresa of Avila had her times of darkness. Paul of the Cross (no relation to John) endured forty-five years of spiritual darkness. The founder of the Congregation of Holy Cross, Blessed Basil Moreau CSC, experienced two months of absolute darkness. He wrote: *"I went from station to station, searching for light, for an inspiration, and I found nothing, absolutely nothing. I knocked on the tabernacle door. I waited and received no answer, not the least encouragement. At that moment I understood something of our Lord's abandonment in His agony... I then understood perfectly the suicide of Judas."*

Compare this with Mother Teresa: *"Lord, my God, who am I that You should forsake me? The Child of your Love – and now become as the most hated one – the one You have thrown away as unwanted – unloved. I call, I cling, I want – and there is no One to answer – no One on Whom I can cling – no, No One. Alone... Where is my Faith – even deep down right in there is nothing, but emptiness & darkness – My God – how painful is this unknown pain – I have no Faith – I dare not utter the words & thoughts that crowd in my heart -- and make me suffer untold agony."*

Thomas Merton's famous prayer captures some of the Dark Night: *"My Lord God, I have no idea where I am going. I do not see the road ahead of me. I cannot know for certain where it will end... you will lead me by the right road though I may know nothing about it."*

Jesus: *"My God, my God, why have you abandoned me"?*

St. Faustina: *"My mind became dimmed in a strange way; no truth seemed clear to me. When people spoke to me about God, my heart was like a rock. I could not draw from it a single sentiment of love for Him. When I tried, by an act of the will, to remain close to Him, I experienced great torments, and it seemed to me that I was only provoking God to an even greater anger... I felt in my soul a great void, and there was nothing with which I could fill it. I began to suffer from a great hunger and yearning for God, but I saw my utter powerlessness. I tried to read slowly, sentence by sentence, and to meditate in this way, but this also was of no avail."*

Padre Pio: *"How difficult, Father, is the way of Christian perfection for a soul so ill-disposed as mine. My badness makes me fearful at every step I take... Peace has been completely banished from my heart. I have become absolutely blind. I find myself enveloped in a profound night and no matter how I turn and toss I cannot find the light. How then can I walk before the Lord? ... He has rightly thrown me among the everlasting dead whom He no longer remembers."*

Now I could keep going, but I don't want to frighten or depress you! You have the idea, I think. It's not the most pleasant experience.

Over my years of ministry, many folks have written or spoken to me of what they called their own Dark Nights of the soul. Were they experiencing that? Or was it something else? It helps to make some distinctions.

First, what some call a Dark Night is really depression. Depression can accompany a Dark Night and increase its intensity, but there is still a distinction. One major characteristic of those experiencing a Dark Night is that they are able to keep up with their daily works and routines. Depression is a serious loss of energy which leaves one unable to get on with his or her life. It can stem from external (death of a loved one) or internal (chemical imbalance) causes. There is sleeplessness (or too much wanting to sleep), loss of appetite, suicidal thoughts, disinterest in everyday things that one used to enjoy, difficulty concentrating and making decisions, bouts of crying for no discernable reason, and so on. Depression is a disease, an affliction of the mind and body.

Not so with a Dark Night. That's an affliction of the soul. Those who are undergoing a time of spiritual purification are able to go about their daily activities, sometimes joyfully. It's only when they move into quiet times of prayer or silence that the flatness hits. As a rule, the Dark Nights do not involve eating or sleeping disturbances and physical symptoms. Depressed people typically look depressed, sound depressed, and make you depressed! Dark Night folks are still able to give much life to others.

To repeat, Dark Nights are an affliction of the soul. In order to experience the pain of the Dark Night, one has to first long for God. Dark Nights *always* deal with the person's relationship to God. The change brought about in this relationship then extends into how one relates to self, others, and the world.

So… people who believe in God but lead sinful lives probably don't care that much about God, and so won't have the pain of absence.

People who believe in God but have lukewarm spiritual practices are not likely to experience Dark Nights either. God just isn't that crucial in their lives.

Folks who go through severe trials may feel deserted by God and experience pain like the Dark Night. But not everyone goes through severe trials in life. And everyone responds to hardships differently. Some may cling to God more tightly instead of disowning him.

People who thirst for God, who have a deep relationship with God, who have experienced great consolations, may or may not be granted the Dark Night of the Senses. God guides each of us uniquely. Everything depends on God's desire for our growth and our mission.

As mentioned above, the Night of the Senses is the departure point for a deeper journey with God. You know you are experiencing it when three things happen.

First, the consolations and good feelings you experienced in prayer are no longer there. You pray, you want to pray, but it feels arid. Sometimes you actually feel rebellious about praying.

Second, you begin to be troubled by a sense that you have done something wrong, or have back-slidden. You interpret the aridity of your prayer as a sign that you have fallen away from God, or that Jesus is mad at you.

Third, try as you might, you just cannot pray or meditate like you used to. You try to use words or your imagination for your prayers, and find you just cannot do it. Instead, you just want to be there quietly.

These three things together indicate that God is moving you from an active, verbal, discursive kind of prayer to a more silent, contemplative one. God is weaning you from all the good things you used to make use of for your prayer and is leading you into a different kind of prayer, one requiring more faith. In short, you're going to be doing less talking, and more listening! The Divine Surgeon is at work.

While the Night of the Senses is the departure point into a deeper relationship with God, the arrival point is what Mother Teresa and the other folks experienced and described in their writings. It's called the "Dark Night of the Soul." This is a phenomenon experienced by many (but not all) of the strongest and greatest saints in Christian history. By the same token, few of us ordinary folks experience it. God alone gives this gift, and God alone determines this Night's length and severity.

Ordinarily, God has a way of reminding us of his presence and his love. But in the Night of the Soul, this consolation is completely taken away. It does not produce a crisis of faith. In some miraculous way faith remains, although it's very deep down. Instead of the ordinary gift of faith, this new faith becomes a complete and total act of the will and a total act of trust in the promises of God. The soul gets emptied of everything that could sustain it. As Mother Teresa said: *"Even though I have no feeling of hope, I will serve You completely, totally, and utterly because I trust in Your Promises and Your Love."*

I realize it's strange to speak of the Dark Night of the Soul as an *arrival* point. It's a scary place, no two ways about it. It's heaven, hell, and purgatory all rolled into one. It feels like a tomb, but ironically a very peaceful one. It's almost as if God is saying: "Be still. Don't struggle or resist. Get rid of your ideas about how this should proceed. Just leave it to me and trust in the midst of absurdity and pain." What makes this "night" the arrival point is that you have become a person who has learned to have absolute faith and trust in God.

I would end by encouraging you not to spiritually self-diagnose yourself. We human beings tend to see ourselves as either better than we really are, or worse than we really are. Only God knows the truth, and seeing the truth about ourselves is one of the great accomplishments of the Dark Nights. Talk with a good spiritual director or confessor -- a man or woman whom you sense is holy, whole, and comfortable with being human. It's a conversation you deserve to give yourself, *especially* if you're struggling in prayer.

Chapter Twenty-Four

"TO REMEMBER IS TO UNDERSTAND"

I'm starting this reflection on September 11th, 2002. All across the country and around the world, heart is joining to heart as humanity remembers a day of mass murder. For Western nations not used to the daily experience of terrorism, this day is also a reminder of just how vulnerable they are to the insane "sanity" of those whose only purpose in life is to hate and kill. But I'm not going to dwell on the events of September 11, 2001. Nor am I going to dwell on forgiveness and reconciliation, important as they are. What I want to reflect on with you is the whole idea of remembering.

The Gospel for today's Eucharist was Luke's version of the Beatitudes. "Blessed are those who are poor, who hunger, who weep; blessed are you when you are hated, ostracized, insulted, and called 'evil.'" These Beatitudes are such a perfect Gospel for this anniversary. It wasn't planned this way; it's just the way it happened.

By way of footnote, it brings an eerie chill which runs down my spine, for the scheduled readings at Mass in the days after 9/11/2001 also dealt with forgiveness and loving the enemy. I remember thinking how glad I was to be at a woodworking class in Maine rather than trying to preach on that topic in a parish setting. Not too many people were in a forgiving mood back then! Many still aren't; we do have work to do, as individuals and as a country. I believe it is the work of Providence that the readings then and now are as they are; it truly is God speaking to us. It's not coincidence.

But back to the idea of remembering. In 1994, Anna Quindlen wrote a book called *Thinking Out Loud*. She tells the story of how she went to a Chinese restaurant and at meal's end received the usual fortune cookie. The fortune read: "To remember is to understand." She then went on to say that "a good judge remembers what it was like to be a lawyer. A good editor remembers what it was like to be a writer. A good parent remembers what it was like to be a child."

"To remember is to understand." Let's chew on those words for a little bit. For us Catholics, remembrance is at the heart of our liturgical life in the Eucharist. We also set aside the month of November as a special time of remembering those who have gone before us. To remember all those people is to understand who I am at this point in time.

Our family history shapes us; it shapes our attitudes. If your ancestors came over on the *Mayflower*, you're going to have a whole different background than someone who came to this country in the late 1800's, and those later arrivals will in turn have a different perspective than those who were offered asylum in this country from the conflicts in Serbia and Bosnia, in the Middle East, or from Central and South America. If members of your family lived through the Depression, that has shaped their whole life, and therefore yours. If your parents, siblings or relatives –or you yourself -- fought in the wars that have scarred our time, you know those conflicts brought very fundamental changes in their lives, and hence in yours. To remember what your family has gone through is to understand their way of acting and reacting in the present time.

Remember your teachers, your pastors, the people you admired from a distance, who were your heroes. All I have to do is close my eyes and a roll call of those people unwinds in my mind and heart. I thank God for their presence, for their challenge and example helped fashion me. Sadly, for many, some people from their past were negative influences. But still, they need to be remembered. In response to their influence, you have adapted certain ways of acting and behaving, ranging from the serious to the trivial. For example, my Dad was not too good about putting his tools back where they belonged. When he needed something, he would tell us kids to go look for it. Sometimes we'd find it, but many times we wouldn't. Well, to this day, I keep my woodworking tools under lock and key and I know exactly where they are and who has them! That was a trivial example, and don't get me started on lima beans! But oftentimes the negative influence is so pervasive and deep that counseling is needed.

Events also shape us, and those events need to be remembered. I asked Carol if she remembered her first kiss, and she did... vividly. So do I (Kristine Kluegh, 4th grade, after school, in the hall between the library and the gym, lasted all of about a second, but I was one happy kid !). Birthdays, marriages, ordinations, professions of faith at the Easter Vigil, deaths, divorces, accidents, phone calls, letters, e-mails, your first crush, that special vacation, and on and on. To remember these things is to understand ourselves.

Now let's move to another level, and this is where I want to bring in the Beatitudes. Can you remember the times when you were hungry – for food, companionship, affirmation, spiritual sustenance? Can you remember the times when you were poor? When income was not enough to pay the bills, medical expenses ate up your savings, you were laid off or unemployed, you couldn't make needed house repairs, and you had to get your clothes from Goodwill?

What of the periods of unhappiness, or deep sadness, or mourning, which lasted hours, days, months, even years? I'm sure there's plenty to remember. What of those times when you were reviled, when you were bullied or hassled, when you received unjust criticism, when you were put down or treated as a non-person by those in authority? Were you ever abused emotionally or physically?

Now take these Beatitude events, remember them; no doubt they have shaped you and formed your behavior and attitudes. Consider what have they done for your empathy for other people who are hungry, poor, reviled, sad and unhappy? To remember is not just to understand ourselves, but it is also to understand other people. So often we make quick judgments on people around us, conveniently forgetting that once upon a time, we faced the same difficulties and tests in our own lives. The blessings promised by the Beatitudes come *to* those who remember what it was like, and then the blessing passes *through* them to those who are presently suffering.

And most important of all, God remembers! Through Jesus' presence in our midst, God remembers what it is like to be hungry, to have no place to lay one's head, to be lonely, to face misunderstanding and false judgment, to mourn the death of a loved one, to have people wanting to kill him, and to weep over the mental density of people who just cannot understand that the only way to peace is through following the ways of God. Our God is not a remote, uncaring, implacable Being sitting way out there somewhere doing nothing. Oh no... God remembers! And because God remembers, he sends blessings to those who suffer as he did.

Chapter Twenty-Five

A PRAYER FOR OUR TIMES

The Second Eucharistic Prayer of Reconciliation is a beacon of hope, an affirmation that there is indeed healing for our broken world. Reflect on it with me. Use my reflections as a stimulus for your own, and draw strength and hope from this prayer. Let that strength and hope permeate your everyday life.

Father, all powerful and every-living God, we praise and thank you through Jesus Christ our Lord for your presence and action in the world.

Every Preface is a prayer of thanksgiving and praise! God is truly present and active in our world. You and I would not be alive otherwise. We wouldn't even exist. Neither would our children or grandchildren, and our pets. We would have no food, drink, or shelter; none of the beauties of nature and the majestic works of human craftsmanship would exist. When you look at the pictures taken by the Hubble telescope, pictures of stars at utterly unimaginable distances, who are we that God cares for us so much? We receive blessing upon blessing. Even in the midst of our sinfulness the blessings still come. Blessings can even be found in our suffering.

In the midst of conflict and division, we know it is you who turn our minds to thoughts of peace. Your Spirit changes our hearts: enemies begin to speak to one another, those who were estranged join hands in friendship, and nations seek the way of peace together.

So much has happened in the last many years! The residents of Northern Ireland are finally living in peace, shaky though it may be at times. Shiites and Sunnis in Iraq are trying to find common ground. Diplomatic conversations are being resumed with various countries, even former enemies. Go back even further: Sadat and Begin, the fall of the Iron Curtain and the Berlin Wall, treaties on nuclear proliferation. Democrats and Republicans can on rare occasions actually cooperate for the common good. Whites join with blacks in rebuilding burned-out churches. Taxpaying middle-classers work side-by-side with welfare folks in "Habitat for Humanity." Prisoners work with neighbors in sandbagging levees. Recent events in the U.S. have triggered conversations about racial relations, abortion, health care, etc. And who among us does not think thoughts of peace? Our yearning for peace and harmony is in fact God's yearning for peace. You and God are yearning with one heart, speaking with one voice, and acting as one body.

Your Spirit is at work when understanding puts an end to strife, when hatred is quenched by mercy, and vengeance gives way to forgiveness.

This reconciliation is happening day by day, hour by hour, in homes and towns, workplaces and churches. A husband and wife are fighting, and one of them steps back and says, "Whoa, what are we doing to ourselves"? Parents are sometimes surprised by how well they handled a situation with their teenager. A victim of crime is moved to forgive the one who committed the crime. Pro-choice and pro-life supporters get together to talk, because they realize that verbal and physical violence are bringing not life, but death to human dignity and goodness. A close brush with death causes someone to re-assess his or her life. A trial-separation makes a couple realize that their relationship is more important than any issue. A worker who is insulted has a quiet heart-to-heart talk with the insulter instead of going off and stewing over it for days on end. You know the Holy Spirit is at work in your life every time you opt for understanding, mercy, and forgiveness, no matter how little it may seem to you. So when you see this grace, give thanks and praise to God. Sing your hosannas, either in your heart or aloud.

God of power and might, we praise you through your Son, Jesus Christ, who comes in your name. He is the Word that brings salvation… the hand you stretch out to sinners… the way that leads to your peace.

The only way that you and I can become peace-full people is to have a strong relationship with Jesus. Inner reconciliation comes when we listen to and believe the words of Jesus telling us how much the Father loves us. Salvation refers not just to something that happens after we die. Salvation is here and now. It is the fullness of heart we feel when we pray or go to Mass, when we love and serve and help others. It is the

111

peace we feel after a good confession, the relief that comes when we make up with someone we've been at odds with. God is allowing you to be one of the people who comes in his name. Every time we have this sense of rightness and peace, we know that we are firmly holding onto the hand of Jesus.

God our Father, we had wandered far from you, but through your Son you have brought us back. You gave him up to death so that we might turn again to you and find our way to one another. Therefore we celebrate the reconciliation Christ Jesus has gained for us.

We wander, we come back. We wander, we come back. Over and over again we take part in the endless cycle of human wanderings and returns. It happens in our relationship with God. It happens with spouses, children, our parents, and our coworkers. We get angry at ourselves, and then make peace with ourselves. Every time we turn back and try to pick up the goodness of life, no matter how large or small it may be, we experience the grace of Jesus' passion and death. In all probability we don't even know this is going on, but truly it is. It's not me alone who's deciding to make peace. The desire to make peace is the felt sign of deep interior calls from Jesus and his Spirit. Jesus calls us and moves us. We feel the desire to be home again with others, ourselves, and God. Or we may feel the desire to pray for peace in our world, country, and church. That too is a response to the stirring of Jesus within.

You have to remember, dear friend, that the normal state of human existence is "Look out for #1." So every time you get the focus off yourself and onto another, you are reenacting in your own life what we celebrate at the Eucharist. You are giving up your own fears and selfish desires so that you and others may have life.

Fill us with his Spirit through our sharing in this meal. May he take away all that divides us.

Do you dare make this request? It's going to mean change, you know. You and I are going to have to let go of our hates and spites and jealousies. We're going to have to let go of our racism and our homophobia and our distrust of anyone who looks like they're going to take what belongs to us. Can we conceive of a life without our pet peeves? Some people cannot. That's why conflict and terror still prevail in the world. Violence has become the center of some individuals' lives. If peace comes, their lives would have no meaning. Can we give up all the pettiness and bitchiness and the "ism's" and phobias that give my life meaning?

May this Spirit keep us always in communion with our Pope, with our bishops and all your people. Father, make your Church throughout the world a sign of unity and an instrument of your peace.

Is our Church a good sign of unity to the world? Is the Church an instrument of peace? Well, rephrase the question. Are you in unity and at peace with everyone (both lay and clergy) in your parish community, your diocese? If you and I can't do it at home, no way can we do it for the world! There is a great tension in our Church today. It comes about because there are three basic groups of people who are afraid to trust each other. (1) There are those who find great peace and meaning in order, law, authority, and doctrine. (2) There are those who find their peace through deep commitment to a personal relationship with Jesus Christ, nourished by Scripture and personal experience. (3) There are also the questioners, the seekers and searchers, who have not yet found a home. Why must we insist on the primacy of one way or the other? If I insist on a particular way, then I make that way the end, not the means. All ways should be a means to the goal of union with Jesus. If the desire of your life and mine is truly full union with Jesus, then we'll use all possible means to achieve that union, and we will refuse to dismiss any of them.

This divisiveness is not a new problem. It faced the people of St. Paul's time. He speaks directly to this issue: *"But now in Christ Jesus you who once were far off have been brought near through the blood of Christ. It is he who is our peace, and who made the two of us one by breaking down the barrier of hostility that kept us apart. In his own flesh… he created in himself one new person from us who had been two and to make peace, reconciling both of us to God in one body through his cross, which put that enmity to death"* (Ephesians 2.13-16).

You have gathered us here around the table of your Son, in companionship with the Virgin Mary, Mother of God, and all the saints. In that new world, where the fullness of your peace will be revealed, gather people of every race, language and way of life to share in the one eternal banquet with Jesus Christ the Lord.

I guess this insight sums it all up. We're all going to be together in the new world that is eternal life in heaven. Saint and sinner, liberal and conservative, black and white and brown and yellow, criminal and victim, homosexual and heterosexual and bisexual, Jew and Christian and Moslem, atheist and agnostic, Pope and dissident, ex-spouses, rich and poor, well-fed and hungry, and on and on. If it's going to happen then, why can't it happen now?

Thanks be to God it is happening. Every day, throughout the world, in large and small ways, our earth is slowly being transformed into a heaven by the good-hearted actions of men, women, and children who are simply and quietly responding to the movements of the Spirit. Some of these actions make national headlines, some the local news. Some actions become part of the family history, while still others are done with no fanfare whatsoever. There is much work to be done yet. That's why this particular Eucharistic prayer praises God for what has been accomplished and recognizes that we have a long way to go until that day when "all glory and honor is yours, Almighty Father, forever and ever. Amen."

Chapter Twenty-Six

GUILTY!

A benefactor wrote: "Your interpretation of distraction in church while trying to pray was very helpful. I always feel guilty about that, but then again, I feel guilty about everything. Some comments in *Cross Links* about 'guilt' might be helpful to myself and many others." I suspect my correspondent is right: some comments about guilt would be helpful. It was helpful to me to sit down and think about it! So many people carry about an unnecessary burden of guilt, and this burden is crippling their growth and their full enjoyment of life.

Anyone who was raised in the pre-Vatican II Church is very familiar with guilt. I know I am. It took me a long time to make some necessary distinctions and get my life on an even keel. A lot of the guilt had to do with sex, of course! But I've come to see that the far more deadly sin is not what is euphemistically called "self abuse," but the self-abuse we heap on ourselves for our human faults and shortcomings. Good religion teaches us to love God; bad religion teaches us to fear God. There's no doubt I was trained to fear God, and that fear caused a lot of unrealistic guilt. Our religious faith is supposed to help us deal with guilt ... not to cause it!

There are two basic kinds of guilt. If you are suffering from any kind of guilt, you first have to ask yourself if it's realistic or unrealistic guilt. *Realistic guilt* is related to something you did that was real and concrete; there was a definite failure on your part or a definite injury to another person. You did it with full awareness of what you were doing. It was your responsibility and no one else's. *Unrealistic guilt* comes when you feel responsible for something you didn't do or for which you had no responsibility. Unrealistic guilt also occurs when your feelings of guilt go way beyond what is reasonable given the nature of what is triggering the guilt.

Realistic guilt doesn't need much comment. You know when you've blown it, when you've caused serious mental, emotional, physical, or spiritual harm to yourself or to another person. Quite frankly, I don't want to take away that guilt from myself or anyone else, because it can be a key to great growth and conversion. This kind of guilt can be a gift from God, and it is most definitely material for the Sacrament of Reconciliation.

Unrealistic guilt is different. It produces great fear and anxiety, much unnecessary suffering, and it drastically affects your relationship with God and others. What are some common examples of unrealistic guilt? In confession, someone says, "I missed Mass on Sunday and feel bad about it." I say, "Why did it happen"? "I was sick," comes the reply. "Were you responsible for your sickness"? "No." "Then why are you feeling guilty over something you had no control over"?

Many parents carry a lot of unrealistic guilt about their children: "Where did we go wrong"? The guilt is compounded when children start blaming parents for their dysfunctions. My response to parents is simply: "You did the best you could with what you had." And if a parent truly did mess things up, say by abusing a child, then I would say: "Yes, that was wrong, and it needs to be dealt with. But your child also has to take responsibility for his or her own life and take whatever steps are necessary for his or her healing, instead of blaming it all on you." God does not hold parents accountable for their children's decisions or behaviors. It's the child who is accountable, not the parent! If more parents could get that through their heads their life would be a lot happier.

Death brings lots of unrealistic guilt: "If only I had been kinder… more loving… spent more time at home… etc… etc." Putting a loved one in a nursing home is guaranteed to cause a lot of unrealistic guilt. Ditto for divorce and separation, not getting a promotion, losing an account. So too for anger or sexual thoughts and feelings and not answering the phone. Even having a bad day can cause some people to feel guilty! I suspect there are some people who feel guilty for feeling guilty!

Every so often there may come a particularly tough one. I think, for example, of Pat, who's driving down a residential street. Pat is going slowly and carefully, driving well within the speed limit. A child suddenly darts into the street and Pat hits the child, causing severe injuries. The child dies in the hospital. Everyone says he's not to blame. Pat himself even knows he's not to blame. He's an innocent person who may lose his mind because of unrealistic guilt.

The best way to deal with *realistic* guilt is through apology, restitution, and reconciliation (with the offended party and in the Sacrament). There is simply no other way. You will not be peaceful until there is apology and reconciliation. Period.

Unrealistic guilt is a bit harder, particularly in a case like Pat's. Believe it or not, one of the best ways to deal with such guilt is through common sense! In most cases of unrealistic guilt, the head says one thing and the heart another. In this case, it's pretty safe to listen to your head. Secondly, talk about it with a trusted friend, priest, or counselor. There's a reason why you feel this way, and if that reason can be uncovered, a major step in personal healing and growth can take place. Third, ask yourself why you feel so guilty. Is it because you didn't live up to your own super-high expectations (you expect more of yourself than God does)? Is it because you didn't behave the way "they" said you should behave (who cares what "they" want)? Is it because you're afraid God's gonna zap you (he is not; he wants to draw you close)? Are you afraid that some kind of heavenly or earthly "Mommy and Daddy" are going to jump all over you (that's just your fearful "child" yelling in your mind's ear)? And for me, there is one central question: does your unreasonable guilt come because you are unable to forgive yourself for being human? Forgiveness may be simply acceptance of your own or another's humanity!

One other comment about guilt. Do you ever find yourself going quietly along, working at something, then suddenly remembering something sinful or wrong from your past, and the guilt hits all over again, even though you may have apologized and gone to confession and worked through it all? If that happens, just know that God is not tracking you down to beat you over the head with past misdeeds. Satan is the one who likes to keep you squashed down under his thumb (how come Satan is always a "he"?).

Look at the rhythm: whenever you do something really life-giving and good, whenever you feel as though you've made great strides in personal growth, you feel great, don't you? Isn't it eerie how quickly the negative thoughts come: "But if you only knew what kind of person I really am." Satan doesn't dare let you feel good about yourself and your goodness, because he knows that if you feel good about yourself, you'll grow closer to God. He wants to take away your peace of mind and heart. My personal response when those things happen to me is to make a prayer of it: "Satan, I know what you're trying to do. I choose not to believe what you say. I *am* a good person. Jesus, keep me close to you and come to my assistance."

If the flashback is over something that involved realistic guilt (for example, an abortion, an affair, killing someone while DUI), then we're dealing with something different. Remember the old phrase: "temporal punishment due to sin"? Well, that's what this is. If something like this has happened to you, chances are good that you've been repenting of it ever since, looking for ways to redress the wrong you did. You've become wiser, mellower, more accepting of other's weaknesses and faults. Maybe you're also volunteering time in an organization with some relation to what you did (for example, giving time to pro-life). But God knows that more "repair work" needs to be done, and this memory may simply be a way of God inviting you to continue in that repair work to your psyche and your soul. If you have those flashbacks, don't panic or despair or lose hope. God is drawing you closer to himself. Simply say a prayer asking for strength and courage, for mercy and compassion. Perhaps ask God if there's anything specific he'd like you to do for others.

When such guilt persists over a long period of time, it might be good to see a skilled counselor or spiritual director. God doesn't want you to live this way. He came that you might have life, and have it to the full. Good counselors are God's healing hands and voice. They are instruments he has given to you, through whom he brings you peace and wholeness. Your guilt is no barrier to God's love. Please don't let it be a barrier to loving yourself and others! Whether realistic or unrealistic, all guilt is an invitation for you to surrender your own self-abusing judgment and accept God's mercy and compassion. God wants to raise you up, not grind you down.

Chapter Twenty-Seven

PRAYER: LOVING GOD WITH ALL MY BEING!

Most of us were not trained in prayer. When we did receive instruction it was very specific. Prayer time was to be totally focused on God, and we could do nothing else during that time! The best place was in church, sitting or kneeling in front of the Blessed Sacrament. Rosaries, novenas, prayer cards, missals, and the Bible were all acceptable helps to prayer. Grace before meals, morning offerings, and acts of contrition at night were recommended practices. Those who wished to practice meditation followed a specific set of guidelines. Distractions were viewed as sinful and were matter for confession. Prayer was a duty, an obligation, and something that we owed to God.

Given this kind of training, no wonder so many people have trouble with prayer! Our hearts yearn to reach out to God, who alone can fulfill the deep longing for loving and being loved that we all have. But if the reaching out is constricted by a whole series of "shoulds" and "should-nots," we'll never get past the "Howdy-do" stage! For sure, we'll not experience the God whose yearning to love us and be with us is infinitely stronger than our desire to love Him and be with Him.

There was a long period of time in the seminary, and also in my early years of ministry, when prayer was sheer frustration. I didn't want to waste time praying because I'd feel guilty that I wasn't doing it right. Instinctively I knew there had to be more, but I just didn't know what it was till much later in life. Some magnificent spiritual directors and retreat directors helped me to grow as a prayerful man, and I'd simply like to pass on to you some of the insights that have worked for me and others. My ultimate hope is that you will feel free enough to pray in your own way and your own style, because you are a totally unique individual, with a totally unique relationship to God that is shared by no one else in the history of the world past, present, or to come.

The most important principle of prayer is that Great Commandment of Jesus: "You shall love the Lord your God with all your heart, soul, strength, and mind." Notice what Jesus says: love God with *all* of you, not just part of you, but *all* of you! Jesus did not want us to go sit in a secluded corner and turn everything off but our mind. He wants all of our being to be involved in prayer. Through his commandment, Jesus encourages us to be creative and open-minded; he asks that we bring everything we are and are not into our times of prayer with Abba, our Father.

The second most important principle of prayer is this: one prays as one can, not as one ought. Loosen your grip on the shoulds and should-nots of prayer, dear friend. It's a grip that will stifle the awareness of God's presence in your life. You and the Father and the Spirit and Jesus are involved in a dance of life that changes from day to day, even minute to minute. To say that I "ought" to pray this way and no other is to tell God that I'm going to do only this one particular dance step and no other. God will dance with you, because he loves you and wants to be with you. But his dancing will be wistful and sad, because he can only do what you allow him to do, and he'd much rather sweep you off your feet and into the universe of his love.

How does one apply these principles in everyday practice? First, be sensitive to what your body is saying. Are you tired, energetic, rushed, relaxed, calm, tense? All these will affect how you pray. If you're feeling rushed, don't force yourself to be still for fifteen minutes… you can't. Just whisper a few short prayers. If you're tired, centering prayer might put you right to sleep, so try a walking meditation. If you're tense, then maybe you just simply need to talk to God about what's making you tense, just as you would confide in a trusted friend.

Be flexible with time. Every person who wants to grow closer to God should set aside some time each day to be with God… at least fifteen minutes. I usually recommend two fifteen minute periods during the day. After all, you don't try to make it through the day on just one meal, do you? If at all possible, stay with your time, both length of time and time of day. But sometimes you just can't do it, because everyday life has a way of breaking into our routines. Some days, all you can do is whisper a quick prayer before you fall into bed… fine… no problem. At other times you yearn for a longer time of prayer. Try to make more time if at all possible. That yearning for more prayer comes directly from the Holy Spirit, and when you yearn for more time, you know that you're growing in love with God. After all, when you're with someone you deeply love, there's never really enough time, is there?

While we're on the issue of time, please do not discount the value of those short little prayers of thanksgiving, praise, and need. A heartfelt "Oh God, that's beautiful," or "Please, God, help me"! or "Thank you, Jesus"! is as significant and as precious as any lengthy prayer period.

Try different body positions. Stand, sit, kneel, prostrate yourself, assume a yoga position. I do most of my praying in a Lazy-Boy with the footrest out and back reclined. But every so often my body is restless, so I might stretch out on the floor. In chapel, I mostly sit, but sometimes kneel with my derriere resting on the seat edge and back straight -- it's a kind of yoga position. Your body will let you know when it's comfortable. Listen to it. Remember: you can love God with your body too.

Be sensitive to what "turns you on." Scholastic theology says that grace builds on nature, and that's definitely true in prayer. When you're really praying, you'll forget about yourself, because you're aware of the feelings of love, awe, praise, unity, wholeness, and gratitude that are coursing through your mind and heart. As Theresa of Avila says, "Do what most stirs you to love."

So if contemplating nature stirs you to an awareness of God's presence to you and God's love of you, then contemplate nature. Sit outside. Go for a walk. Visualize nature scenes in your mind's eye as you're sitting in your chair. Look at a painting or hold a nature book in your lap as if it were a Bible. Sometimes I lay flat on my belly and just lose myself in the universe that is that little patch of grass right below my eyes (actually that's a misnomer, because my belly is such that laying flat would be an accomplishment!).

If it's music that turns you on and helps you to lose yourself, go for it! Put on the i-Pod or the radio, close your eyes, and allow God to love you through the medium of music (he created it, didn't he?). Ditto for art, reading, silence, incense, candles. If taking a hot bubble bath or getting a massage causes you to sigh with a deep delight: "Oh God, this is wonderful," then that "Oh God, this is wonderful" is pure prayer. It's loving God and allowing God to love us through his gift of the warm water or the skilled fingers of the masseuse.

I encourage you to develop a repertoire of prayer. We change. What works today may not work as well tomorrow. Remember that the goal of prayer is to love God and allow ourselves to experience God's love. Love is multi-dimensional. There is no one way to express love. When I love another human being, I have to adapt my ways of showing love to what that person may be feeling at any given time and to what I may be feeling. So too with prayer. Fortunately God feels the same way towards us all the time, but we human beings can't say the same about ourselves.

A repertoire of prayer allows us flexibility. My usual form of prayer, for example, is a kind of quiet listening in the darkness. But sometimes my mind is chaotic, and not restful and quiet. So I'll pull out the Bible and turn to the Psalms… and pray them. Pray the rosary. Whisper your aspirations and ejaculations. Use a scriptural or devotional mantra (for example, "Jesus I love you and need you") and let it repeat over and over again. Concentrate on your breathing or heartbeat. Let your mind and heart roam the world and pray for whoever pops into mind. Sing your prayer, hum it, dance it, play it on a musical instrument. Cry it, weep it, paint it or carve it. There are times when I'm so filled with an ache for God or for something of God that all I can do is groan my prayer. There's no words that can capture the feeling. That groan is prayer too!

Or growl out your prayer (either for real or in your mind). Again, we're to love God with our whole being, and if I'm really steamed at God, an insipid little "Jesus, I don't like this" isn't really going to hack it. It's dishonest prayer, because we're not loving God with our whole being. Our whole being wants to roar out our pain and frustration! If you still think this is improper prayer, then be aware of the fact that many of the Psalms are this kind of gut-roaring prayer.

Maybe from this you can see that there is no right way or wrong way to pray. There is only *your* way. Give yourself the freedom and the joy of being able to love God with all your heart, mind, soul, and body. When you give yourself this freedom, you will see with a striking clarity how the love of Abba, our Father, sustains the universe and permeates your life. You'll be able to appreciate ever more the totally unique relationship God has with you, and you with God.

Chapter Twenty-Eight

LIFE IN THE WILDERNESS

Every other summer, the first readings at daily Mass are taken from the Old Testament books of *Genesis, Exodus, Numbers,* and *Deuteronomy.* These books contain the stories of our ancestors in faith.

How I admire Abraham! Here he was, comfortably settled in Ur, when this voice from nowhere told him to pack up everything and move to a new land. Little by little, this voice revealed itself to be Yahweh. What acts of trust this man made! Now, remember, you and I have always known that there is a God. Abraham had no such knowledge. He was placing his life and future into the hands of a totally unknown being.

Then we have the stories of Jacob, Isaac, Joseph, Moses, and Joshua. We follow the Israelites as they leave Egypt, wander in the desert, and long for the good old days of safety and security. These are, in short, the stories of men and women who were forced to leave what was familiar and venture into a desert wilderness where God would transform them.

The stories had particular meaning for me beginning in the summer of 1997, when I moved to the "Solitude of the Savior," where I lived alone for the next five years except for the occasional guests who came for a retreat or day of recollection. This move was freely-chosen, and it was the first time in my life that I had ever lived alone -- really alone -- the nearest neighbor was not even within shouting distance. It was leaving what was familiar and having to learn all over again what it means to trust God.

Actually, that move to the Solitude had its beginnings some years prior, when God pulled me into the wilderness. Everything I had valued, cherished, and built my life on was uprooted and re-examined, discarded or revised. My understanding of self, God, priesthood, religious life, friendships, and ministry were thoroughly revamped. The only analogy

I can draw is that of remodeling a house: the exterior remains the same while the interior is gutted.

It was not a pleasant time. It was a vast and howling wasteland, to use Scriptural terms. I wanted to "go back to Egypt" in the worse way, and yet I intuitively knew that to do so would destroy me. Now, many years later, I can look back and call it a time of extraordinary grace and growth.

You too have had your wilderness experiences, times of darkness when there seems to be little or no light. You were called to leave what was familiar and comfortable, to go through a period of painful testing and purgation. You were invited, in other words, to enter the Paschal Mystery, to die to the old self in order to become a new creation.

Many things can catapult you into the wilderness, or cause darkness to settle like a pall over your life. The death of a significant person, serious illness, rupture of a relationship, unemployment, the empty nest, retirement, a significant birthday, and new living situations are examples. You can be the victim of unjust accusations, or it can be the other way around: your sinful behavior finally backfires. A lessening of religious fervor can bring you to the desert, as can the inability to pray as you used to, or the sense of being abandoned by God, or unanswered in prayer. At other times there seems to be no apparent reason why you find yourself in the wilderness. This desolation I can only attribute to the direct action of God.

What is it like in the wilderness? It's not pleasant, that's for sure. There can be a loss of personal identity. You don't know who you are, or what the meaning and purpose of your life is. There is loneliness, because you feel that no one else has ever experienced this before, and besides, all your usual props are either crumbling or gone. You think about all the decisions and choices you've made, and find yourself thinking: "If only...." There is anxiety. Am I making this up; is it really happening? Am I losing my marbles? Do people think I'm nuts? Your whole being cries out to God, and there's only silence. You're jumpy, nervous, and tired, because your nights are filled with restless thoughts. Your relationships suffer, because the other person can't figure out what's going on with you, and you can't really find the words to tell them. You can't even find the words to tell yourself what's going on!

Because it's such an unpleasant experience, we human beings tend to avoid the wilderness by whatever means possible. We numb our spirits and bodies with drugs, drink, sex, shopping sprees, sports, and working long hours. Some may read voraciously, trying to find a book that will tell them what's going on and how to get out of it as quickly as possible. Still others will look for someone or something to blame. You will find yourself daydreaming for the good old days when life was simpler, or being so afraid of the future and of your inability to cope that suicide seems like an attractive option.

But I write this as one who made it through the darkness and who survived the wilderness. There *is* light after dark, the Promised Land *can* be reached, and it is a land you never began to imagine. There will be new responsibilities and new awareness, because there is a "new you." Many things such as relationships will have to change to meet the new reality of your life. Your prayer will change because your understanding of God, self, and the world will change. I do not know how, when, where, or through whom God will deliver you, but what I do promise is that it *will* happen, *if* you don't run away from it, and *if* you remain faithful to a faithful God.

So when you find yourself in the wilderness, what can you do? Accept the reality of your situation. You are in darkness; you are in the desert. It's the pits, no doubt about it. Don't run away, don't blame, just accept.

Seek a spiritual director, a counselor, a trusted friend – someone who will be your companion or guide. This is a trip you cannot make on your own, because there are no landmarks. Nothing is familiar. At the very least, talk with your family physician, because you want to make sure that what you're going through isn't being triggered or complicated by a physical or chemical imbalance in your body.

Try not to start anything new for the time being. Not only can this be a form of running away, but this journey through the wilderness is going to sap a lot of your energy. You can feel very good about yourself if you just get through the day having fulfilled your basic responsibilities at home and at work.

Believe that God is with you. Perhaps the greatest pain of the darkness is the feeling that God has abandoned you. I assure you that the contrary is true. Notice how God likes to come at night: the night of the exodus from Egypt, the night when the beloved is discovered in the "Song of Songs," the night of the birth at Bethlehem, the night when Jesus walked on the water, the night that fell over the earth on Calvary, and the darkness of the tomb.

What you must do, and this is an absolute must, is to let go of your old images of God. One of the most significant graces of the wilderness experience is the deeper discovery of who God truly is. Remember the experience of Elijah in the cave? At the very moment you begin to see God as God is, rather than as you wish God to be, the wilderness and night cease to be places of terror and fear. They instead become the womb of a rich new life. And eventually, either in this particular wilderness or in any wilderness that comes later in your life, you will come to the realization that "God alone suffices," as Theresa of Avila discovered.

Closely related to letting go of images of God is letting go of patterns of prayer that may no longer be needed. As you come to know God, your way of being with God in prayer changes. To hang onto the old ways of prayer when they may no longer be needed is akin to taking a journey across the back roads of the USA using a map from 1950. Here the advice of a spiritual director can be of immense assistance.

Let personal and communal prayer and the Eucharist be your food and drink for this journey. Pray the psalms especially. Poetry can capture your feelings and moods in a way that no other prayer can, and those psalms have been the prayer support of God alone knows how many people who have made the same wilderness journey that you are making. I don't think I would have made it through my own wilderness without the help of Psalm 42 in particular.

Be patient. God alone knows what lies ahead and how long you will be in the wilderness. If you try to rush things, then you'll end up doing harm to yourself. All in God's good time. With God's hands forming and shaping you, you know you'll be a magnificent work of art. God won't be rushed, and that's hard for us to accept.

Be as open as you can with others. As I said above, chances are that your family, friends, and co-workers will not understand what's going on, unless they've been through a similar experience. If they have, they'll be happy for you and also sad --sad because they know of the pain but happy because they know what's waiting on the other side. No one needs to know all the details. Oftentimes all you can say is a simple: "I'm having a tough time today and I need your patience."

Be prepared for change. You will see things in our society and our Church that you instinctively know are not quite right. You will become aware of what sin really is, particularly your own sin. Your possessions will not become ends in themselves, but means by which you can draw closer to God and help others do the same. The boundaries of your heart and world will widen. You will put on more and more of the heart and mind of Jesus and his Father. I know this sounds scary, but remember: none of this happens on your own. The Spirit helps you every step of the way as you're birthed into a new life.

Chapter Twenty-Nine

"O LORD, I AM NOT WORTHY"! THANKS BE TO GOD YOU'RE NOT!

In India, there's an old story about two earthen jugs that a water bearer carried to his master's house each day. He would loop the handle of each over a pole across his shoulders, fill them at the river and carry them up the mountain path.

One of the jars was badly damaged. It had a crack down one side that caused it to leak half its water before they arrived at the master's house. The defect was plain to see, but the water bearer did not discard the jar. He was careful to put it on a different side each day to ease the ache in his back caused by the uneven load. Because of the poor performance, the cracked jar felt inferior to the sound jar. It was ashamed of how it wasted the efforts of the water bearer.

After a year of daily trips to the river, the cracked jar could no longer keep silent. "I am so sorry," it confessed to the water bearer, "for my flaw. It is unfair that you work so hard and only get the result of half as much work because of my imperfection. You should find another jar that is as sound as that one, so your efforts are not wasted."

"You should not compare your work to the work of the other jar," the water bearer replied. "I need both to accomplish the master's work. I know of your imperfection and have put it to good use."

As they made their way up the mountain path that day, the water bearer pointed out the beautiful flowers that grew on each side of the path. "For many years, nothing could grow here," he said. "The soil is dry and no one could take the time to provide water for plants to grow here. But you have found a way that takes no extra work to nourish the flowers. You please the master not only with the water you bring to his house, but the water you spill along the way."

I read this story last May, and immediately filed it away to use in a Lenten reflection. It spoke to me in so many different ways. Now perhaps it can speak to your own heart as well. I grew up in a Church where we were encouraged to choose Lenten penances for ourselves which would demand some sort of sacrifice. I actually believed making the sacrifice (and sticking to it for more than a week!) were more important than any personal change or conversion. Nowadays, however, I sense that folks are at loose ends. They know Lent is supposed to be a special time for renewal and conversion, but don't really know how to go about it except by making some sacrifice. The thinking goes like this: if it hurts, it's gotta be good for my soul.

I propose something different for your reflection: this Lent, make an effort to stop laying a guilt trip on yourself for what you think are your faults, your failings, your shortcomings.

We are constantly being bombarded by messages about our worth and value. These messages come from within ourselves, and also from our environment: "I'm not good enough. I lack self-discipline. I don't pray enough, and sin way too many times. I'm fat... skinny... tall... short... lazy... old... boring... bald. I drink too much, sleep too much, smoke too much, spend too much time on the Internet. I'm not rich enough. I don't drive an SUV. My home is shabby compared to my friends. My kids are struggling in school and they can't get into Notre Dame. I'm on a limited income, and I'm ashamed not to have all the extras that everyone else has. I'm too dependent on what other people think of me, and if people really knew me they'd be appalled; and God knows me, so God must really be disgusted with me. My prayers aren't answered, and there's too much suffering in my life, so I must not be doing something right, but I don't know what it is. My children and grandkids have all fallen away from the Church, their marriages are kaput, the kids are in trouble, so I must have done something wrong as a parent. I don't feel attracted to my spouse anymore, so what's wrong with me?

You get the idea, I'm sure. If you didn't see something above that fits you, I know for sure you thought of a few personal failings and shortcomings. If you didn't think of anything, that means one of two things; you're dead, or you're in denial.

Why is it that we must heap ourselves with guilt and shame? So many of those things are not our fault. I'm bald because it's a genetic thing. A grown child's religious choices are his or hers alone. It's part of growing up and making adult choices. I don't have an SUV because I realistically can't afford one. We inflict so much needless suffering on ourselves – physical, emotional, and spiritual – because we persist in this unneeded blame game.

On the other hand, many things *are* our fault. If I have chronic illness because I chose not to engage in healthy behavior, that was my choice. If my marriage is suffering because I spend too much time at work, then I must bear the consequences of that choice. Guilt and shame can be effective tools in bringing about personal change. Guilt and shame, however, are *not* to be used to viciously cut yourself into little pieces. No matter what you or I do, we still remain God's beloved child. No sin of ours will ever be bigger than God's love and forgiveness.

Use your shortcomings and faults – whether real or imagined – not as whips to flagellate yourself, but as stepping stones from which you can launch yourself into the arms of God. Over the last few years it has become more and more clear to me that I need my sinfulness and my flaws. I need those cracks in the water jug that I am. Now this does not excuse my sins. They do real damage to myself and to others and, when possible, should be avoided, and I must always make amends when possible. But as Jesus himself said, we sin seventy times seven times a day despite our best efforts to the contrary. It is our sins and shortcomings that keep us running to the arms of Jesus for help and consolation. If we were not flawed people, we would not need God.

So perhaps instead of working to eradicate your faults and flaws, simply hold them up and look at them. Observe the cracks, explore them. But then, instead of smashing yourself, see how God has used them to help you grow. Conversion, after all, is not getting rid of faults by your own powers. No… conversion is turning to God for help, to a God who wants to show you not only how your goodness is a blessing to the world, but also how your faults can be a blessing.

Chapter Thirty

THE END IS NIGH!

Back in March, during dinner with some friends from St. Joseph Parish in South Bend, the table talk turned to the end of time. Chris asked me if I believed we were in the End Times, when the world would end and Jesus would return to glory. Her husband, Jim, and another guest, Peggy, believed that we were. I was the only holdout.

In early July, *TIME* magazine's cover story was "The Bible and the Apocalypse." It detailed the success of books written about the end of the world. Using ideas from books of the Bible (especially Revelation), from the prophecies of Nostradamus, and various other works, many people today are convinced that we are very close to the end of time. They point to the 9/11 attacks, the wars and terrorist violence around the world, the cultural wars in various countries, the upheavals in the financial markets, and the chemical and biological scares and threats. Freakish weather patterns and destructive storms fuel the conviction. Some people will point to the rise of hate groups who attack Christian values and beliefs. Growing sexual immorality and permissiveness (including such things as the clerical pedophilia scandal) are seen as a sign that Satan's rule over this world needs to be ended, and soon.

In short, many folks look around the world and see evil upon evil. They raise the arms of their hearts in anguished prayer, wondering how long God will permit this evil to continue unabated. The sheer massiveness of evil reminds them of events in the *Book of Revelation*, and so they look avidly for signs that the Second Coming is upon us.

Other folks take a slightly different approach. They look for the Second Coming as a time when God will bring justice to the world, punishing evildoers and rewarding the good. For example, in this scenario all the corporate executives who made their millions on the backs of their workers and then sold out their workers are going to be punished by a just and vengeful God. Ditto for terrorists, for tyrannical world leaders, for drunk drivers who kill loved ones and get away with a slap on the wrist, and for those who favor abortions. Folks firmly expect Hell to be a place of wall-to-wall people, and Heaven will be occupied by the select few who lived righteous lives.

At the other end of the spectrum are those who view all this apocalyptic talk as nonsense. They firmly believe that the world has millions of miles left on it. If the world does come to an end, it will be long after they're dead, and thus beyond their caring. So eat, drink, and be merry! Now don't get me wrong. Yes, some of these folks couldn't give a hoot about anything or anyone other than their own little lives. But there are still many people who are very much aware of the great problems facing our world, our country, our churches, and they are concerned for just and fair resolutions. They just don't think that it all adds up to the imminent end of the world and the Second Coming of Christ.

Now we come to the folks in the middle, among whom I count myself. We know that the world will one day come to an end. That's going to happen for sure when our sun burns out a few billion years from now. We also have the teaching of Jesus, who said several times that the world will end, and that he will come again. We believe Jesus when he said that no one knows the time when this will happen -- not even Jesus himself knew. We also know and believe that those who did evil to their brothers and sisters will be punished, if not here, then in the hereafter. The only problem is this: when, where, and how? Do the End-Timers know something we don't? Could they be right? Is it a matter of months instead of centuries?

My own personal reflection on the topic has five aspects to it: First, I do believe the world will come to an end, but I also believe we have a long time until that happens. By the same token, I'm not gonna bet my life savings on it! I have that belief because of the extraordinary patience God has shown to his people over the centuries of human existence. That is so evident in both Old and New Testaments. God gives us time to repent, to convert, to change our lives. God wants everyone to be saved, and I believe that he will give us the time we need to make our lives right before him. Will humanity use that opportunity? Who knows? Many were the times when God would have been totally justified in saying, "Enough of this nonsense"! and totally squashing the world. However, that would have harmed the innocent as well. Will God harm his beloved children just to prove a point? I mean… just look at the numbers. How many really evil people do you know? Not many, eh? How many good decent people do you know? Lots, right? Well, if you were God, would you destroy the world because of a few?

Second, the end-of-the-world theme has come up many times in world history, and usually it is a regional phenomenon. If you were a citizen of the Roman Empire facing the barbarian invasions, for example, you knew the feeling of impending catastrophe, but a citizen of China could have cared less. If you were a Jew in the sixth century B.C. and saw your beloved Jerusalem being razed and your neighbors being deported to Babylon, it was the end of the world for you. For the Celtic tribes, however, life went on as before. The Black Death scoured Europe, but Native Americans lived gently upon the land. The Flu Pandemic, the Depression, the explosions of the first atomic and the first hydrogen bombs, the Cuban missile crisis… folks were pretty sure things were gonna end right then and there. In every case, it was a sudden and catastrophic change in the everyday life of a given region of the world that precipitated this end-times fear in that region.

Now move to the present day. The end-times phenomena in the U.S. reached a crescendo because of September 11. This was a sudden and catastrophic change in American life. But following that regional pattern, the end-times discussion is raging in the U.S., but in Europe (which did *not* directly experience 9/11) it's not a pressing matter of concern.

Third, the end of the world was not a topic of pressing concern in the 1990's. Those were good years in the U.S.A. Prospects for peace seemed to be improving around the world. Several wars were waged with minimum loss of American life (but I venture to say that those on the losing side didn't feel quite as good as we did).

It's a bit different now. Terrorism, financial struggle, loss of faith and trust in civic, religious, and business leaders, attacks on religious values (such as "One nation under God") are real hammer blows to the national psyche. I believe that the end-times talk crescendos when folks feel most powerless and unable to control their lives. In times like these folks either lash out with blame and punishment, or they isolate themselves behind protective walls. Basically, when people feel that they have some say in their lives, then the end-of-the-world scenario doesn't have as much power.

Finally, I believe the world is ending every day. When we go to bed at night and fall asleep, we die to that day. The next morning we rise to a new day, with new possibilities, new opportunities. When someone loses a loved one to death, their world ends, and a new one must be fashioned, which does not include the physical presence of the loved person. Divorce, retirement, layoff, firing, serious illness or injury, bankruptcy, foreclosure—those are all moments when someone's familiar world comes to an end and something new must be birthed into being. Marriage, ordination, religious vows, graduation, the birth of the first child, a falling in love—all these bring an end to one world and the creation of a new.

Sure we fear all these things. Humans are nervous about change. But, our life experiences tell us that we have nothing to fear, because God walks with us through the change. In addition, family and friends are present too, and oftentimes, one meets new people who turn out to be profound companions on one's life journey. So we don't have to wait for the end-times. We're experiencing it every day!

A frightening view of the end-times feeds on fear. There is one sense in which fear can be a good thing. It will help us to make necessary changes in our life and re-arrange life's priorities. But, by and large, fear is an evil thing, for it paralyzes us into inaction, causes us to make judgments about other people, and fosters violence to oneself or to others. Those are not the signs of God's presence. Negative fear is *always* the work of the Evil One—*always.*

Let's remember a few words from the prayer we pray right after the "Our Father" at Mass: *"Protect us from all anxiety, as we wait in joyful hope for the coming of our Savior, Jesus Christ."* It's far better to live our lives in joyful hope as opposed to traumatic fear.

Chapter Thirty-One

IS THIS A CRAZY WORLD OR WHAT?

Muslim extremists stir chaos in the Middle East, Pakistan, Thailand, Sudan, Somalia. Closer to home, there are extremist governments in South America, drug lords terrorizing Mexico, Cuba in transition. In cities across the United States murders are at a new high.

Governments are strapped for cash, forcing them to cut services to the poor, to schools, to the youngest and oldest citizens. Computers have us at their mercy. Vital records are lost or stolen, crashes paralyze businesses and homes. Try finding a human being on the other end of a phone these days when you need service!

Oil companies make billions in profits while many families have their budgets wrecked by high fuel costs for home and auto, job worries, health crises. Last month I read an article where several scientists say that carbon dioxide emissions are going to have an irreversible influence on the world's climate by the year 2010, unless drastic measures are taken.

I could go on, but you read the papers. You watch the news. Aren't you just a little bit scared about what the future might bring? Do you feel that anyone is in control or that anyone really knows what's going on?

Less well-covered have been the trends in religion, and for many folks these are just as worrisome. The growing strength of militant fundamentalism is a major concern. This trend is not restricted just to Islamic terrorist organizations, but even Christian fundamentalism has a certain militancy about it.

There is a major shift to non-white Christianity. Sixty percent of all Christians now come from outside Europe and North America. Between twenty-five and thirty percent of the U.S. Catholic Church is now Hispanic. This change is happening even within religious communities. Last year in Holy Cross, for example, there were thirty-two men in formation in the U.S. In East Africa and Chile, there were fifty-five in formation.

There is continuing controversy over the proper relationship between church and state (religious activities in public schools, evolution vs. creationism, displays of the Ten Commandments). There is much more God-talk than ever before from public figures. Some such talk is sincere, some is merely a cloak of righteousness ("By their fruits you will know them.").

Bio-technology raises new moral questions. From stem cell research to cloning, religious groups are grappling with – and divided by – the ethical dimensions of scientific advances.

Sexuality and gender debates divide congregations. Southern Baptists are arguing about the role of women. Protestant denominations are deeply split over same-sex unions and the ordination of practicing homosexuals. In several denominations, there is talk of possible schism. Catholicism is not immune to these conflicts either.

Strong religious leaders on the national level are few and far between, and the ones who are prominent have their own agendas. Some Catholic leaders, such as Cardinal McCarrick of Washington, D.C. and Cardinal Mahoney of Los Angeles have regional influence, but I think the U.S. Catholic hierarchy is so consumed with the pedophilia scandal and other matters of sexuality, finances, the priest shortage, and liturgical changes that it is almost invisible when it comes to moral and spiritual leadership (the recent stand on immigration being an exception to this contention).

In spite of or because of all this, there is a greatly renewed interest in spirituality, both within religious traditions and also outside them. Protestant Christians, for example, are rediscovering the ancient Catholic practices of meditative prayer, retreats, and monasticism. Many Jewish congregations are putting more emphasis on traditional spiritual practices. Catholics are looking for different ways to express their relationship with God and each other in addition to Mass and the sacraments. Meanwhile, other Americans are seeking a spiritual life without specific religious ties. Through a blending of worship styles, they are crafting their personal, more individualistic spirituality.

So what does it all add up to? We're in a time of massive change, which is accelerating at a pace too fast for us to comprehend. Our whole culture is struggling to understand how the institutions of government, church, education, and family life came under such upheavals at about the same time. There's very much an "out of control" feeling. The natural reaction to this confusion is fear, and because of fear we want to do what human beings have instinctively done since Day One: fight back at that which threatens our physical, mental, spiritual, sexual, or material comfort zone.

I've been reading a fascinating book. *Cosmos and Psyche: Intimations of a New World View*, written by Richard Tarnas, starts off by saying that we are presently in a time of history that has its parallel in the time of Copernicus, Galileo, Newton, et al., when it was discovered that the earth was not the center of the universe – a discovery that set off a tremendous reaction among the peoples of Europe. On the one hand, it led to the great discoveries of the Enlightenment and the Renaissance, and to a multitude of new insights about human life and the natural world. On the other hand, there was violent resistance, led by the Church, to all changes these new insights and discoveries brought about. This back-and-forth between insight/discovery and resistance continues even to our own time. Using my own words, I can summarize what Mr. Tarnas said in this way: When it was discovered that the earth was not the center of the universe around which everything revolved, the new center of the universe became 'me,' around which everything revolves ("me" can be an organization, person, or group). Now we're starting to see the insufficiency of 'me as center of the universe,' and we're looking for alternatives.

On the one hand, this awareness is good. We've learned a lot about the uniqueness of every human being and about what makes us tick. The discoveries of science have made life easier and safer in so many different ways. On the other hand, we're now seeing the havoc that "me as center" has wreaked on marriage, family, church, social values, the environment, the allocation of resources, and the sense of community. To use the words of Jesus: "What does it profit one to gain the whole world and lose one's soul?" (Luke 9:25). I really believe that we are now engaged in a search for our souls -- for union with God, others, the world, and yes, with ourselves.

I don't know what further conclusions Mr. Tarnas might draw, or what he will suggest as alternatives, but let me share some thoughts of my own on the matter. These reflections come from prayer, from reading, from letters that benefactors write, conversations, etc. They're not gospel – just the thoughts of one human being.

Am I pessimistic or optimistic? I would come down on the side of optimism. It is the extremists that are causing most of the troubles in our world, but they are a very tiny minority. They just seem to have a lot of power because the news media feed on and encourage (by their very presence) these shenanigans. The vast majority of men and women in our world are sensible, moderate, thoughtful people. All they wish for is the respect due them as human beings, a decent living, a roof over their heads and food on the table, safety and education for their children, good health care, a spiritual home, and a happy old age. Sooner or later, radical agendas collapse from the weight of their own inconsistencies, their inability to speak to the needs and dreams of the common person, and their lack of hope and love. Just in 2009, look at Hezbollah's electoral defeat in Lebanon, the massive unrest in Iran, Pakistani tribes turning against the Taliban, Hamas losing support amongst the Palestinians, Tibet's rebellion against the Chinese government.

I am optimistic because we have seen the power of non-violence to topple governments that do not respond to human need. We've seen in our own country how public outcry can affect the inertia of government, or change its direction. The demand is not going to stop either. There are just too many basic human needs that are not being met or are being ignored. They *can* be met, and that's the tragedy of the whole thing! It just takes a re-arranging of priorities.

I am optimistic because civil and religious authority is being questioned as never before. The days of "Trust me"! or "Because I said so"! are giving way to the demand that those in power be accountable, take different viewpoints into consideration, and credit people with enough intelligence to weigh pros and cons and make their own decisions. If people feel they have been heard, if they sense they are being treated with respect and consideration, the chances of good, sound solutions to problems are greatly increased.

Optimism blooms when I see the actions of Bill and Melinda Gates, and Warren Buffet and others like them. The actions of these folks is a prime example of how "me" is giving way to "we." College kids are volunteering in droves for a year or two of service and assistance to the poor in the U.S. and around the world. A large group of evangelical ministers recently presented a petition to the Administration urging that the threat of global warming be taken seriously. We're learning what it means to share our world with diverse peoples, animals, plants, etc. We're learning that when the basic needs of the Earth and all her people are honored, everyone and everything benefits.

I have seen a great increase in the number of people seeking solid spiritual growth, a deepening of their relationship to God, the world, and other people. Traditional religious practices alone do not suffice; folks want the traditional practices *plus* personal spiritual depth.

Recent DNA genealogical research is showing how we are related to each other genetically. All of humanity can trace its deepest ancestry back to East Africa. Truly we are bone of each other's bones, flesh of each other's flesh. I'm not altogether optimistic that this discovery will reduce racial and regional prejudices, but hey – gotta start somewhere.

I am optimistic because on the local level people continue to reach out to others in need. We do care for each other; we reach deep into hearts, pocketbooks, and pantries when necessary.

Above all, I am optimistic because God has promised through Jesus that evil will not win. I've seen this in my many decades of life – what goes around does come around. Oppression fails. Abuse fails. Lying, cheating, selfishness, and narcissism fail. War and violence fail. Authoritarian rule fails. Extremism of any kind fails.

So yes, I have optimism. There are just too many good people. Recent history is showing a drive for human dignity and a compassion for the Earth and all her creatures. There remains also a God of extraordinary compassion, kindness, and justice. Love always wins… always!

Chapter Thirty-Two

FORGIVENESS

At the end of the year we are very much aware of past and present. With various emotions, we look back over the year and look ahead to the coming year. If there has been any kind of rupture or hurt in our relationships, then it seems as though it's felt most strongly around this time of year, as we think of what was, what is, what could have been, and what will be.

In other words, the new year is a time when we look at our personal history. I am what I am because of what I have been and done, good and bad. My self is woven out of a mass of tangled threads. My motivations and intentions are mixed. I have allowed people to influence me for better or worse. I have trusted other people, and at times the trust is worth it, while at other times it brings a broken, angry heart, because I have been betrayed. Some of the things I have done have turned out to be creative, while other things have been destructive for myself and for other people. To deny my past is to deny my self; I am my history. As a mature person, I try to accept that. As a Christian, I believe that my history does not absolutely determine my future. I am free to choose alternatives. I am free to forgive. If I cannot or will not forgive, then I consign myself to a "hell," to a life of alienation from God, others, and self.

So what is this thing we call forgiveness? It is not the same as acquittal – leaving the courtroom without a stain on our record. Acquittal is saying: "Forgive and forget." In other words, let's simply pretend it never happened.

But we know this isn't true. We can't forget. If you have been badly hurt by someone, then the scars and memories will always be there, even if you "forgive" them. If forgiveness is forgetting, then it mocks the depth and seriousness of the suffering that we humans inflict on one another. If forgiveness means forgetting, then forgiveness is a trivial and profoundly offensive idea, for there are things that should never be forgotten.

Now some folks will agree that the past can't be changed and it shouldn't be forgotten. So, they would say that forgiveness is an agreement not to forget, but at least to suspend judgment on the past. In other words, I have hurt you, and I deserve your anger. I deserve punishment, but you kindly excuse what I have done. This forgiveness is a very New Testament approach, and many Christians think this way. I am a sinner, but God graciously treats me as if I were not.

This is an advance on the "forgive and forget," but it's still not true forgiveness. What this kind of "forgiveness" is saying is this: I know exactly what you are and what you have done. But I'll say no more about it. Do what you like, I won't make any difficulties. This is in fact a terribly negative judgment, because I'm not taking you seriously enough to do anything. You're in kind of a limbo… always looking over your shoulder waiting for me to bring up the subject. You *know* I haven't forgotten! And chances are very good that in some serious argument, I'm going to forget myself and bring it up.

A good example of this would be infidelity in a marital relationship. It is very hard for couples to talk about this, even after the infidelity has become known. This silence nurtures the growth of mistrust and suspicion. If Pat says he's going to work late, or Chris says she's going to have lunch with a friend, all the suspicions come right to the surface, but no one speaks about them. You always wonder what the other person is *really* thinking, or *really* doing. You can't even have a decent honest disagreement, because you're afraid it might spin out of control and you'll say things in the heat of the battle that you'll later regret. It sometimes feels like you're walking on broken glass in your bare feet. If it's not living in hell, you're certainly in the outer vestibule.

Real forgiveness is something that gives us hope. It recognizes the reality of the past and gives hope for the future. The occasions when we feel genuinely forgiven are the moments when we feel that someone *does* care what we do because she or he loves us, and that such love is strong enough to cope with and survive the hurt we have done. Forgiveness like this is enormously creative, because it reveals new dimensions to a relationship, new depths, new possibilities. We can find a love that is richer and more challenging than before.

Real forgiveness is me saying to you, "Yes, you have hurt me, but that doesn't mean our relationship is all over. I forgive you. I still love you." That is a moment of enormous liberation. It recognizes the reality of the past, and the seriousness of the damage that was done. The "I still love you" is a mature and serious love, without illusions. It is a love that looks at and fully *feels* your weakness.

One of the best examples is the forgiveness that results between a genuinely recovering alcoholic and his or her spouse and family. The disease of alcoholism produces a terrible amount of destruction within a family. I have known several families who have faced the issue head-on, and through AA and Alanon have reached the point of genuine forgiveness. These families and individuals speak openly and honestly about the hurt, but they also speak of how they have grown in love. The hurtful reality of the past is not denied or forgotten. The future is in God's hands. The present is filled with hope and love.

There are times, however, when forgiveness seems almost impossible. Can survivors of the concentration camps forgive the camp commandant? Can Arabs forgive Israelis and vice versa? Can innocent victims forgive terrorists? Can you forgive a drunk driver who killed your spouse or child? There are simply those times in life when we run smack into the human limits of love, and we cannot forgive.

The same holds true for individuals who have done something for which they cannot forgive themselves. It's a lead yoke around their hearts and lives, a screaming inner voice which daily reminds them that they're a lousy, no-good person.

At those times, it's well to remember what Jesus said: "For mortals it is impossible, but not for God; for God all things are possible" (Mk 10: 27). God forgives, and God has the right to forgive. The Gospel says that God-made-man is the ultimate victim of human cruelty. God bleeds for every human wound, suffers every human pain, and weeps for every life that is needlessly, senselessly ended or altered. Inasmuch as we do good or ill to any other person, it is done to God. Forgiveness is not just a human affair – it is God's affair too.

The good news of Jesus is that there is beyond all our sin a love that is utterly inexhaustible. God's love for us never reaches a point where God will say: "Enough! That's the last straw. I can't love you any more"! So God can always survive the hurt we do to him via the hurt we do to others and to ourselves. God's love is always there, waiting for us, a home whose door is always open. Nothing we do can ever shut that door. The only thing that keeps us out is our own personal refusal to ask for and to trust in that mercy and compassion.

To fully understand how God forgives, all we have to do is look at Jesus on the cross. We believe that Jesus crucified is God crucified. The cross is a terrible act of violence. It represents the total human rejection of love. And not even *that* can destroy God's love; he returns to his disciples and wishes them peace. God cares what we do, because God suffers what we do. God is forever wounded, but forever loving. The possibilities of relationship with God are new each day.

So the hurt that I do to myself or to others need not be a stopping point in growth. It need not be a reason to flagellate myself unmercifully. By the same token, neither do I need to flagellate other people for the hurt they've done to me, or silently hold them accountable for their sin. Sin and hurt can become a *starting* point, not a stopping point. Our sin can be the occasion of a fresh and wider vision of the grace of God as well as a fresh and wider vision of the possibility of human love. I personally am becoming more and more convinced that my sin is a stepping stone to greater and greater understanding of the endless endurance of God's love. Beyond every failure, God's creative mercy waits. We have a future because of this love.

Now all this is a matter of faith. It takes faith to see God in Christ crucified. It takes faith to believe in the unyielding and inexhaustible love of God. It takes faith to believe that there is a future for us despite the reality of our sins. And it also takes faith to believe that God can forgive those whose violence has shattered the lives of individuals, families, and societies.

This is hard to comprehend. We find it extraordinarily difficult, if not impossible, to forgive murderers and tyrants. The most frightening thing about this inability to forgive is that we consign ourselves to a living hell of alienation. If I have an unforgiving heart, it's going to eat away at every aspect of my life. I will know no peace. My days will be filled with thoughts of revenge and vengeance. My heart cannot heal and cannot mourn. The capacity to love slowly gets dried up because love is killed by pain.

But, remember, at the heart of our existence is a love that cannot be killed by pain. God can forgive and does forgive. So this is a warning against treating or regarding any human being as unforgiveable. If I hold someone else's sin against them, and expect God to punish that person, then I have to hold my own sins against myself and expect God to punish me. If I forget how much hurt I have inflicted on God present in others, and cling to my "rights" and nurse my unforgiven injuries, then I'm in mortal danger. That's the whole point of the parable of the unforgiving servant (Matthew 18.23-35). We must somehow use God's grace to forgive the unforgivable so that we can live. Through forgiveness, you and I help God create the future of our love.

Chapter Thirty-Three

GOD AS MOTHER?

Before I begin this reflection, please note the following: Given the nature of the topic, I know there will be some reaction. Please be assured that I am not a radical liberal feminist, a heretic, a child of Satan, a far left-wing nut, a New Ager who defied Church teachings, or whatever else pops to mind. Nor do I speak for all of Holy Cross. And above all, I don't want to cause you apoplexy or urticaria or trichotillomania or hyperventilation. In other words, now that the gate is down, the bells are ringing, and the lights are flashing, you go past this point at your own risk! So chuckle up... the life you get could be your own! (I know, I know... that was a real bad groaner.)

Why this particular topic?

Well, in late October, I received an email from a benefactor who shared with me an excerpt from a theology book he had been reading. The book was given to Ed by his niece or granddaughter – I can't remember which – and the excerpt reported on a poll of Catholics in Ireland. The poll showed a sharp increase in the number of those who saw God as mother. There was an equally sharp increase in the number of those who imagined God as spouse or lover rather than master.

Ed went on to write: "What kind of sheltered life have I lived? My only recollection of God as mother came from some of my niece's objections to Scriptures that God isn't necessarily a male and that the use of the male pronoun isn't appropriate. But the percentages for the motherhood of God and the spouse astonish me"!

Ed is an older man, and discussion of the motherhood of God is relatively new. It is a beloved image of feminist theologians, yet all too often it is wielded as a sword against males and I have a hard time with that. Many times in spiritual direction I have encountered women (and some men) who have great difficulty praying to God as Father, because for them, "father" is a word that carries many psychological scars. I've encouraged them to use the image of God as mother, and that often seems to help.

Now it's important to realize that in reality, God is neither mother nor father. Nor is God friend, spouse, or any other term we choose to use. God is God... God just IS. Our application of human terms is simply our poor attempt to try to understand the unknowable, to personalize a relationship with someone we see as very important in our lives. God knows this is the way we are (he created us this way, after all) and so is quite comfortable with our efforts to ascribe human characteristics to the Divine. We also have to deal with the poverty of the English language when it comes to talking about someone with no gender. Our language leaves us with only three possibilities: he, she, or it. Since God is most certainly not an "it," we're forced to use one of the other two pronouns.

Though the image of God as mother – or as others would say, the feminine face of God – has not yet hit the mainstream of modern Catholic thinking, there is ample precedent in Scripture and in spiritual theology. It begins right in the opening chapter of Genesis: "God created man in his own image, in the image of God he created them; male and female he created them." Both male and female are required for God's image to be complete.

As a general point of fact, over and over again the Old Testament speaks of God's compassion and mercy. Believe it or not, the word which is consistently used as a metaphor for the divine compassion is *rehem*, which means "womb, uterus."

In *Deuteronomy*, Moses told the people: "You were unmindful of the Rock that begot you, you forgot the God who gave you birth." The Hebrew verb translated as "begot" refers to the specifically male function in reproduction. At another time, as recorded in the *Book of Numbers*, Moses is fed up with the complaints of the Israelites, and says, "Why are you so displeased with me you burden me with all this people? Or was it I who conceived this people? Or was it I who gave them birth, that you tell me to carry them at my bosom"?

Isaiah has beautiful descriptions! God asks: "Can a country be brought forth in one day, or a nation be born in a single moment"? Consider this line: "Thus says the Lord: as nurslings, you shall be carried in her arms, and fondled in her lap. As a mother comforts her child, so I will comfort you." God speaks, "But now, I cry out as a woman in labor, gasping and panting" and "Can a mother forget her infant, be without tenderness for the child of her womb? Even should she forget, I will never forget you."

Psalm 90 hints at God's maternity: "Before the mountains were begotten, or the earth and the world were brought forth, from everlasting to everlasting you are God." Psalm 22 contains another reference: "You relied on the Lord, let him deliver you." Again the word used is not as we commonly understand it. "Deliver" does not mean "free from." The original language uses the word for delivery of a child.

Jeremiah has the Lord asking, "Is Ephraim (i.e. the Hebrew people) not my favored son, the child in whom I delight"? All the language here is feminine, according to the commentaries.

In the *Book of Job*, God gives a tremendous speech to Job, one of the most beautiful passages in all of Scripture. Among other things, God asks Job: "Has the rain a father; or who has begotten the drops of dew? Out of the womb comes the ice, and who gives the hoarfrost its birth in the skies"? (38:28)

The *Book of Proverbs* speaks of a person who shared with God in the creation of all things. This person is consistently given a female gender, by the writer of the *Book of Wisdom,* and also by Jesus himself, e.g., Matthew 11.19 and Luke 7.35. Many scholars have identified the person of Wisdom with Jesus or with the Holy Spirit. The ancient Hebrew word *ruah* is feminine gender, and means "breath" and "spirit." In the Bible, *ruah* is the power of God which brings creative life out of chaos.

Jesus uses motherly imagery also. Listen: "O Jerusalem, Jerusalem… how often have I yearned to gather your children, as a mother bird gathers her young under her wings" (Mt 23.37). Speaking of birds, the dove has always been a feminine symbol, and for centuries the dove has been a sign of the Holy Spirit. Something I did not know before, but which ties perfectly into this reflection, is that the first tabernacles in the ancient church were always in the shape of a dove. There's powerful symbolism there!

Ancient Syrian Christians, such as Macarius, spoke of the Holy Spirit as "our Mother." The 13th century mystic Mechtilde of Magdeburg offers this image: "God is like a great mother, who bends and takes thy child from the floor to her bosom." Blessed Julian of Norwich is one person in western spirituality who consistently reflects on this image. Time and again she refers to Jesus as a mother who nourishes us with himself. In her *Revelations*, she also says: "And thus I saw that God enjoys that he is our very spouse, and our soul is his beloved wife. And Christ enjoys that he is our brother, and Jesus enjoys that he is our savior." Julian refers to these five roles – father, mother, brother, spouse, and savior – as the five joys of God. Julian proclaims that "our Savior is our mother, in whom we are endlessly borne and never shall come out of him."

Two recent Popes have both referred to God as mother. John Paul I made the statement that "God is Father, and even more, he is Mother." I still remember how that made the news, because it was such a radical statement from a Pope! John Paul II praised God as Mother. He commented on the parable of the Prodigal Son: "The father who embraces his lost son is the definitive icon of God.... The merciful father of the parable has in himself all the characteristics of fatherhood and motherhood. In embracing the son, he shows the profile of a mother."

Let's take a different way of looking at God as Mother. If we – male and female alike – are made in the image of God, then who better to reflect that image than the Blessed Virgin. Mary gave life. Her child is flesh of her flesh, and bone of her bone. God gives us life, not just at conception, but also through Baptism and the Eucharist. Life doesn't happen just at birth. I can look back over my life and see four significant events where God gave me new life, new vision, new hope. These events were such turnarounds for me that I can truly say they were a new birth.

Mary sustained her young child's life, and provided what was needed for her child to grow. How does the God who loves us as a mother reach out to us, touch us, offer us nourishment? Mary wept. She experienced sadness when her child faced danger, or sadness, when she saw danger ahead but could really do anything about it except pray and hope that what she and Joseph have taught their son will endure. Do you believe God weeps for you -- not only because of what you have done, but also because God knows the pain and hurt in your life? Much of our pain comes from sinful people and broken nature, but much of it is also self-inflicted through the choices we make. God takes no more delight in your pain and suffering than you would in your own child's pain.

Mary made great sacrifices. She left behind, permanently or temporarily, things she would like to have in order to make sure Jesus had what he needed. Mothers know intuitively the full meaning of the words of Consecration: "This is my body, given up for you." We see on Good Friday how much Mary had to sacrifice so that we might have the life we need free from fear.

I might add, by the way, that all these things are also done by fathers. It's just that we guys do them in a different way. Women have a "very unique capacity for the other," linked to their capacity to give and bear life. Men are also capable of living for others, but it's different. I don't know enough psychology or anthropology to speak fluently to these differences, but I know they're there.

Mary yearned to be present. Remember that scene from the Gospel when Jesus was told that his mother was outside? Remember Cana? This desire to be present is absolutely a universal characteristic of motherhood. God's heart yearns to be present to us also. To think that God is distant and unconcerned about the events and practicalities of our life is to think wrongly. God searches daily for ways to mother us.

Mary's heart delighted in her child. When the shepherds visited Mary and Joseph in the stable, Luke says she pondered all these things in her heart. Mothers ponder all the moments of a child's life, from the first little coo, to marriage, to the first child of the new generation. They delight in all these things, and so does God.

So as you can see, the feminine and motherly images of God have been very much a part of the Church's spiritual heritage. It's just that they have not been talked about a whole lot. John Paul I and II were not breaking new ground when they each spoke of the motherly nature of God; they were simply resurrecting ancient images.

I hope this reflection has been of some help to you. If you remain comfortable with the male imagery used of God, then by all means let that continue to nourish your spirituality. But if you would like to experience another dimension of God, or if your spirituality is in a kind of limbo stage, or if you have difficulty with the male imagery because of inner scars, try praying, meditating, and reflecting using the feminine images of God. You might be surprised by the results!

Chapter Thirty-Four

RANDOM MUSINGS ABOUT THIS AND THAT

I love driving the back roads of the USA when traveling. The pace is slower, the countryside unfolds in a way it doesn't on the Interstates, and you meet the most interesting people in their home setting. You not only see more, but what I always marvel at how Mother Nature so quickly reclaims what is hers. Abandoned homes or barns, parking lots, driveways, once-tilled fields… it's amazing how quickly things revert back to nature. At one point, this led to a very sobering thought: Mother Earth does not need human beings. She'll get along quite fine without us. But we human beings definitely need Mother Earth. So it pays to take good care of her.

***

I like to post thought-provoking sayings on my bulletin boards. In the office, one is: *"Today is the tomorrow you worried about yesterday."* In the shop, I've posted: *"Those who complain a lot will have a hard time seeing blessing."*

It took years for me to learn that most of the time the things that I worry about and plan for never come to pass. Or if they do come to pass, either they're not as bad as I thought they would be, or they come in an entirely different way than anticipated.

And as far as complaining, what good does it do? Yes, there can be legitimate reasons to complain, such as shoddy service, dangerous prod-

151

ucts, etc. But most of the time complaints are about picayune things, silly things, and end up only making myself and others miserable.

I might add that I've noticed something interesting about myself. Instead of being thankful for what God has given me, I too often look around to see what others have. It's a violation of the 11th Commandment ("Thou shalt not make comparisons."). As usual with a violation of that commandment, the result is envy, jealousy, perhaps a little spite and malice. Thanksgiving and gratitude go out the window!

**

Here in Fatima House where I live, we have community night on Thursdays. In nice weather some of us sit out on the patio. Not far from where we sit is the path around the lake, which is populated by ducks, geese, swans, turtles and the occasional jumping fish. A multitude of walkers and joggers file by. It's a lovely path, filled with natural beauty. I was so surprised one evening when I saw a young lady walking along, reading a book, with an I-Pod plugged into her ears – seemingly oblivious to the beauty. One of my fellow residents goes over to St. Mary's convent daily to say Mass for the infirm sisters. One day at lunch he said: "I saw something today I haven't seen in awhile: a young lady *not* talking into a cell phone." I know of small offices where a boss uses e-mails to communicate with staff instead of walking down the hall to speak face-to face. It also seems as though text messaging has replaced actual conversation. I mentioned that to my boss once, and he said: "Sometimes it's safer to text message than to talk on the phone." Maybe so. but still....

I don't know. As good and as convenient as all these electronic marvels are, would we not cope without them? What will happen to normal human conversation, to intimacy, to an awareness of our surroundings, and to the daily contact that sand-papers us into the image and likeness of God? We need community and communion to grow, as well as aloneness and solitude.

**

Following on the above, why this fear of solitude and silence? So many people fill their lives with noise. I am so grateful that I have two hearing aids I can turn off and gain instant silence. Of course, silence and solitude mean that the inner noise crops up, and it's that which most people fear: "Who am I"? "What is my life all about"? "Do I make a difference"? "Am I *really* loved"? "Why do I always act this way around certain people"?

There's also the raging noise that comes from the humiliation of being rejected, over-looked, ignored, or left for another. There's inner crying when we feel unable to be ourselves, to fully use our talents, to fulfill our dreams in the way that we would like. When we sin and do wrong, or betray what's best in ourselves, guilt hisses. Inside each of us, there's always a frustrated artist, musician, poet, writer, athlete, politician, lover, and saint. All this noise assaults us.

The right question to ask is not "Are we hurt"? but "Where are we hurting"? We all carry a lot of disappointment, frustration, and sadness inside. Solitude enables you and me to look squarely at these facts of our life. Along with suffering, silence and solitude are life's greatest teachers. In that quietness, that void, we meet God. We achieve depth and wisdom, perspective and compassion, and above all, we discover that we are loved deeply by God, just as we are.

***

One of the really fun things about getting older is having to get up at night to use the bathroom. Sometimes I can go right back to sleep; at other times, I lie awake. I can't help but wonder sometimes if this is a part of God's plan for our growth. When we lie awake during the night, our mind just won't shut up. The inner phantoms just chatter away about life's journey, death, guilt, despair, blame, revenge, lust, and so on. They keep up awake and force us to deal with them, because we won't deal with them during daylight.

Being awake when the world sleeps has a long tradition in spirituality, for all religious traditions say that night is the time we can gain the most insight about ourselves as we really are. When we can't sleep at night, we're forced to recognize that our lives in the light have not been shadow-free and perfect. So what better time for prayer and for encountering our Divine Physician?

***

Turning sixty and having parents who are in their early eighties, each day is seen more and more as a gift. I'm at the point now where I say: "Well, I didn't see my name in the obits this morning, so I know it's gonna be a good day"! Those who speak of "new day, same old stuff"! just aren't paying attention to the extraordinary opportunities to be found in daily routine. It helps me to recall a Buddhist saying: "Put your finger into the river. Take it out. Put it in again. Are you putting your finger into the same river"? The answer is "No." It may look the same, feel the same, smell the same, but it is not the same river. Nor are you the same person you were when you started reading this paragraph.

***

Perfection is not an option in human life. Human beings are inherently imperfect, and nothing we do will ever change that. I deeply believe that God deliberately made us imperfect so we would always need to grasp a stronger hand. And if God made us this way, surely God gives us slack, grace, understanding, compassion, and forgiveness. To accept one's imperfectness is perhaps the surest way to inner peace and a deep relationship with God, self, and others. It can also lead to a healthy sense of humor and perspective.

***

Time and speed... oh man, are we obsessed by it! "Now, right this moment"! "Get outta my way"! "Why didn't you fill the check out while you were standing in line"? "Which is the quickie Mass"? "Isn't she or he done yet"?

It's always been one of my secret delights to watch someone in a hurry pass me. Inevitably, if it's city driving, I'll catch up to that person at a stoplight ahead. If I see someone constantly looking at their watch, I'll wait till the next time he does it, and then innocently ask, "What time is it"? Almost always, he has to look at the watch again!

The faster we go, the more we leave behind the simple joys of life. Getting things done quickly doesn't lead to relaxation; it just means we do twice as much work in the same amount of time. Letting our time be constantly controlled by others or by external circumstances leads to resentment, rebelliousness, and a multitude of physical ailments. Taking control of our use of time and earmarking some time for ourselves is absolutely necessary for mental, physical and spiritual health.

And please don't say: "It can't be done." Yes it can. How about some prayer or deep breathing at stoplights? Looking at and enjoying your surroundings while you're waiting in line? People-watching in the airport? Doing some spiritual reading while in a traffic jam? Standing or sitting outside for a brief moment, savoring the beauty of it all?

Each moment of the day has the potential to teach us something about ourselves and God. If at the end of a day I haven't learned anything new about my world, my self, my God, then basically it was a wasted day as far as human growth goes. Sure, maybe I got a lot of things done, but is "getting things done" the source of happiness and contentment?

**

In nature, there are ceaseless cycles of activity and growth, followed by dormancy and hibernation. Activity must stop in order for new growth to happen. We are a part of the natural world, right? I'm not going to advocate hibernation, attractive as it sounds sometimes! But dormancy is another story. This is something you can do several times a day. Dormancy is Sabbath time. It's a brief moment in the day when you choose **not** to do something productive, so as to give your soul, mind, and body a chance to quietly take in nutrients so that you can *remain* productive. Push back from the desk, close your eyes for five minutes, and observe your breathing. Buy a rocking chair and sit in it regularly, not thinking, not praying, not talking to a friend, just sitting. Go someplace where you just cannot be reached. Trust me, the world will get along without you for a few minutes. Dormant times make for a marvelous human being!

**

In the Gospel of John, the first words out of Jesus' mouth are: "What are you looking for"? The entire Gospel basically tries to answer that question: water from heaven, bread of life, healing of blindness, the way, the truth, the life, etc. On Easter Sunday morning, Jesus asks Mary Magdalene the exact same question: "What are you looking for"? After hearing her answer he simply says, "Mary." And everything changes for her. That's what we're looking for too: to hear the Lord call my name with such incredible love. Until you hear it, you will always be dissatisfied and incomplete. All the musings above give you clues to ways you can prepare yourself to hear your name.

Chapter Thirty-Five

DO I REALLY NEED YOU?

Our Eucharistic celebration offers a brief glimpse of the Kingdom of God, the time when people "of every race, language, and way of life will be gathered together in one eternal banquet with Jesus Christ the Lord." How is it possible that such a diverse group of people could come together in peace for a brief time, sharing one bread and one cup?

I'd like to move out of the walls of your parish and mine. Let's broaden our vision a bit. As you know, whenever politics is as usual, you and I will be assaulted by incessant appeals to our fears. You're going to be told that "Unless you vote for me, our country is going to be taken over by *them*"... whoever "*them*" happens to be in the candidate's mind. I use the word "assault" deliberately, because that's what it is. The last thing the candidates and interest groups want you to do is take time and think through what they're saying.

Debate in Congress over the budget and over issues like welfare, immigration, and health care is following the same pattern. Each side accuses the other of this, that, and the other thing. Interest groups mount assaults that often turn vicious, and disclaim any responsibility for the destructiveness of their words and actions.

In short, there is a constant tension in our country between a concern for the common good on the one hand, to something called "tribalism" on the other. One of the dictionary definitions of *tribe* is "*any group of people having the same occupation, ideas, habits, etc."* *Tribalism* is defined as *"tribal organization, culture, loyalty, etc."* The media, politicians, and interest groups are formed into various tribes, each with its own culture, loyalty, and expectations. These tribes are trying desperately to recruit the rest of America. If you won't allow yourself to be recruited, then you are classified as "them" and subjected to isolation, ridicule, and verbal assault (sometimes physical assault). It's the same thing that happened to Jesus.

Actually, we all have a bit of tribalism in our lives. It's unavoidable simply because you and I have biases and prejudices peculiar to our skin color, gender, and economic status. We have things we want to protect, values we want others to share, certain habits, routines, and loyalties that we want to preserve. To a certain extent, tribalism is good. If I have strong values, for example, it's a comfort for me to live, work, and pray with people who share the same commitment to those values. But the danger of tribalism is that I can become exclusive, excluding any person or alternative value system or philosophy of life which does not fit into my personal or tribal view of reality. There is a total lack of trust in anyone or anything else. One who is caught in negative tribalism says, "I have all that I need within my tribe; I do not need anyone else; I do not trust anyone else."

Even our Church succumbs to tribalism. It happened in the early part of the century with waves of immigration. People who spoke a common language gathered in certain parishes. Nowadays tribalism manifests itself in tensions that exist, for example, between charismatics and non-charismatics, between those who have differing views on authority and dogma, and in the way people choose sides between different models of church or ministry.

Is there an antidote to tribalism? Sure… it's called interdependence! Like it or not, we are terribly dependent on each other for the basic necessities of life. To say that I don't need anyone else flies in the face of reality. Not a day passes that you and I don't have to make an act of faith in someone else. Take, for example, our drinking water, our dependence on police and fire department, and, yes, even our dependence on the Federal government for good roads, air traffic control, and Social Security checks.

Every single thing I have comes because hundreds, perhaps thousands, of people, have worked to make it possible. Take this book you're holding, for example. Someone planted and cared for the trees. That "someone" does not exist independently but has a huge support system. A lumber company chopped down the trees. That lumber company has people who make and supply the chain-saws, people who make and supply the trucks, folks who provide its utilities and machines. The chain-saw makers and truck makers have their own suppliers. A trucking company took the logs to the paper mill. Both the truck company and the paper mill have their suppliers and banks and insurance firms, and these banks and insurance firms have their own suppliers. From the paper mill, another trucking company brings it to the printer, and this truck travels on roads maintained by local, state, and federal street departments. The printer has its own support system. And all the employees of all these companies have their banks, grocery stores, gas stations, insurance agents, doctors, hospitals, child-care centers, and so on. Can you comprehend how many thousands of people were directly or indirectly involved in the making of a sheet of paper? And if that holds true of this paper, what of every other tangible and intangible item in our lives?

And I dare to say, "I don't need anyone else"? How can you say, "I did this on my own"! I've really been trying to think if there is anything in my life that came to me without one bit of human intervention. I can't think of a thing! Can you? Every single bit of my inner and outer life depends on contact with other people, past, present, and future. A major step in human and spiritual maturity occurs when we are no longer able to say, "My life and my salvation is the work of my own hands."

The genius of Catholic Christianity has always been an emphasis on communal salvation. We are in this together. In two of his letters (Romans and First Corinthians) St. Paul uses the organic human body to describe our relationship with one another. Jesus tells his disciples to depend on other people for their basic needs. He uses images of seeds, yeast, fishing nets to show how God gathers all into one. The news of Jesus' birth was proclaimed to local shepherds and to Oriental astrologers. At his last supper, Jesus prayed that "all may be one."

Modern Popes have spoken forcefully about human interdependence. The *Catechism of the Catholic Church* devotes a chapter to the subject. Nor is it restricted to human relationships. Our relationship with the environment is one of the fastest-growing areas of theological reflection today. The sum total of these reflections is this: to repudiate another human being is to repudiate God. To dismiss our environment as unimportant is to dismiss the creative wisdom and activity of God.

Science as well makes a contribution. It's generally accepted that our universe began with a big bang. Stephen Hawking, the British physicist, tells a beautiful story of the creation of the universe, and he also tells how we came to be what we are. "We are all made of the ashes of dead stars," he says, and "we" here means every created thing in the universe, from slugs to viruses, to elephants to mosses, and from cereals to trees and human beings. We are all connected with each other by common origin as well as by need. Try to imagine life without green plants and water.

More and more people are beginning to comprehend that all life is one. If you spend any significant amount of time in prayer you'll know exactly what I mean. I feel nothing but the deepest sorrow and sympathy for those who take refuge in labels and stereotypes, who refuse to listen to alternative points of view, who litter and pollute, whose only god is their bank balance, and who insist on their right to say and do what they want regardless of how it may affect others. Whenever life isn't to their convenience, they glibly blame immigrants, Blacks, feminists, the poor, gays, Hispanics, the Pope and bishops, and the Federal government. These are fearful people, so insecure that all they can do is attack and gossip and blame. They say: "Nothing has value in itself. Everything in the world, including people, exists to serve me or to entertain me." These folks are missing out on an incredible experience of life, of beauty, and of communion.

Why do I write this way? I do it because I have to. It's an expression of care for you and for myself (because by putting these words on a public document I acknowledge my own need for conversion). God knows, I'm not sinless. I'm a white clerical male (boy, talk about belonging to the Big 3 of tribes!). I'm prejudiced and a racist. I'm a Democrat who can't stand the agenda of the GOP. What the Christian Coalition and the NRA and some of the talk-radio folks are doing frightens the hell out of me -- excuse the language. I don't know whether to weep or curse over some of the things that go on in our Church. I'm a long ways from interdependence. Yet I want to get there, and I suspect you do too. Can't we do it together? Can't we help each other? Are you really happy with the way things are now?

In classic spiritual theology, you must name the demon in order to gain control over it and exorcize it. I write these reflections because I care about you and our world. I write these words as an expression of my faith and hope that someday soon, a critical mass is going to be reached in which good men and women like you are going to rise up and say, "ENOUGH"! no more the verbal, spiritual, and physical abuse and violence that marks so much of our life. If what I say can help you stop and look at your own actions, as it is helping me to stop and check my own, then the day of that critical mass is that much nearer, and the advent of the Kingdom of God is that much closer.

I close with a quote from St. Paul: "*God has given us the wisdom to understand fully the mystery, the plan he was pleased to decree in Christ: namely, to bring all things in the heavens and on earth into one under Christ's headship*" (Eph 1: 9-10). God, grant us the wisdom to understand this unity, and the courage to do our part to bring it about! If we can't do it with each other's help, then God help us.

Chapter Thirty-Six

MUSINGS, MEANDERINGS, AND UNCERTAINTIES

As I write these reflections, a little TV behind me is tuned to CNN. Reporters describe the scene at the crash of AA Flight 587 into Queens, New York City in November of 2001. My first reaction was– as I'm sure it was for every American: "Another terrorist attack"? The very fact that we ask that question shows how much life has changed for us since September 11th. For a country reeling from the deaths of September 11th, the loss of another two hundred and fifty lives is almost too much to take. In the past, airplane crashes could elicit a sense of horror and sympathy. But as I type this, there's a deeper feeling… a deeper sorrow… because the family of people that we call the United States is grieving once again. September 11th seared our national heart, and now this crash is also searing our national heart. It's no longer a case of anonymous people losing their lives; it's people with whom we somehow, someway have kinship. We "feel" this crash differently.

That bond of solidarity is one of the great blessings to come from September 11th. It's almost like the United States has suddenly become a small neighborhood where everyone knows everyone else, where people pitch in to help those who have suffered loss, where folks keep an eye out for each other, where neighbors, co-workers, parishioners take a little more time to talk with each other instead of rushing off to work on the day's agenda. Our suffering is not being wasted, thanks be to God. We are learning something about ourselves as a nation.

Reflecting on the events at the close of 2001, what have I learned about myself? About this country, this world? About God's presence to us?

The image of those two planes slamming into the World Trade Center will forever be seared into my mind and heart. It is the image of implacable evil, of a massive violation of the sanctity of human life. We've all had confrontations with evil in our lives, but this was something so far beyond the pale that words fail – it was mass execution, period. A few weeks later, I thought to myself: "Now I can identify a little with the victims of the Holocaust."

I was in Maine when the attacks took place. Driving home, I passed over one of the Hudson River bridges, and was nervous as can be. I took the Bay Bridge/Tunnel across the Chesapeake, and found myself looking for ships and planes. On the way back to South Bend, I-77 goes through two tunnels in Virginia, and again the nerves struck. Once again, identification took place: this is what people in Israel, Palestine, Iraq, or Afghanistan live with every day of their lives. Ditto for those people who live under oppressive regimes who stifle every form of dissent.

When I returned to South Bend, there were several letters waiting from benefactors, telling me of lives lost in New York and Washington. A husband, a son or daughter, an uncle, a cousin, an in-law, a dear friend -- letter after letter came in, and as of this writing I have written forty condolence letters to families directly affected by the attacks. Nothing in my pastoral experience ever prepared me for this. And then it occurred to me: this is my identification with the men and women who labored at ground zero. They had no experience of this either.

We are no longer as isolated or as ignorant as we used to be. The things that would always happen in other parts of the world have now happened here, and there's no telling what the future will bring. We've been insulated from many of the world's problems; we've seen them but we haven't felt them. Now we feel them, and we don't know what to do. Every one of us is trying to adjust to new realities in our lives, to think about things we've never thought about before. Change is difficult in normal circumstances. But when it slams into our existence with barbaric ruthlessness, the vulnerability is truly frightening. Nothing is taken for granted any more, be it travel, mail, water, food, whatever.

163

Many folks have mentioned how their faith is shaken, even as many say that their faith is providing some support. One elderly benefactor made a beautiful statement: "God will take care of our nation because we have helped others so much." Yes, that's true. Another person has asked, "How can the same God be invoked by Osama bin Laden as being "on our side" and invoked by the USA as being on *our* side." Well, it's been that way for centuries when it comes to war and violence. People love to find reasons why God is on "our side" rather than "the enemy's." Another person wondered what God thinks about killing the Taliban and their leadership. Is it right or wrong?

Well, it seems to me that God made things pretty clear: "Thou shalt not kill." Every major world religion has a prohibition against killing other people. God did not say: "Well, you can kill if this or that condition is met, or if the other guy shot first, or if you're defending yourself." No conditions. Just four words: "Thou shalt not kill." God does not favor killing people. Our God is a God of life, not death. Yes, in the Old Testament God urges the Israelites to wipe out the inhabitants of Canaan. But Biblical scholarship agrees that this is simply a case of people putting words into God's mouth to justify their action. God cannot contradict himself. He cannot say on the one hand, "Thou shalt not kill" and then on the other hand give detailed instructions on how to kill people. It's impossible. So, whose side is God on…?

Well, look at it this way. President Bush is exactly right on target with the food-drops to the Afghan people. This is the will of God. It's the right thing to do. Sometimes I think that if the allies took even half the money they're using for the military exercise and gave it as a grant directly to the Afghan people for food, shelter, employment, and infrastructure, the Taliban and Osama bin Laden would be right out of business. Ditto for any area of the world where there is terrorism. Terrorism feeds on poverty, desperation, hunger, and mistreatment. Terrorism can be the outward expression of the inner rage of a desperate people who feel they cannot make their voice heard in any other way. That doesn't make terrorism right. It's just recognizing that people can be pushed just so far before they'll strike back.

Terrorism can also be a way for sociopaths to justify killing simply for the enjoyment of killing. I've often thought that one of the big reasons why peace is so difficult to come by in the Middle East and in Northern Ireland is that we have men who find the meaning of their lives in killing others. Peace will leave them with meaningless lives. They fear that emptiness, so they work against peace as much as possible. They kill and maim in order to provoke a reaction, which gives them the justification for more killing and maiming.

Now having said all that, I still find myself conflicted. I have not suffered a direct loss from violence. So it's easy for me to sit here and type, "Thou shalt not kill." Yet I also know that if someone dear to me were deliberately hurt or killed, I'd be in a rage and ready to retaliate in full. It's OK to have that anger… that is not forbidden us. Anger is the sign that a fundamental personal value has been affected. Anger demands redress; it demands that things be put right somehow. What needs caution is the feeling of rage. Rage demands revenge, it lashes out unthinkingly, and that only leads to more evil.

I also know that a nation has the right and obligation to defend itself against outside attack. But how does one defend in a way that promotes peace and security, instead of sowing seeds of hatred that will blossom into future terror and violence? I don't know.

Secondly, there's a conflict within on ways to deal with Osama bin Laden and others who think similarly. The truly Christian response is to capture the man and his cohorts, bring them to court of justice, and put them behind bars for the rest of their lives. Yet part of me says we should kill him, because if he is imprisoned, terrorists will demand his release and will commit terrorist acts till their demands are met. How do we reconcile or deal with all the possibilities? I just don't know. God forgive me, but I've thought sometimes that it would be so easy if the man just committed *hari kari*. That way, no one gets blamed.

Third, why did I react so strongly to the events of September 11th, as opposed to other events? The reaction came because these were "my people," and I saw it on TV. And then I thought: where was I with the genocide in Rwanda? In the former Yugoslavia? I saw it all on TV. But they weren't "my people," so I was silent. How easy it was to forget that they are bone of my bone and flesh of my flesh because we are all children of God. So… what will I do in the future?

There are no easy answers. This is tough, because we're a people who are accustomed to the quick fix at minimal cost. I know violence isn't the answer... it never has been. Every act of violence breeds more hatred, creates new victims (usually the innocent), and encourages future attacks. Now this reflection is an area where people of good will can disagree. I am not presenting this analysis as the whole truth and nothing but the truth. This is only a little piece of the truth. You have a piece, and he has a piece, and she has another piece, and somehow, some way, we must listen to each other's wisdom without attacking the other person or the other group. Refusing to listen is only sowing the seeds of anger and frustration which will break out in rage and anger somehow, someway.

That logic is important to realize. Even though the brute fact of violent terrorism hit home on the 11th of September, many people have already been victims of it in smaller ways. Think of road rage, for example. Think of abused women and children (yes, and men too), and of the violence that results when a person is pushed too far and sees no other recourse than to strike out. A boss who bullies his or her employees is a terrorist, as are civil and ecclesiastical servants who abuse their power. Whenever people feel that they are not taken seriously, whenever people feel that they are not being listened to, whenever people struggle for the basic needs of life while others live in relative luxury, sooner or later there is going to be a reaction of anger and rage. You know that's true! Look inside your own heart. You *know* you'd react strongly if faced with the conditions above and it appeared as though no one gave a hoot. The fact that you haven't reacted strongly is a credit to your cooperation with God's grace.

One more set of thoughts. On the morning of September 11th, only a tiny handful of people woke up knowing what kind of day it was going to be. Ditto for all those folks who boarded Flight 587. Today, even as you're reading this, there will be fatal accidents and heart attacks. People will get a phone call or a visitor at the door, telling them that someone they love has been killed or is seriously injured. Babies will be stillborn, a child will die of disease or accident or abuse, and hopes and dreams will plummet like a dying meteor.

In other words, the fragility of life hits us hard these days. We're suddenly asking a lot of questions about life that we've managed to ignore.

At the root of it all is our fear of death. Am I ready to die? Am I ready to let go? Am I afraid of meeting God face-to-face? Is there any unfinished business in my life? Are there unfulfilled dreams that could be realized if I changed my priorities? Is my turning to Jesus for help simply a band-aid to cover the pain of the present moment, or is my turning to Jesus done with a much broader outlook on the rest of my life and into the next?

How best to respond? I like to remember what my spiritual director once told me: "Pray as if everything depended on God; work as if everything depended on you." May we pray deeply, take each other seriously, open our eyes to the needs of the world, and share what we are able to share so that others may have the basics of life. May we see how God walks with us, stands with us, weeps with us, and suffers with us. And when we see this compassion, may we with one hand cling to this loving God and with the other reach out to all the peoples of the world who yearn for a normal life, free from fear.

Chapter Thirty-Seven

DISTRACTIONS IN PRAYER

I hear it so often in confession: "Father, I was distracted in prayer or at Mass." It's probably in a close tie with anger and impatience for second place (first place, of course, goes to you-know-what kinds of sins). And each time I hear this, I try to help folks realize that distractions are not a sin.

To understand distractions, you have to understand how the human mind works. All through the day, we're storing up all kinds of things in our brain -- things we see, hear, feel, taste, etc. Constant mental stimulation goes on because of our work and conversations. Our poor brain stores all this stuff up as it comes in. It piles one thing on top of another as fast as we think or sense it.

When we slow down, the brain starts sorting out all that stuff. Some is stored in memory; other stuff it throws away. Even when we think we're doing nothing, the brain's still working a mile a minute. Even when we're sleeping, the work goes on. That is one of the purposes served by our dreams!

So when it comes time to pray, or when it comes time to prayerfully listen to Scripture or the Eucharistic Prayer at Mass, what happens? We slow down from our normal activity. As soon as we do that, the mind starts its instinctive sorting-out process. It doesn't know we want peace and quiet for prayer. All it knows is that it has a quiet time to do some work, and it gets to work! Your slowing down to pray is like pushing a "GO" button.

And does it ever go! First off the top comes the inconsequential stuff. But the longer we're at prayer, the more deeply the mind goes. Once past the everyday stuff, there arise thoughts about our future, our rela-

168

tionships, our fears and concerns. There may also be sexually-arousing thoughts. Maybe there was a fight with our spouse or co-worker that we keep replaying, or you're planning a special evening with someone special, or you're replaying the Notre Dame football game.

The list goes on and on; you know how it is. It seems as though we just cannot still our minds and focus on God, and the harder we try to be quiet, the worse it gets. The worse it gets, the more frustrated we get, until finally we stop praying with a shrug of the shoulders or a heartfelt blast of self-criticism. Then we go to confession and talk about distractions.

As I said, distractions are not a sin. The brain is not under our control. We don't freely will those distractions, so how can they be sinful? To say our distractions are sinful is the same thing as saying that our breathing is sinful. The brain must do what it has to do, just like our lungs must do what they were made to do!

So how do you handle distractions? Here's a recipe that is one-hundred percent guaranteed to produce perfect prayer, every time. First, when you start to pray -- whether it be Mass, a rosary, contemplation, your assortment of prayer cards -- make a simple act of faith, placing yourself in the presence of God, and expressing your faith that God will be with you during the period of time you have chosen for your prayer. It could go like this: "Dear God, here I am, ready to pray this Mass. I want to be with you, I want to pray from my heart. I know that distractions will come, but that's OK. I believe you and I will still be present to each other."

Second, start your prayer, whatever it may be. Realize that it will take a few antsy moments for your body to get settled and comfortable. Once you're settled, you'll be able to concentrate for a few minutes, and then the distractions start! When you become aware that you've stopped your prayer and are thinking about something else, do not get mad or upset! Simply say to yourself: "Oops, Lord, I've stopped my prayer" or "My brain's doing its thing again" or "I will go back to my prayer." Then pick up your prayer where you left off. A few seconds later another distraction will come. Do the same thing. Simply say: "I've stopped my prayer, Lord; I will return to my prayer." Keep doing this till Mass is finished or your prayer time is over.

That's all you have to do. I give you a one-hundred percent guarantee that you'll have perfect prayer every time! You are either praying like you want to, or you are making another kind of prayer: "Oops, Lord...." If you have to make the "oops" statement a hundred times in fifteen minutes, well, that's a hundred acts of love, for you are telling God that you really want to pay attention to him but your silly brain won't shut up. So, you never stop praying. And even in those times when your mind has really wandered off into the boonies, you're still praying, because your act of faith is doing the job. Remember what St. Paul concluded: even when you can't find the words, the Spirit will still pray within you (Romans 8: 26-27). You are either saying the prayers yourself, or the Spirit is saying them for you while you're temporarily distracted by a strong-willed mind.

I might add this: Do not judge the effectiveness of your prayer by the distractions or lack of them. Judge your prayer by its effects in your daily life: are you more kind, gentle, charitable, patient, long-suffering? In other words, the fruits of the Spirit will be manifest in your life. That's how you judge prayer, not by distractions or numbers of prayers or length of time spent praying. "By their fruits you will know them," said Jesus (Mt 7:16).

There are, however, some distractions that are worth paying attention to. Sometimes a refrain from a liturgical song will come to mind, and try as you might, you can't get it out of your head. That's OK. Go with it. That could simply be a song the Spirit wants to sing with you! Let go of your own prayer agenda and follow the guidance of the Spirit.

Sometimes a Scripture quote or something padre said in his homily will really sit with you, and you keep coming back to it time and again. That too needs to be looked at. Let go of your own prayer agenda. Ask Jesus: "What are you trying to tell me with this quote or phrase"? The very fact that it caught your attention means that it's making a connection with something deep within your soul and heart. Play with it gently. Come back to it in quiet moments throughout the day if necessary.

Pay attention also if you're angrily obsessed with a situation or a relationship. If you're on the outs with someone, the quiet time of prayer is going to bring all the negative energy to the surface. You'll find yourself stewing, replaying a fight, plotting revenge or punitive action. No matter how many times you try to return to your prayer, these "angries" will come back and need to be dealt with. You will not have peaceful prayer until you are reconciled with yourself or with the person or situation causing the angry reaction. And even if you manage to get by without reconciliation, it only means you've repressed the anger. It's going to come back somehow, someway.

I hope this helps you to enjoy your times of prayer a bit more and to be more relaxed about the inevitable distractions. It's so important to keep a sense of humor. Watch how your brain scampers all over the place. No wonder a spiritual writer coined the term "monkey mind"! The only time you will ever have a one-hundred percent distraction-free prayer is if God directly intervenes and pulls you into the state of infused contemplation, and that's pretty rare. So relax and enjoy!

Chapter Thirty-Eight

I'M RIGHT, YOU'RE WRONG... NO YOU'RE WRONG, I'M RIGHT... YOU'RE WRONG, I'M RIGHT...NO, YOU'RE NOT! I'M RIGHT... NO WAY! YOU'RE WRONG!

I really wanted to write something about suffering. Yet for some reason, it wasn't coming together. Nothing was flowing and I was getting close to Panicsville, because this was due at the printers!

The day after Labor Day, however, an idea glimmered as I reflected on the Scripture readings for that day's Mass. St. Paul criticized the Corinthians because of their penchant for going to court and suing each other over minor disagreements. Luke tells us how Jesus spent the entire night in communion with the Father before choosing the apostles.

My first thought was that things aren't much different today. In society and in religion, there are unremitting efforts to force people into specific ways of thinking and behaving. The result, of course, is constant tension and turmoil -- in short, a lot of needless suffering. So I guess this essay is about a unique kind of suffering, after all.

Jesus faced the same problem. Just prior to the Gospel passage mentioned above, Jesus had several verbal battles with the Pharisees. They were all over Jesus, claiming that he was not from God and was not teaching God's ways. And they were saying this of a man who spent all night in communion with God and did it frequently. So there's the conundrum. If Jesus spent so much time in communion with God, how could he be teaching or doing un-God-like things? It doesn't make sense!

More and more I am seeing a growing lack of respect for the religious experience of other people. It actually assumes the proportions of intolerance. Have you also sensed it? It's frightening sometimes to see how the experiences, thoughts, and feelings of truly good, prayerful men and women are totally dismissed as irrelevant, unorthodox, or even demonic, and it's just as frightening to see how easily I can fall into that trap.

If not intolerance, there's moralism. Moralism is when I try to dictate another person's behavior with no reference to that person's unique circumstances. It's not a dialogue, but a series of glib "ought's" and "must's." Moralism is a copout. It's a way to avoid grappling with the reality that there can be many choices for any given situation.

So, if men and women of good will spend time in communion with God, then how can they teach or do un-God-like things? It's a cardinal rule of the spiritual life that when a person spends time each day in prayer, their minds and hearts are gradually transformed into the mind and heart of Jesus and his Father.

Now let me add two qualifications here. First, I am defining "prayer" as two-way communication with God, where you listen just as much, if not more, than you speak. There must be dialogue for growth to take place and for two people to become one mind and one heart.

Second, remember the teaching of Jesus: "By their fruits you will know them." If I spend two hours a day in prayer, and during my waking hours am the meanest, most critical SOB that ever walked around, then I don't know what it is I'm doing in that two hours, but it sure ain't praying! It may look like prayer, and may sound like prayer, but if my words, thoughts, and actions do not manifest the fruits of the Spirit (love, joy, peace, patience, kindness, goodness, faithfulness, gentleness, and self-control) and a deep, abiding respect for all of God's creation, I cannot claim to be in communion with God. Yes, I do sin, and so do you; we all have those times when the fruits of the Spirit are not evident. This does not affect our communion with Jesus if reconciliation and forgiveness are sought. All I'm saying is that one who *truly* prays does not have a *habitual* attitude of meanness, intolerance, criticism, and moralism.

Let's go to some real-life examples. Our Holy Father spends a significant amount of time in prayer. So does my local bishop. So do I. Yet our views of the Church are very different. Am I wrong and they right? No! Let's get rid of those labels! Pope Benedict, Bishop D'Arcy, and Herb Yost have very different experiences of God. We have different cultural backgrounds, and we've all had to deal with major handicaps in our life. Grace builds on nature, says Thomas Aquinas, and all these different things influence our communion with God, and God's communion with us.

Are all of those men and women who signed the "Open Letter" to Pope John Paul on contraception "wrong" (*New York Times, 9/6/94*)? Not if their convictions and values arise from deep communion with God. How can those women and married men asking for ordination be "wrong" if their plea comes from a deeply-felt experience of God's call? On the other hand, was John Paul II "right" when he says that women and married men cannot be ordained? Yes, because his conviction came from his experience of God and his understanding of Church! Was Paul VI "right" in penning *Humana Vitae*? Yes, for the same reasons.

Is Pat "wrong" to ask Fr. Joe for an open parish meeting to discuss the way authority is exercised? Is Fr. Paul "right" when he insists that all decision-making power is in his hands? Are older Catholics "right" in bemoaning the loss of reverence in the young? Is it "wrong" to converse in church before Mass?

Were the ND alumni who protested the awarding of an honorary degree to President Obama "right" in what they did? Yes, if values nurtured by prayer were deeply offended. Was Fr. Hesburgh "wrong" in accepting the co-chairmanship of President Clinton's Defense Fund? Not if it came from a mind and heart shaped by long periods of communion with God.

The list goes on and on, but I think you get the point. What you and I must ask ourselves is this: Is my notion of "right" or "wrong" dictated by my personal preferences or fears, or is it the fruit of communion with God and an understanding of what the Church is all about? If it's communion with God, then the fruits of the Spirit will be present, which means that

— I'm Right, You're Wrong... No, You're Wrong, I'm Right

I will be very hesitant to blast anyone else's thoughts, words, and actions. I can challenge those words and actions, question them, dialogue about them, but to assail them or to dismiss them—never. To put it as simply as possible: where there is intolerance, God is not present.

Now if good-hearted men and women can truly hold differing opinions and beliefs, where does that leave us? What are the alternatives?

First, it leaves us in tension. But it's good tension. A violin and cello can only make beautiful music when the strings are tuned tightly. We Americans are geared towards quick and easy solutions. Unfortunately, many times the quick solution is achieved by shouting others down or ignoring them, and if this happens often enough, verbal or physical violence will result. Tension can give rise to enormous creativity and deeper understanding if we allow it to exist and accept it as a part of human growth.

Second, you and I need to realize that we have only a piece of the truth. No one person can experience all of God; no one person can fully comprehend the message of Jesus. Not even our Holy Father can claim this for himself. That's why he calls synods, councils, meetings with the Cardinals, and so forth. My experience of God is unique, yours is unique, so are Pat's and Chris's, and Fr. Sam's and Sr. Monique's and Pope Benedict's. Rather than claiming that "my experience" is normative, why not listen to each other? Why not share our experiences, so that we can all appreciate just how vast and infinite God is?

Following from this is a third point: if you hear God saying one thing, and I hear God saying something else, is God contradicting himself? No. I believe it's God's way of saying: "Hey, folks, look at the *whole* picture"!

Fourth, remember that, generally speaking, the more viciously individuals or groups are attacked, the greater the possibility that they are indeed saying something that God wants us to hear. It has been this way from the time of the prophets until now. Those who unsettle the status quo and afflict the comfortable are mercilessly harassed and even killed. Careful discernment is needed.

Fifth, we can pray for each other and with each other. For example, I mentioned that I have different beliefs on some things than our Holy Father and Bishop D'Arcy. Do I "write them off"? I try not to. Instead, each morning, during the Eucharistic prayer, I pray fervently that I may be "in communion of mind and heart" with them, and I also pray they will be in communion of mind and heart with those they serve.

Finally, you must trust your own experience of God. This is another way of saying that you must "follow your conscience." If your experience of God is such that you need to spend an hour a day in front of the Blessed Sacrament, but the church is closed during the day, then trust that experience, see your pastor, and ask for access to church through the rectory. If you feel that God is calling you to a more active role in the parish, and that urge comes up again and again in prayer, then trust that experience of God and volunteer. If your prayer helps you to see that a civil policy or a church policy is something Jesus would not advocate, then trust that and communicate with your religious and civil authorities. And whatever you do, do it gently, with respect and reverence, as befits one who possesses the fruits of the Spirit and who realizes that others may be acting out of their own communion with God.

"Be reconciled with one another," said St. Paul in one of his letters. That's my plea too. Life is too precious and God is too vast! Besides, I'm going to be in heaven with the folks I dislike so intensely. Why not start now learning to live with them, for they also are members of the Body of Christ. As we pray in the Fourth Eucharistic Prayer: *By your Holy Spirit, gather all who share this one bread and one cup into the one Body of Christ, a living sacrifice of praise.* Oh God, grant us such communion!

176

Chapter Thirty-Nine

REFLECTIONS FROM AN ORDINATION CEREMONY

While sitting with the other priests during the ordination of Fr. Nate Wills, C.S.C. (April 22, 2006), I found myself wandering back to my own ordination thirty-one years ago. Because I was behind the ordaining bishop, I couldn't lipread, and so I didn't know what Bishop Dan Jenky was saying to Nate and the congregation. But I remember that the charge from my ordaining bishop was read right from the book. The ritual words focus on three major responsibilities that priests have: preach the Gospel, shepherd the faithful, and celebrate divine worship.

Walking back home, and during prayer in the days following, I found myself wondering what I would have added to the official rite (the bishop is permitted to depart from or add to the ritual text if he so desires). Thirty-one years of experience does count for something. I've lived with and worked with new priests and old priests. Benefactors have written to me about their wonderful and not-so-wonderful experiences with their priests.

The very first thing I would tell a new priest is that he must devote a significant amount of time each day to prayer. I am convinced this is the single most important thing he can do for those he serves. People really hunger for an experience of God-with-them. I deeply believe they are looking for men who have a sense of the sacred, who can show how God is present in all the gritty and grotty details of everyday life, to show how a relationship with Jesus and his Father is possible in this hectic world of ours. Only through constant faithful daily prayer can one find God this way. There is just no other way of doing it. I might add to this a word about celibacy: the more one prays, the more he is able to be a deeply loving celibate.

I spoke of the "gritty and grotty details of everyday life." I would remind the new priest that he is a human being who happens to be a priest, and not the other way around. If he does not allow himself to experience the heights and depths of his own broken humanity, to bring his failings and short-comings before God in prayer, and to seek counseling when necessary, how is he going to know what other folks face? This ranges from allowing himself to experience tiredness and frustration, anger, futility and rejection, living from paycheck to paycheck, weighing competing demands on time, etc. It means allowing himself to fall in love if that be what God desires, to experience the conflict between the original choice and the new attraction. A priest is a human being. If he is not, then there is no way he can relate to human beings. He's not superman. He's just an ordinary man entrusted by God and the Church with an extraordinary opportunity for service.

Along this same line, I know we priests are a pretty sheltered crew. We don't have to worry about employment, health-care, food, housing. If something breaks or leaks, we call the janitor or the maintenance department. For religious priests, there's ample time off if we want it; less so for diocesan priests, who must find someone to cover for them in their absence. And my question is this: given all these freebies, what do we do with them? These things are gifts of the People of God, given to us so that we may facilitate their growth in holiness, and our own as well.

I would suggest that in today's world, a priest cannot be all things to all people, twenty-four hours a day, seven days a week. He has to set some boundaries for the sake of his own physical, mental, and spiritual health. This is especially necessary since there are so few priests. This can range from being faithful to a day off, to moving from the rectory to a house a couple blocks away. A priest also needs to find something that grounds him and centers him, and to spend some time with that. For example, that is why I like my woodworking.

This conviction is a hard one to deal with. To many folks, these hobbies and outlets sound so un-priestly. I remember back in 2000 telling the Provincial that one of the things I wanted to do on my sabbatical was attend some woodworking classes. He didn't like that at all, saying instead that a proper sabbatical was one that has theological updating, etc. My response was that if something makes me a better, happier, more well-rounded human being, *de facto* it makes me a better minister to the folks. Priests need to get out of their heads and to do something with their hands in order to nourish their creativity and to ease stress.

In terms of relationship to the parishioners and the folks with whom he ministers (key word right there: *"with,"* not *"to"*), I would propose a variation of the real estate maxim: "Listen, Listen, Listen." And when you're done listening, listen some more (and can you see the connection with prayer, which is listening to God?). It has been my experience, particularly on contentious issues, that when people know they have been heard, things have a way of turning out OK, even if the eventual course of action is something they disagree with. Yes, there will always be those who just won't stop pushing and picking. You can explain things to them over and over, and listen for hours, to no avail. Eventually there will come a point where you will simply have to say "Enough"! and move on. Maybe you've made a new enemy; but, remember, even Jesus knew when to shake the dust from his feet and call it quits.

And by the way, speaking of Jesus, he knew when to play with children and when to teach adults. The modern Church seems to do just the opposite. True, much prudence is needed in spending time with children, but the little ones have such a wonderful way of energizing you, confounding you, and helping you to escape the reality of the messy adult world. Theirs is a different sense of time. I always think of how Wisdom plays eternally at the feet of God.

Ah yes… time. A suggestion: when celebrating Mass or any other liturgical or sacramental function, take off your watch and put it in your pocket. This insight came to me shortly after listening to a homilist deliver a loooong monotonous sermon. I looked at my watch after the Prayer of the Faithful, and decided to use Eucharistic Prayer II so folks could get out on time. That's when it occurred to me: "Hey Herb, this is God's time, sacred time. What's with this watch bit"? So ever since then I've not worn a watch while presiding. What's the rush? This is precious time with the Lord and with each other. You only look at your watch when you're with someone you don't love very much or doing something you don't like.

New priests are invariably gung-ho. They have all the latest theology and know-how. I would call them to remember that the grace of God has been working in the parish or the assignment long before their arrival, and it will be working a long time after they leave. They do not have to revolutionize the parish and upset the folks. In our parishes and organizations, there are many gifted people of generous heart. Listen to others, take their wise counsel, and work in harmony with them. Be willing to learn from them. Be open to their suggestions. Trust them. After all, they are your fellow-workers in Christ. "Because I said so" just will not work anymore as a style of leadership.

By the same token, however, a parish or organization that remains static will die. Even while building on the work of his predecessors, a priest must be alert to the need to move his flock to a different pasture, so to speak, if he sees that such is necessary for their growth in holiness.

And to the People of God, I would say this: I told the new priests to "listen, listen, listen." I would tell the People of God to "affirm, affirm, affirm." Why do you think I have cherished this ministry with the Holy Cross Association for almost twenty-two years? It's because you folks have let me know, very frequently and in very specific ways, that I have been a help on your journey. It energizes a human being to know that he or she is making a difference in the lives of other people.

So too with your parish priests, with any priest you know. Affirm them often, and in specific ways. In other words, "That was a nice homily, Father" is a nice thing to say, but so is "Good morning, Father." But if you say, "I really liked how you pointed out this or that," or "Your advice in confession gave me a whole new insight," then you are truly being a blessing to your priest. The guy's gotta be good at something. Seek it out and affirm it.

I would also remind you of the 11th Commandment: "Thou shalt not compare." Priests come and go in your life. We are not clones of each other; we're highly unique individuals. We will help you grow in a different way than the priest whom we replaced. We may think that assignments are made by bishops or provincials, but they're really made by God, who sees all and knows all. Accept us as we are; receive what we have to offer and love us into new growth. That's why God gave us to each other; we're responsible for each other's growth in holiness.

Be willing to challenge, to criticize, and to share your wisdom. But, back up your words with action. If, for example, you feel that religious education is suffering or insufficient, volunteer to be a teacher or assistant. Commissions, committees, and councils are always in need of personnel. I know your time is precious; so is your pastor's. Would you rather have him visiting the hospitals and shut-ins, or spending hours on the phone searching for help?

Be aware that your priests are not there to please you. Sometimes they have to do and say hard things, or to make decisions that leave you feeling disillusioned and unhappy. Now I have to be careful here. You may have a pastor or administrator who rules by fiat. So maybe there is reason to be unhappy or angry, and that needs to be processed and dealt with. But if you've had a chance to voice your piece of the truth and wisdom, and the outcome is different than what you hoped for, try to be at peace. You don't know all the factors that entered into the decision. By the very fact that he listened to you, padre deserves the benefit of the doubt.

In sum, pray, listen, affirm, work together. For both priests and people, these are the foundations of a healthy, happy community. You could almost call them the four legs of the Eucharistic table, for those are also the things that Jesus does for us, and with us. And please, dear Father, raise up more men and women for ministry in our Church!

Chapter Forty

WHY DOESN'T GOD ANSWER MY PRAYER?

I'm writing this from the perspective of a man who has been reading correspondence from Holy Cross Association members for twenty-four years now. When I first took over this work, I had "head knowledge" that prayer was answered. Now I speak from the gut-depth of my conviction that Jesus meant it when he said that prayer would be answered.

I have seen how God answers "Yes" to prayers. It's been a joy. But I have also witnessed two other answers that God gives to our prayer: "Maybe" and "No." When God's answer seems to be some version of "Maybe," I counsel patience, perseverance, and promise my continued support as we watch and wait and hope. If God's answer turns out to be "No," then I try to help with the heartbreak as best I can, given the limitations of the written word and the miles between us.

It's very hard for you and me to deal with the "Maybe" and the "No." No way do I have all the answers. Folks, I have just as many questions to ask God as you do! For example, Chris Smith and Pat Jones both have the same kind of cancer. They share the same hospital room. Their spouses and families pray for healing and health. Both families go to St. Joseph's Oratory in Montreal, begging the intercession of Blessed Brother André. As far as we know, both families have the same degree of faith. Pat dies; Chris goes into remission.

Why did Pat have to die? I don't know… I really don't. God's the only one who does. Perhaps the passage of time will reveal the answers, perhaps not. But for now, it hurts deeply, and one's faith is scarred. I can't answer the questions that Pat's family has, for they're my questions too! Real faith will say that Pat's death is for the greater honor and glory of God, but humanly speaking that can be small consolation. It's a poor way to give glory to God, they say!

Why does God say "Maybe" or "No"? There are several possible answers, and I'd like to share some of them with you. Sometimes God delays an answer just to see how badly we want what we're praying for. Remember the Gospel stories of the persistent widow, or the story of the man who begged for bread to feed his children? They persisted and persisted in their requests, and finally received what they wanted. We give up too quickly. God doesn't run fast-answer franchises! His sense of time is infinitely different than ours!

Sometimes the timing is not right to give an answer, according to God's plan of salvation. God asks us to patiently wait, and in the meantime, keep praying. A beautiful illustration of this is in the biblical *Book of Habakkuk*. The prophet looks around him and sees the Chaldean armies overwhelming his people. He wonders why God is allowing this to happen. *"How long, O Lord? I cry for help, but you do not listen! I cry out 'Violence,' but you do not intervene"* (1:2). So Habakkuk decides to position himself on the city watchtower, and he will not move till God answers his complaints. Finally God does: *"The vision still has its time, presses on to fulfillment, and will not disappoint; if it delays, wait for it, it will surely come, it will not be late… the just one, because of faith, shall live"* (2:2-4).

In the Gospels, whenever Jesus answered the prayer of people who were begging for help, he always stressed the necessity of faith. In some cases, his first response was "No," but the person's persistent and deep faith transformed the negative answer to a positive one.

How does one know when they have reached the point of persistent and deep faith? To be honest, I'm not sure. I suspect the answer has to do with how deeply we mean it when we say: *"Thy will be done."* When we can truly and sincerely say that, then we will be happy with the answers God gives to our prayer, for our prayer will always be answered.

Most of the time, however, it's our lips and head that say: *"Thy will be done."* The words have not yet become part of our heart and soul. If an individual says: "Chris's prayers were answered; why not mine"? or if another person says: "I'm angry at God because God didn't answer my prayers," then these people are focusing on their wills, not God's. The very fact that we question why God didn't answer our prayers says that we're not saying a wholehearted: *"Your will be done."* As I said, if we truly believe those words, whatever answer God gives our prayer will be totally acceptable.

Sometimes an answer is delayed till our motives are purified. Why do I want someone to get better? For their sake? For my sake (so I won't have to live alone, for example)? Or for God's greater honor and glory? Why do I want a job... money... health? Why do I want to pass the driver's test, or want Leslie to be accepted at Notre Dame? Most of our praying has mixed motives. Let's be honest with God and with ourselves. Make the mixed motives a part of your prayer. For example: "Lord, I really want to pass this driver's test. I want to be independent, I need to be able to get around. I also hate having to ask people for help and assistance; it hurts my pride to have to ask for help."

Many times God will say "No" or prayer will seem unanswered, because he's not going to do for us what we can do for ourselves. God will not end world hunger and war, because that's something we can do. Leslie goes to daily Mass and prays for a job. If Leslie then stays home all day, or goes to interviews with a lackadaisical attitude, then Leslie's prayer isn't going to be answered. If I pray for health, and continue to smoke, drink, keep excessive work hours, or worry about this and that and everything else, God's not going to answer the prayer. God will assist our efforts with his grace and gifts, but he will not do the work for us.

God will say "No" or "Maybe" because he has a greater perspective than we do. Maybe God has greater gifts in mind than what we're praying for, ranging from personal conversion to eternal life. You know the story of St. Monica and Augustine. The story is told of how Augustine one day came to Monica and told her he was going to Italy. Monica about fell through the floor. Augustine was living an extremely immoral life, and Italy was not noted for its sanctity. So Monica asked God: "Don't let my son go to Italy; he'll be lost forever." Well, Augustine went to Italy. Monica thought God didn't answer her prayer. But, when Augustine got to Italy, he met St. Ambrose, and Ambrose was the instrument of Augustine's conversion! Unanswered prayer? No... just proof that God usually knows what he's doing!

Or take my own vocation as another example. When I decided in high school to pursue the priesthood, I applied to the Diocese of Harrisburg, but was turned down because of my hearing. Ditto for several religious orders. Unanswered prayer? No... because I was encouraged to give it one more chance, and here I am, a member of the Congregation of Holy Cross. God got me where he wanted me. God's perspective was greater than mine!

Yet another example of a greater good might be the case of a family who is praying for one of its members who is critically ill. In the course of this prayer, the family draws closer and closer together. Relationships between the individuals reach incredible depths of care and concern for one another. The sick person dies. Was that person's death in vain? Was prayer unanswered? No... no more than the death of Jesus was in vain, for his death brought incredible riches of life to the human family. God's grace and the family's prayer brought about a win-win situation: the sick individual now has eternal life with God; the family has new depths of life with each other.

Many times prayer is being answered, but we're just not looking in the right place. We become so fixated on receiving a certain specific answer that we can't see how God has been and is answering our prayers. I remember my first vocation crisis, about six months after ordination. Day in and day out I prayed: "Give me a clear, unmistakable sign that you want me to continue being a priest." I was looking for a vision, or a dream, or something like that. In the meantime, people were complimenting me on my homilies. Some were saying how helpful I had been in confession or in counseling. I was receiving lots of affection, love, and affirmation from the parishioners. Then it finally dawned on me: these were the signs that God was giving me. I was just looking in the wrong place!

It pays to take the blinders off. Most of the time, God will answer our prayers via human beings and the circumstances of our daily life. That's been his track record all along. He always works through human beings. He even sent his Son as one like us to continue his work. Doctors and nurses, poets and letter-writers, street people and executives, people of other races or religions, friends and strangers, the Bible and phone calls, sunny days and gray days, sinful moments and graced moments, 3AM or 12 noon, driving or walking, in the bathroom or in church: you just never know where or when God will answer your prayer, or who he will chose to bring the answer!

Faith is the key to living with unanswered prayer. It's the only thing that keeps us from going nuts or from writing God out of our lives. Somehow, we have to believe deep down that God has his reasons for the answers he gives, and that the reasons are honorable and for the greater good. Yes, there are still angry and negative feelings and emotions. That's normal. Tell God how you feel! But follow that with as heartfelt a "Thy will be done" as you can manage. That's what Jesus did in the Garden: "Father, I really don't want to go through this... I'm frightened. But your will be done." Believe that whatever God does is motivated by love for you, for those you love, and by love for the world. Note the three arenas of love – God's answer is never just about you. If you keep your focus on that love, on God's will, and God's greater honor and glory, then your prayer will always be answered. Even a "No" will bring you peace!

Chapter Forty-One

REFLECTIONS ON THE SACRAMENT OF RECONCILIATON

O f all the sacraments, the Sacrament of Reconciliation is one which finds most Catholics wondering: "What is its purpose in my life? Where does it fit"? For some, there is consolation, freedom, a sense of deliverance and hope, and a feeling that all has been set right once again. For others, perhaps the great majority of Catholics, there is fear, anxiety, nervousness, puzzlement and uncertainty.

I share that confusion too. Here I'm speaking as penitent, not as confessor. I do not receive this sacrament frequently, even though my own sinfulness is very much akin to the "seventy times seven" that Jesus spoke about. Like you, I went through the whole range of experience. Once a month in grade school we were herded over to church for confessions. All mortal sins had to be confessed before going to communion, and of course every sin was a mortal sin! In my teenage and young adult years, shame and guilt over my sexual drives and behavior drove me to confession once a week, if not more frequently. I often found myself wondering: "What good is this doing, because I know I'm going to go right out and commit the same sins again"? So on top of everything else there was shame and guilt that perhaps I had made an invalid confession! There finally came a point when I stopped going to confession completely because I always felt worse afterwards and was never sure I was forgiven.

I have returned to the sacrament, but now I approach this moment of grace out of need rather than because someone says I'm supposed to! But there's still some uncertainty. In sharing these reflections with you, I'm writing as much for my own clarification as yours.

Even the new *Catechism of the Catholic Church* has some uncertainty. The first question it asks about this sacrament is: "What is the Sacrament called"? Five answers are given: the sacrament of penance, of conversion, of confession, of forgiveness, or of reconciliation. Each one of those words has a very specific meaning, and it's going to affect our attitude towards the sacrament. The *Catechism* then goes on to say that there are other ways to obtain forgiveness of sin: prayer, fasting, almsgiving, efforts at reconciliation with one's neighbor, and tears of repentance. Also contributing to forgiveness of sin is reception of the Eucharist, reading Scripture, observing with a full heart the seasons and days of penitence, and making pilgrimages. (It should be noted that the *Catechism,* in the Section on the Eucharist, says that the Eucharist wipes away *venial* sins; the forgiveness of mortal sin is still reserved to confession).

If there are so many ways to look at the Sacrament of Reconciliation, and so many other ways to obtain forgiveness of sin, no wonder there's confusion! So what's a person to do? This is a sacrament after all, one of the means by which God draws us more deeply into his life. Not to make use of the sacrament is to deny ourselves a great experience of the mercy and forgiveness of God. But most of us have enough integrity that we don't want to misuse the sacrament either. We want it to be something more than a rote repetition of a "shopping list" of sins which we know we're probably going to commit again.

The *Catechism* gives us a possible way out of the tension. The discussion of the Sacrament of Reconciliation is part of a chapter called: "The Sacraments of Healing." There are two of those sacraments: Reconciliation is one; the Anointing of the Sick is the other.

Now, I believe you have a deep and intuitive knowledge of when you would most need and profit from the Anointing of the Sick. You'd ask for it when facing surgery, in times of serious illness, when the stresses and strains of life have beaten you to your knees, when you are undergoing severe mental or spiritual chaos, when chronic illness is depressing your spirits. Most people who have received the Sacrament of Anointing at those times can testify to its profound effects in their lives. You most definitely feel and sense the power of this sacrament and the presence of Jesus. This is not a sacrament you'd receive every week. You normally wouldn't request it for the common cold, or the ordinary aches and pains and stresses of everyday life. No, you'd seek other remedies. You'd take the correct medication, or have a heartfelt talk with someone, or take a day off.

So what I'd like to suggest is this: why not apply the same reasoning to the other sacrament of healing? I believe that you can have an intuitive sense of when you most need the Sacrament of Reconciliation. You **know** when you have committed major sin, when you have caused a serious rupture in your relationship with God, the Church, other people. You can rationalize and try to run away or hide from that knowledge, but you can't. It's always a part of your consciousness that you messed up big time! Even if you succeed in not thinking about it, your body is going to remind you of the seriousness of your sin *via* headaches, neck, shoulder, and back pain, excessive outbursts of impatience and anger, sleepless nights, gastro-intestinal problems, etc.

In addition to the above, I also believe the sacrament could be used to celebrate and consecrate major renewals and conversions in your life. Two examples come to mind. First, let's say you've had a serious illness and you've been in the hospital for a couple of weeks. You've done a lot of thinking, and you realize that some major changes have to take place in your life. When you leave the hospital, you start making those changes, and the result is a great new sense of meaning and purpose in your life. At some point, it would be good to receive the Sacrament of Reconciliation as a way of closing one chapter of your life and celebrating the beginning of a new chapter. Or, you've had marriage difficulties, and you have gone through extensive counseling. This has resulted in new directions for your relationship. This would be a great opportunity to receive the Sacrament of Reconciliation, for reconciliation and conversion and repentance have taken place!

Now, the two things I've just talked about do not happen that often. Some could take what I've written and say: "Well, that means you're saying that confession is needed very sporadically, maybe even three or four or five times in my life. But there's still a law on the books about confession 'once a year, if you have mortal sin to confess.'"

Yes, that rule is there. And yes, some people will still feel some need or obligation or compulsion to receive the Sacrament of Reconciliation frequently. Many folks find weekly and monthly confession quite satisfying, and it is indeed a source of strength and healing. That's a real grace from God. But the point remains that an enormous number of people are looking for ways to make confession more meaningful. If you are in this latter group, let me share something that I've started to use for myself.

It begins with the premise that every human being experiences life and death, pleasure and pain, success and failure, happiness and sadness. We love and cherish the positive experiences, and we run away from or avoid the negative. I am starting to see that my sins are in effect unhealthy ways of dealing with my fears, with the feelings of pain, emptiness, failure, death, and sadness. Chances are good that there are two or three things that you do over and over again. These sins are like arrows pointing directly to an area of your life where there is great fear, emptiness, loneliness, etc. -- to an area that needs healing. These sins are going to keep repeating themselves until you deal with or come to grips with the underlying cause.

Let's take the example of anger. Anger at your spouse for not being there for you could be an arrow pointing to your fear of being alone or your fear of rejection. Is your nit-picking criticism of your co-worker an arrow pointing to your realization that you are not the worker you could be, and thus at risk for being laid-off? Is your anger at homeless people really an attempt to deny and smother your intuition that you are really too deeply in debt and thus risk losing it all? Are you angry at me because of something I said or did, or is it really because I remind you of someone who hurt you badly in the past, but you're afraid to look into that past and deal with the hurt?

As I said, the sins we commit most frequently point directly to areas in our life where we most need healing and reconciliation. So I have two choices. I can go in and do the usual thing: "Bless me, Father, for I have sinned. It's been one month since my last confession. I was angry at my wife and kids and co-workers twenty times this past month." Father gives me a little ferverino, a penance, and absolution, and I leave feeling OK, but not really OK either.

Or, I can add something else to that confession of sin: "I've thought about it, and I think the anger is because I'm really afraid of getting older. I can't do as much as I used to, and many of my friends are having heart attacks or getting sick. I'm scared that the same thing will happen to me, and I'll be useless and not worth anything. Rather than facing that fear of aging, I'm taking it out on someone else." Holy smokes… if I have a good confessor or spiritual director, can you imagine how he or she can help me! Talk about an experience of reconciliation and healing!

I hope these reflections are helpful to you. You do need the sacrament when you have committed serious sin, sin that mortally wounds your life with God and others. Outside of this, trust your intuitions. You'll know when you need the Sacrament of Reconciliation. When you do go to confession, take advantage of its full power and grace of healing by using your sins as signposts. There is a reason you're doing the things you do, and if you can find that root cause, you can be healed.

Above all, dear friend, enter fully into the Sacrament of the Eucharist. This Sacrament does forgive the everyday garden-variety sins we commit. Be heartfelt in the Penitential Rite at the beginning of Mass. Be heartfelt in your *Amen* to the prayers of the priest, which so often speak of forgiveness and mercy. Pray the *Our Father* and *Lamb of God* with your whole soul, and do the same for *Lord, I am not worthy to receive you.* God will never refuse your heartfelt prayer for wholeness, reconciliation, and forgiveness!

Chapter Forty-Two

THE POWERLESSNESS OF GOD

That title kinda grabbed you, didn't it? It's such a different way of looking at God. When going through grade school in the *Baltimore Catechism* days, there was no doubt whatsoever that God was all-powerful. That was pounded into our heads from day one. That was one of God's primary attributes. It is repeated in the modern *Catechism of the Catholic Church.* Quoting Psalm 104, the *Catechism* affirms that God can do whatever he wills to do.

Now, of course, that will immediately bring the question: Then why doesn't God stop war and suffering? Why didn't God cure Pat's cancer? Why was my baby born dead or disabled? Why is it that one crappy thing after another seems to be happening in my life, 'scuse the language'? On and on the questions hammer at heaven's door: why, why why? When there is no answer, some people become bitter, and write God or the Church out of their lives. Others mutely accept the status quo, saying: "It's God's will." But inside, there is grief and anger at the unfairness of it all. Still other folks acknowledge the grief and resentment, but know deep within that somehow, someway, life will come from suffering, pain, or death. These folks are the ones who will say: "I hate what's happened, I don't like it, but I trust that God is with me in this and will draw good out of it."

I am not denying that God is all-powerful. I accept that teaching and believe in it. One has only to look at the marvelous unity in all of creation and the intricacy of the universe. There *is* a divine order in creation, a goodness and beauty that persist despite the best efforts of humankind to upset it all. What I do *not* accept is a definition of power that makes God into a capricious vindictive tyrant, concerned only with punishing us for our sins, and inflicting suffering on the innocent, or on those who step "out of bounds." I reject that totally. Unfortunately, that's the kind of God many of us grew up knowing! I also reject the notion of power that sees God as kind of an almighty sugar-daddy, one who is supposed to be there to take care of my every whim and fancy. I see God's power as that which brings life and wholeness to his children. In that sense, yes, God is supremely all-powerful, for God is Life and Wholeness personified. Everything God does is meant to give life and restore wholeness -- everything. It is we humans who frustrate the divine intention with our selfishness and fear.

It is only in recent years that I've begun to wonder about and reflect on the powerlessness of God. This reflection was triggered by years of listening to parents, either in person or through their letters. Over and over again they talk about a time in the parent-child relationship when the parent ultimately becomes powerless to affect or guide their child's life. There's a recognition that the child has to make his or her own decisions and suffer the consequences. Parental experience of life enables them to see that certain courses of action are ruinous, yet what can they do? Parents know that certain moral values have a sound rationale behind them, and that they are necessary for good order and happy relationships. But, if the child chooses different values, what can they do? If a child is critically ill or dying, parental powerlessness strikes home with all the force of a Mike Tyson punch to the emotional gut. In all these situations, and more, what can a parent do except be there, pray, hope, weep, make gentle suggestions?

There finally came a point when the parallels between parents' relationships with their children and God's relationships with us became too obvious to ignore. In so many ways, I think God is powerless. If I decide on a certain course of action, for example, what can God do? If I am the victim of someone else's sinful behavior, what can God do?

There's plenty of evidence in the Old Testament that God certainly tries to exert influence on our life and behavior. That's an obligation of love. Loving parents do that all the time. But, if we decide to go our own way and do our own thing, God can only stand by. In the Gospels, there are many instances of powerlessness. Remember the father of the Prodigal Son? Or the rich young man -- Jesus was saddened when the man refused his invitation. He wept over Jerusalem. He beat his head in frustration against the intransigence of the Scribes and Pharisees. He could not sway Judas from betrayal.

And finally, there are the two ultimate examples of the powerlessness of God. The first is what we celebrate at Christmas -- the Incarnation. What is more totally powerless than a baby? The second is what we celebrate at Easter -- Jesus' death on the cross. God could not prevent the death of even someone he loved, and Jesus willingly submitted himself to execution.

By now you may be wondering, "How can God be all-powerful yet powerless"? Well, you know, that is indeed a paradox, yet somehow in God the two truths co-exist with each other. It's hard to find the right words to express it. I could be a good old-fashioned cleric and say, "It's a mystery, so accept it and don't question it"! But I know that's not enough for you. Even as you're reading this, you're probably trying to draw some conclusions of your own.

For what it's worth, here's how I think the all-powerfulness and the powerlessness hang together. A way to understand it is to use Paul's words: "It is when I am weak that I am strong" (2 Cor 12:10). To use the most obvious example: what is more powerful than a baby? He cries, people respond immediately. She smiles, people get all goofy. Babies have extraordinary power! They can transform us. So too I believe God's powerlessness has the potential to transform our relationship to him. As one of my seminary classmates said: "When I think about it, it's a lot easier to relate to a God who knows what it's like to be powerless than to relate to one who is all-powerful."

Powerlessness is powerful... extraordinarily so. The powerlessness of Calvary was transformed by Easter Sunday morning. Frightened apostles were strengthened by the Spirit. God is powerless until we turn to him for help, and then God's power will lead us to life and wholeness. And how is this power manifested? Sometimes there's a direct grace from God, given to us without human intervention. We've all had those insights which seem suddenly to help everything make sense. At other times there's an outright miracle of physical, mental, or spiritual healing. But most of the time, God's power transforms our human powerlessness through the assistance of human beings.

When you are feeling powerless, what happens? Isn't it true that a lot of times people will rally around you to support you and strengthen you? How many times has a letter or phone call come at just the right time? Maybe you picked up a book on a whim, or one was given to you as a present, and it was exactly what you needed at that time. When you or someone you love is fighting illness, doctors and nurses and medical science are God's agents. Hospice workers are God's ministers helping a dear one make the transition from this life to the next. Again, I go back to the parental experience: a parent is helpless until their child says, "help me." Those words unchain all the power of love in your heart and that love flows forth in action. As with a parent, so too with God.

Because of our freedom, God is powerless. The deepest desire of God's loving heart is that we walk with him, moving day-by-day towards the fullness of life and wholeness. Should we decide to sidetrack, God can only say: "OK, have it your way, but I'll be here when you need me. You'll just have to learn on your own that apart from me life makes no sense at all."

Because of our neediness and helplessness, God is powerful. When we call on God for help and assistance, it's there. Sometimes we see it vividly and clearly. At other times we need a bit of time and distance to see how God's power affected our lives. May the powerlessness of the Infant of Bethlehem move you to a deeper relationship with the God who loves us deeply, so deeply that there's really no reason to fear him or his power.

Chapter Forty-Three

HEALING AFTER ABORTION

Over fifty million men and women in the U.S. have lost a child to abortion. It is estimated that close to fifty-percent of the U.S. population has been affected directly or indirectly by abortions. This number does not include those who have suffered a miscarriage, a stillborn child, or who have carried an unwanted pregnancy to term because of fear or pressure. These folks have several of the same negative effects.

Most people agree that abortion is wrong. Of those who have actually had or participated in an abortion, seventy-percent will acknowledge that they felt what they were doing was wrong. No matter how much they may have tried to rationalize, they knew deep down that a human life was being taken away. Some manage to keep the demons at bay for years, but eventually the guilt and grief do work their way to the surface. It's a rare man or woman who has no aftereffects whatsoever from an abortion.

These folks are really caught between a rock and a hard place because of the politics of abortion. I think we lose sight of that. No matter how one feels about abortions, the fact is they do happen. It means that there are a lot of folks out there who are deeply hurting. But to whom can they go? On the one hand, they're afraid to share their feelings and fears with their pro-life family and friends, because they fear rejection, condemnation, and alienation. On the other hand, when they turn to family and friends who are pro-choice, their grief is not acknowledged as valid. They walk away from their pro-choice friends feeling that their grief is irrational, unimportant, or even abnormal.

You've got to remember – as I said above – that over seventy-percent of women who have had an abortion believe that abortion is immoral. Most of these women thought they would never have one. But at some point in their pregnancy they were faced with an overwhelming fear. They feared not being able to raise a child, feared losing their partner, losing control over their lives, and so forth. They felt pressured by families and partners, either directly or in more subtle ways (for example, "it's your decision, but…"). Some feared for their mental health, others for bodily health. Others looked at their economic circumstances and feared that another child would deeply affect the well-being of present children. In other words, it is rare woman who takes a cold, calculating, matter-of-fact attitude towards an abortion.

Anyone who wants to protect the unborn must understand the pressures that most women faced when they made an abortion decision. This decision is made in fear, isolation, and often with the manipulation and coercion of others. Furthermore, avoid stereotyping. Men and women who have had abortions are found in all religions, all ethnic groups, and all income levels. They can be grade-school students or Ph.D's. Every profession is represented, from stay-at-home Moms to ministers. Every age group is represented, whether it be having the abortion or facilitating one. Couples can be committed to each other in marriage, or they can be single, divorced, dating, separated, playing the field. The child can come from consensual or casual sex, rape, or accidental insemination ("We were just fooling around."). The one common denominator is that nearly everyone makes their decision based on force or fear.

What are some of the aftereffects of abortion? I attended a workshop presented by an organization called Rachel's Vineyard, which is a tremendous resource for those who have had abortions. What surprised me were two major points the presenters made. One: the aftereffects of abortion strike not only the woman, but also her male partner, and anyone else who was involved in it (such as the father who drove his daughter to the clinic). Abortion affects existing children. They feel "survivor guilt" because they feel they were the ones "chosen" to live. Some may feel responsible for the abortion – if they had not been so much trouble to their parents, maybe Mom would not have felt it necessary to "get rid of" another child. It affects children to come, also. Moms who have had an abortion feel compelled to be perfect mothers, so they may stifle a child. Or they're afraid to love their child too much, for fear they'll lose them, or they fear they'll lose the child as punishment for the abortion. *Everyone is affected.* That is crucial to know.

The other surprise was how the presenters used the model of post-traumatic stress syndrome to describe the emotional aftermath. This is something we usually attribute to those who have been in battle, or to the victims of crime. But again… remember… for most human beings, abortion is an extremely traumatic event.

Everyone responds differently. There are common reactions: feelings of guilt, shame, remorse, helplessness, bitterness; lowered self-esteem; avoidance of babies or problems bonding with other children; a fear of future pregnancies, or a desire to have a "replacement baby"; flashbacks to the actual abortion experience; sleeplessness or nightmares; sexual dysfunction; eating disorders and substance abuse; broken or abusive relationships; self-destructive behavior; suicidal thoughts or tendencies.

The timing of the emotional response varies too. For some, it will come swiftly… perhaps even as the abortion is being performed. For others it is delayed. Delayed responses often come with the birth of another child, or the death of a loved one, the end of a relationship, a spiritual conversion. Sometimes the reactions take place on the anniversary of the abortion, or on what would have been the child's birthday. Many women have reported actual abdominal cramping on those occasions.

On average, it takes about ten years before a woman will seek help to heal this profound wound. With the proper assistance, a woman can find a deep emotional and spiritual healing of her pain and a healthy reconciliation and spiritual connection to her aborted child. As groups like Rachel's Vineyard educate the public about the effects of abortion and the need for healing, women and men are coming forward earlier for help. The earlier one finds healing, the earlier the self-destructive behavior can be transformed into life-giving and hopeful attitudes.

Every Friday morning in Morning Prayer, the Church prays from Psalm 51: "A broken, humbled heart, Oh God, you will not scorn." Jesus himself gave countless examples of how his compassion and love extended even to those we would call the worse of sinners (notice that Jesus himself *never* calls anyone a sinner.) And time and again, you've heard me say that no sin of ours is ever going to be greater than God's love. God's love cannot be negated ... by anything. Anyone who has had an abortion absolutely needs to keep that in mind and heart. You are loved deeply by a God of extraordinary compassion and understanding. Reconciliation to God is not the hardest part of post-abortion recovery. It's reconciliation to yourself that requires the most work.

With that in mind, how can you respond to someone who has had an abortion. There are several do's and don'ts. Don't shut off conversation. Allow the person to talk as much as she or he needs to. Listen patiently. They're trying to sort out their feelings and they are also testing the waters, so to speak (saying one thing to see how you'll react, and then sharing something else if they feel you're accepting). Don't diminish it. Allow them to regret their choice. Yet at the same time remind them that every human being makes mistakes – some severe – but that God's forgiveness is there for the asking. In addition, we can all learn from our mistakes and become gentler, more compassionate human beings towards others. Don't sugarcoat ('Well, it was best for you at the time'). Don't suggest that another child can make up for the one who was lost. Do encourage them to find a support group or to seek counseling.

If you yourself have had an abortion or have directly or indirectly participated in one, know, above all, that you are still loved by God and are forgiven if you ask for that forgiveness. Recognize that it's going to take time and effort to come to healing and sort out all your feelings. Overcoming the constant doubt and despair, as well as the thought that others are always judging you and condemning you ... these are going to take time. Allow yourself to mourn deeply. Your grief is normal; it is real. Admit your personal responsibility and learn to forgive yourself. Recognize that others were also involved, either by encouraging you to have the abortion or by failing to help you avoid it, and learn to forgive them.

Place your child in God's care and make sure you have named your son or daughter. Members of your family are in heaven. Ask them to care for your child until you get "up there" to do it yourself. Because your son or daughter lives in God now, he or she will not condemn you or blame you for anything. Your child loves you unconditionally, and wants only for you to be healed and restored to joy and happiness.

Above all, do not try to heal yourself alone. Others have had this experience and want to help you. The people you will talk to have been there and know exactly what it's like, and they will be able to walk with you through your suffering and help you arrive at a place of joy, relief, and freedom. Be sure to ask lots of questions. Make sure you are comfortable with a counselor or a group. Some counselors may be hostile to those who have had abortions or do not have experience in dealing with post-abortion trauma. Listed below are some resources where you can ask for help. Please note that this includes not just the mother of the child, but the father, the grandparents, anyone who was actively involved, or who refused to be involved and now regrets it. Just recall the words of Jesus while standing in front of Lazarus' tomb: *"Untie him and let him go"*(Jn 11:44*)*. That's what it's all about. Recall too these words to the woman caught in adultery: *"Neither do I condemn you"*(Jn 8:11*)*.

The workshop I attended was sponsored by *Rachel's Vineyard Ministries*. I was very impressed with their work. Their phone number is 877-467-3463. The web site is: www.rachelsvineyard.com. There is also a special connection for men: www.rachelsvineyard/men, and there are several men available with whom you can talk or exchange e-mails. I'm not on their staff, nor am I being paid to write this, so this is not an advertisement. Based on what I learned and experienced, I do not hesitate to recommend these folks. They are Catholic in orientation, but anyone is welcome to use their services. Other resources would be:

• National Office of Post-Abortion Reconciliation and Healing (800) 593-2273 or www.marquette.edu/rachel

• Carenet (800) 395-4357 or www.care-net.org
• Hope Alive USA (479) 855-0072 or www.HopeAliveUSA.org
• Fathers and Brothers Ministries (303) 494-3282. No web site that I know of.
• Men's Abortion Recovery. E-mail wfbrauning@aol.com
• *Forbidden Grief; The Unspoken Pain of Abortion*, written by Theresa Burke and published by Acorn Books (ISBN is 2001135181), is a truly excellent book. She is the founder of Rachel's Vineyards Ministries. Her book covers in greater detail the counsels I mentioned above and includes personal stories from many people who have been involved in abortions.

Chapter Forty-Four

WHAT IS THE CROSS
WE MUST CARRY?

ime and again in the Gospels, Jesus says: "You must take up your cross if you would be my disciple." Those words chill your heart and mine. So too with Jesus. He knew he had to endure the cross, and with every iota of his humanity wanted to run the other way. Yet, with the assistance of Abba, his Father, he endured the pain of the cross and broke through into a whole new realm of life.

What exactly is this cross that Jesus is asking us to bear? As I've matured chronologically and spiritually, my understanding of the cross has changed. I've come to believe that our crosses are highly individual and personal. They can also change over time. The definition of the cross depends on my spiritual, emotional, and physical health. It depends on family (both natural and religious) circumstances, including one's financial circumstances.

Consider my deafness, for example. For a person who's had normal hearing all his or her life, to suddenly lose it would indeed be a cross. But I can't remember what it's like to hear normally. I was stricken with measles at age seven, and that's what caused my deafness. So for me, the deafness is not a cross. In fact, it's oftentimes a luxury. To be able to get instant silence at the flick of two switches is definitely a joyful thing! However, since I depend on lip reading to communicate, to lose my eyesight would definitely be a major cross.

We certainly have mental images of what a cross is. If I were to do a word association test and say, "cross," one of the first associations would invariably be "illness." Any life-threatening illness is a cross. We see people in wheelchairs, and we know they carry a cross. Alcoholism or any other addiction is a cross, both for the victim and his or her family.

"Death" would be another word that comes to mind. People who have lost loved ones suffer enormously. Life is never quite the same after the loved one has died, particularly if it was a child. And of course, we have our own death to consider, and for some, this is a terrifying prospect.

"Fear" is also a cross. Those afflicted with phobias (fear of crowds, of open spaces, of enclosed spaces, etc.) suffer terrible agonies. People are afraid of their neighbors, afraid of change, of God, of confession, of opening themselves to others and sharing feelings or thoughts. Abused children and spouses live in daily fear.

"Lack of meaning in life" is a cross. So is "the struggle to make ends meet." And "caring for a disabled child, spouse, or parent" is another cross whose weight can press an individual or a family to the ground.

"Shame and guilt" is the name of another cross that some folks carry. Each of us has an abiding sin that has marked our lives. Try as we might, it seems that we'll never be rid of it. We hope and pray for God's forgiveness, for understanding and compassion.

So for many folks, there's no doubt about carrying their cross. They feel its weight every day. Some collapse under its weight and take their own lives, or they become bitter, unhappy, disillusioned people. Other folks carry on with dignity and heroism. They have become truly beautiful, transformed people. You know who they are. You have family members, friends, fellow parishioners who are like this. You yourself may be one of those people who have cooperated so beautifully with God's graces. With Jesus you have passed from death to life.

But what if you have good health? What if you have enough income to meet life's necessities with some left over for enjoyment and for good works? What if your normal fears are minor irritants rather than paralyzing weights? What if you've learned to come to terms with your illness and have learned to live with it? What if there's no one who is totally dependent on you for his or her very existence? Where then is the cross?

I would like to suggest two possibilities. First, the everydayness of life can be a great cross. If you want to use an analogy, you know what Monday's are like! Life is full of Monday's. There are plenty of times when you just don't want to keep on doing the same old thing, day in and day out. You deal with the same old cranky spouse, the same young bratty child, the same unending bills (and appeals for money!), the same aches and pains and yakky neighbors. You feel used, taken for granted. A succession of gray, rainy/snowy days dims your spirits, and day after day of heat makes your hair frizzle. Little things go wrong in bunches, and you start looking around, wondering "What next"? You're in a hurry, and you hit every red light or get behind some doofus who's going ten miles below the speed limit. Your prayer seems fruitless. Distraction after distraction flits across your mind. You go to Mass, hoping for some peace and quiet, and there's a screamer in church. You look forward to a night for just the two of you, or to a quiet soak in a hot tub, and sure enough, something always comes up.

Bearing the cross of everydayness oftentimes means gritting your teeth and doing what has to be done. You find yourself digging deep down for those extra human and divine resources, and amazingly, you find the patience, strength, or cheerfulness you need. You pray for help, and somehow, someway it's there. You get through five minutes, five hours, a day, a week… and life comes. The dawn breaks through. You sense that you've changed and grown, and you have. With Jesus, you have passed from death into life.

Second, let's say you're able to do all of this. Say you're able to deal with all the goofiness of life with equanimity. Does that mean you've arrived? No, I don't think so. I've come to see that there is another cross that Jesus may challenge you to carry. It's this: to look at the world and act towards the world with the mind and heart of Jesus Christ and of God who is Abba/Father. Notice that there are two parts: look and act. The first is easy; the second is crucifyingly hard!

Looking and acting with the mind and heart of Jesus comes when Jesus and his Father are heart and soul of your life, when you truly have a relationship with them. As you enter more and more into this relationship, you put on Christ, as St. Paul says. You become a person who never judges or condemns the sin and imperfection of another (this humility is the most typical characteristic of a truly religious person). You look at our world, our country, and our church, and see that all is not according to the mind and heart of Jesus. You begin to understand what Jesus was feeling when he wept over Jerusalem.

Once you see the pain, sorrow, the selfishness, and stupidity of our world, the Spirit moves you to act. You act first in your own life; you become aware of your own selfishness and need for salvation. Coming to see your utter poverty and inability to save yourself is an enormous cross to bear. You see that the world and the Church need help, and so you offer your help, whether it be through prayer, letter writing, voting, and participating in religious, social, and civic activity. You begin to speak out, and as you do this, you will experience crucifixion of one kind or another, because people do not like to hear the truth. They do not want to hear challenges to change their ways of thinking and acting. So, as it has been since the beginning of the world, they kill the messenger.

We all have a cross in our lives. We're tempted to run away from it or ignore it. That may work for awhile, but sooner or later it has to be carried. But how to carry it?

First, if you are laboring under a particularly heavy cross, try not to look ahead to the future because worry and fear will only increase the weight of your cross. God has promised to be with you, and that promise is in full force in the *present* moment, *not* in future moments. You can get through five minutes of anything with God's help. Yes, you must make prudent provisions for the future. What I'm talking about is the looking ahead and worrying that you won't have enough resources or strength. I sometimes think that most of the weight of our cross is in our heads!

Second, admit your fears and anxieties. Seek help. Jesus did in the Garden. He made it clear to his Father that he would rather not go through the passion, and on the cross, he cried out to a God who had apparently abandoned him. In the Garden of Gethsemani, Jesus wanted Peter, James, and John to pray with him. He was not reluctant to accept help from Veronica or Simon of Cyrene. This carrying your cross with a stiff upper lip stoic acceptance is a buncha hooey, which will eventually harm you and others.

Third, look beyond yourself. Again, Jesus is the example. Remember his care for the women of Jerusalem, the good thief, Mary his mother, and the beloved disciple. There is something about doing good for others that has enormous power to lighten the burden of your cross. Sometimes, the "other" to whom you must do good is you yourself. May God give us all the strength to carry our cross with the dignity and humanity of Jesus, so that with Jesus, we may experience new life.

Chapter Forty-Five

THE MEANING OF CHRISTMAS

We believe that God took on human flesh, becoming the man whom we call Jesus of Nazareth. This mystery is what we celebrate at Christmas. But why? Why did God become human? Why were the circumstances of his birth so pathetic? What does it mean for you and me?

It's easy to answer the question about the circumstances. Jesus *had* to be born in a stable in order to have credibility. Now, remember, this is a stable -- a reeking, cobwebby, dark stable. It's not the cozy little straw-filled things we have in our homes and churches. Chances are there was not even a fire and perhaps little or no light... only a fool would have any kind of open flame in that environment.

God chose this situation for credibility. It was providential that there was no room at the inn. If Jesus had been born in a mansion, most of the human race then and now would not have been able to identify with him. They would not have been able to say: "Jesus is one of us." Had he been born in the inn, there would still be a hefty percentage of people who did not have the luxury of being born in comfortable surroundings, let along living in such a place. But Mary, Joseph, and Jesus started their life as a family in a stable -- the meanest, most grungy conditions possible.

You can't get any lower than this! Jesus can look the poorest person in the eye and say, "Yes, I know what it's like. I was there." He continued to live in poverty right up until the moment of his death. "Foxes have lairs, and the birds have nests, but the Son of Man has no place to lay his head." He even had to borrow someone else's grave.

But that still leaves the question: "Why did God become a human being"?

The *Catechism of the Catholic Church* gives four answers. The Word became flesh in order "to save us by reconciling us with God... so that we might know God's love... to be our model of holiness... to make us partakers of the divine nature" (#456-460).

In other words, before Jesus came among us, people did not really know God. They knew all kinds of things *about* God, or worse yet, they made God in their own image and likeness (in other words, they took their biases and prejudices and canonized them by saying that they were God's will). As a result of all this distortion, God became a terrifying figure. You could no more get close to this figure than you'd want to get close to a nest of swarming yellow-jackets.

Jesus showed us a God who was tender and compassionate. Rather than inflicting ills and punishments on his people, the Father of Jesus was right there with the folks, battling the ills and setbacks of life. Jesus showed us a God who had a special love for the poor and the outcast, a God who would cry over his people as Jesus wept over Jerusalem. How can you be afraid of a God like this? So Jesus came to take away that fear of God, which is a more down-to-earth way of saying "He came to reconcile us to the Father."

Jesus was our model of holiness. In his life, we see what God wants. In every age people have worried about what they must do to save their souls. Jesus' answer is simple: "Do what I do. Spend your life giving, not getting. Love the sinner, heal the sick, spend time with the outcast, be patient with those who are 'slow.' Spend time in prayer. Lay down your life." For Jesus, eternal life is contingent on how you and I treat our brothers and sisters. Holiness is not centered on how much we pray, how often we go to Mass, or what church we attend. What God looks at first is our relationship with the human race.

Finally, Jesus came to make us "partakers of the divine nature." This happens through Baptism and the Eucharist. By Baptism, we become sons and daughters of a loving Father, brothers and sisters of Jesus, "bone of my bone, flesh of my flesh." Through the Eucharist we become one with Christ, who is one with the Father. That's an awesome truth. We become like God! The Father, the Son, the Spirit, united with all of us. Awesome… utterly awesome!

To the above reasons why God took on human flesh, I would add one more. When you look over the history of God's relationship with his people, you can't help but wonder, "How can people be so dense"? From the time of Adam and Eve and Noah, through the patriarchs and prophets, God constantly and continuously reached to his people with love: "I will be your God and you will be my people, dearer to me than all others." Yet with a dismaying frequency folks turned their backs on God and went after false gods, or put their trust in weapons of war, military and political alliances, or personal power and wealth. Sometimes people would change for the better, but it never lasted long. Folks always seemed to go back to the old ways.

And so, God had to ask himself "Why? Why are people so afraid of me? Why do they constantly refuse the life, peace, and happiness I offer to them? How can anyone be that foolish"? So, God decided to become a human being to see what we were afraid of. And through Jesus, he discovered in the flesh that people were afraid not of God but of death in all its forms. They were afraid of physical death, because to them that was the end of it all. There was no life after the grave. So the prevailing philosophy became: "Get what I can to enjoy this life and the heck with anyone else." Those who could not get anything because of their powerlessness lived lives of quiet desperation, convinced that they were worth nothing in the eyes of God because they weren't prosperous.

Not only were folks afraid of physical death, they were also afraid of change, of letting go of the familiar and comfortable. Jesus ran across that fear time and again in his ministry -- the rich young man, the Jewish attitudes towards non-Jews, the obsession of the leaders with meticulous observance of the Law.

So, when God saw this fear of death, it was like an "Aha"! experience. He knew what he had to do. That's why he raised Jesus from the dead. Now, remember, Jesus was fully a human being of his time, so that means he had no idea of the resurrection. Like any pious Jew, he but hoped there was an afterlife in which the just were rewarded and the evil punished.

Why else was he so scared of dying? Why else did he feel abandoned by God? He thought it had all been a waste of time.

But the Father would not let Jesus stay dead. Through the resurrection we now see and believe that any kind of death can always bring new life. There is no reason to despair. There is no reason to get it all in this life regardless of what happens to others. There is all the reason in the world to trust God. Death is not the end of anything now, but simply a transition time, a moment of passage from one life to another and infinitely greater life.

So, as you go through Advent and Christmas, celebrate not just the baby, but celebrate the man Jesus. Celebrate with gratitude and thanksgiving what Jesus and his Father have done for us. Let the Christmas season be not just a memorial of Jesus' birth, but also a memorial of your birth, for you are significant to the world as Jesus was. Through you, people are reconciled to God. Through you, folks know of God's love. Other people look to you as a model of holiness, and you help others become aware of their participation in the divine nature. You're not doing it perfectly, and neither am I (that's why we need reconciliation and conversion), but we are doing it to the best of our ability at any given time. God will compensate for our human limitations. All God needs is a willing heart! Once God has that, nothing is impossible! God had that heart in Jesus, in Mary and Joseph, in the prophets and patriarchs. Does God have it in you and me?

POSTSCRIPT: *Many folks today are concerned about the meaning of Christmas being lost in the hustle and bustle and in commercialism. That is a valid concern, and no doubt you're trying to do something about it. Children love Christmas, but for adults, it's different. Sometimes this season is more of a problem to be faced than a season of joy. The house has to be decorated and munchies baked. Gift lists mean countless trips to crowded stores. Too many parties impinge on precious time. And then there's the problem of how to pay for all this. Children do not know about the hard work, the bills, and the problems and stress all this causes in adult relationships.*

Trust that God understands. Even in the midst of the most hectic schedule, there are always those few moments when you're able to sit back, experience a bit of peace and quiet, and ponder the meaning of it all. There are moments when you're able to pause and give thanks for your family, your blessings, for your ability to celebrate this season. There are the memories of Christmas past with loved ones who are no longer here. Perhaps you have mixed feelings. Someone you love may not be here next year because of illness, age, or other reasons.

There's really no way to avoid the hustle and bustle of the season, so cherish those thoughtful moments as gifts from God. And if nothing else, take comfort from the example of the Lord. Just as Jesus pours himself out so that his people can have life, so too you all pour yourselves out, so that your family and friends may have life. In other words, dear ones, you don't have to go far to find Jesus in Christmas. You are living it!

Chapter Forty-Six

WAS IT REALLY "GOD'S WILL"?

We so often pray: "Your will be done, on earth as it is in heaven." When tragic death or natural disaster strikes, we say or think: "It was God's will." Yet we inwardly rebel: "What kind of God would will innocent death and human tragedy"? Using the phrase "the will of God" is a way of explaining the unexplainable, and it is also a statement of piety. Yet it leaves many with an uneasy feeling, primarily because we can't fathom how God's will could include what we call "evil."

What exactly is this reality we call "God's will"? First, let's make a distinction. I'm not going to write about "What is the will of God for me"? That's amply documented in the Gospels. Through Jesus, God has told us what we need to do: *What I want is mercy, not sacrifice. Whatever you do to the least of my brothers and sisters you do to me. It is the will of him who sent me that I* [and by extension, you and I] *should lose nothing of what he gave me. Take up your cross and follow me.* A whole way of responding to life is also outlined in the Beatitudes.

My objective is to talk about what people mean when they ask: "Why does God will this or that to happen"? That's a very different question than "What is God's will for me"? And yet, they're two sides of the same coin.

In reflecting on the will of God, the first thing to remember is that God's creation has two characteristics. First, it is good; and second, it follows the law of cause and effect. Creation is good, but it is not perfect. Only God is perfect. Because creation is not perfect, that means that every created thing, including humanity, has a weakness in it somewhere. The principle of cause and effect applies to that which is good and to that which is incomplete, and God cannot intervene to stop the orderly progression of events.

Let's take the weather. It was created by God, therefore it is good. It follows clearly defined natural principles. So when a certain set of conditions exists, we have snow. When another set of conditions exists, we have a gloriously sunny day with low humidity. Bring in another set of factors, and we have destructive weather like tornadoes, hurricanes, and typhoons. God does not directly will the hurricanes or tornadoes. They happen because of the principle of cause and effect. By creating the world with specific natural laws, God accepts the fact that disasters will take place. He doesn't will them or inflict them on his people; he accepts them as consequences of those natural laws.

The same principle applies to us. We are good, but we're not perfect. You and I are unfinished people. For sure, we all suffer the effects of the spiritual imperfection called original sin. We each have one or more physical, mental, or emotional stumbling blocks that get in the way of our complete happiness. They are there simply because we're not perfect. The weakness can come through genetics, upbringing, lifestyle, the sinful choice of another, or environment.

Now, dear friend, here's a point that may be hard to understand or accept. Remember, creation is good, and creation is incomplete. Now I would like to suggest that even that incompleteness can be good! The faults and stumbling blocks are not good in themselves. They are good because they lead us to a greater dependency on God and help us to become better human beings. In the Easter Vigil, the Church speaks of the sin of Adam and calls it a "happy fault," because it merited for us a great Redeemer. I'm applying the same principle to our lives. The pain and suffering we experience because of human sin or natural disaster are not good in themselves. They are good only because they help us become the people God intends us to be. It's like surgery. The pain is not good, and the surgeon does not deliberately inflict the pain on you. But by enduring the pain, we become healthier.

Another point to remember is that a lot depends on perspective. Way back in the last sentence of my first paragraph, I put the word "evil" in quotes. That was done deliberately. God looked at all creation and said that it was "very good." Even the serpent in the Garden was included in that evaluation! We are the ones who make the distinction between "good" and "not good." If, for example, you were living in Bangladesh, you would see a torrential monsoon as a threat to your livelihood and your life, because of the flooding it brings. If you lived in central India, that exact same monsoon would be a great blessing, for it prevents drought.

Most people would call a gloriously sunny day "wonderful"! But if you have a problem with skin cancer, you wouldn't enjoy it as much. Skiers love snow; but that same snow is a threat to someone struggling to keep a job, because it might prevent them from getting to work. Or, to use a personal example, take my hearing handicap. Many people would think it "not good." There are times when I feel that way, but by and large, I call my deafness "good." At the flick of two switches, I get instant silence! That gives me a good night's sleep for sure! But more to the point, in the silence of my prayer, I hear God in a way that I probably wouldn't were I able to hear normally. As I said, what some would call "good," others would call "not good." Which one is the "will of God"? Do you see the fix we get ourselves into?

I've come to believe that when we say "It must have been the will of God," it invariably means that we've come face-to-face with a flaw or an incompleteness in our lives, and we're having trouble accepting it or putting it into perspective. Deep down, we're all perfectionists, and we cannot abide something that isn't right. Rather than going through the pain and struggle of acceptance and adjustment, we turn to God in hopes he will fix it up. Some, however, will turn away from God in anger, but what they're really doing is being angry with their own imperfections.

Ironically, God will fix it up, but not in the way we expect. He will say either "You fix it" or "Learn to live with it, for through this physical, mental, spiritual, or emotional weakness, you will gain salvation." Along with the challenge will come the grace necessary to overcome the effects of the "not good" thing and to grow from it. Here's where we touch on the other side of the coin: "What is God's will for me"? To help us, he sent Jesus, who perfectly illustrated the will of God. He healed the sick; he fed their physical and spiritual hungers; he befriended outcasts and had parties with them. He did all he could to restore and heal those who were broken. There was a principle of cause and effect at work. Because Jesus so deeply believed he was the Son of God, because he so deeply believed in his mission, he was able to do these things. Because people like lepers had so much faith in Jesus, because they were willing to do whatever was necessary to believe in Jesus, they were healed: "Your faith has saved you," said Jesus.

Jesus also had to learn to live with sin and imperfection. People like the rich young man who could not let go of his riches broke Jesus' heart. He had to learn to live with Judas and with intransigent religious leaders. He also had to learn to live with the knowledge that he would die violently. Did he get bitter at people? No. Angry with God and others? Yes. He was honest with his feelings, but then he simply did what he could and accepted the unchangeable.

Whenever possible, you and I are to work with God in the work of mending imperfect creation, frail people, and yes, mending our own broken hearts. Since we're made in the image and likeness of God, we share God's desire for wholeness and good order, and we have power to contribute to that wholeness. It's the cause and effect principle again. If we do all the good we're capable of doing then good will come. God wills that!

Similarly, if we do harmful things, or if we choose not to turn to God or others for help, God will allow the consequences of our choices to unfold. Once they're set in motion, God will not intervene to stop the progression of events. That's the only thing he can do. He's powerless to do anything else. Sure God could change things around. But if he does, he upsets the whole natural order and becomes not a God of freedom and justice, but a God of arbitrary, capricious whim and injustice. God must accept what he has created, or else he contradicts himself.

So, on a practical level, what do you say, for example, to a couple who have deeply longed for a child, have conceived one, and then the child is stillborn? For many, the standard response would be: "It must have been the will of God." They say it out of the goodness of their hearts. But when I hear that, I utterly rebel. The God I believe in does not will suffering, violence, death, and pain on his people. No way! If God were like that, I'd be an atheist overnight. God is handcuffed by his own natural laws! God did not will the baby's death; some natural development caused the death. God asks us to mend the hearts that are broken and to look for the seeds of hope that are present in every tragedy. He wants the couple to pass through their pain and enter into their mourning with faith that somehow, someway, meaning will come from the tragedy. And God is right there with those who are grieving. God mourns also. After all, he had dreams too for that child, that adult, those people. The lovely thing about God is that he brings extraordinary comfort to those who mourn, but you have to go through the mourning in order to receive the comfort. Jesus showed us what to do. He had to suffer to reach the resurrection.

When it comes to the natural order, God is powerless; but when it comes to the ways of love, God is all-powerful. God supports us with incredible grace when we try to bring about healing and reconciliation or to work toward serenity and peace. So a situation where we would normally think, "It's God's will," is in reality an invitation to conversion and to a deeper awareness of our dependency on God. We can ask ourselves: Where did I go wrong? What kinds of wrong decisions were made? What can I do to prevent something like this from happening again? How can I help those who are affected by the tragedy, sickness, whatever? If every tragedy has within it a seed of hope, what can I do to help God bring it to life within me? What does my helplessness teach me about the necessity of having faith and depending on God for help?

It's God's will that we try to answer these questions. Thus we help him bring about the triumph of good over evil, to bring wholeness where there was brokenness. The threat of harm and the consequences of sin (our own sin or another's) will always be an inevitable part of your life and mine, but we can conquer it! God permits imperfection to exist because he must remain just and faithful to his own laws. Those imperfections and flaws, however, do not have to lead to despair or sin. God's will is that life and growth come from suffering or death. Jesus' resurrection is proof of that! "You may for a time have to suffer the distress of many trials, but this is so that your faith, which is more precious than fire-tried gold, may by its genuineness lead to [your] praise, glory, and honor when Jesus Christ appears" (I Peter 1: 6-7).

Chapter Forty-Seven

WHEN YOUR CHILDREN DO NOT GO TO CHURCH

Don't you sometimes feel that New Year's Day is misplaced? We're so tied into the school year that oftentimes I've thought that New Year's Day and Labor Day ought to be switched! For some reason, seeing everyone go back to school makes me feel a sense of new beginnings, and much more so than January 1st. And we are coming up to another celebration of new beginnings... November 1st... and the special month of remembering our dear ones who have entered the new life of heaven.

The waning days of autumn combine with the traditional Catholic specialness of November to direct our thoughts to the afterlife. We think about our loved ones. We think about ourselves, wondering what our passage will be like. We find ourselves hoping that we'll be "in good shape" when God calls us home.

And sometimes, folks worry about their children or grandchildren, or nieces and nephews. And I'll give you three guesses as to what parents or grandparents or aunts and uncles worry about most. If you guessed "worry about their children not going to church and receiving the sacraments," you're right! That's a special pain, a special purgatory... and that's what I'd like to write about this month.

I hear it time and again: "Father Herb, please pray for my child's return to Church; that the grandchildren will be baptized; that my nephew or niece won't join the church of his or her fiancé." There seems to be a fear that if the younger generation is not in good standing with the Church, then they're not in good standing with God.

I understand how you must feel, for several members of my own family are not church-goers. You and I love our Church. We cherish all it stands for, and it's a natural hope that those we love will share our attachment and love of the Catholic Church. But sometimes it is just not meant to be, either permanently or temporarily, primarily because Faith is a gift, and God distributes his gifts as he wills.

Now, am I worried about my kin's salvation? No, not at all. They're good people. They're living the Gospel. Nowhere in the Gospels does Jesus make Mass attendance a prerequisite for heaven. He does want us to keep the Sabbath holy, but never specified how it was to be done. For one member of my family, who usually has a very stressful work week, playing a round of golf on Sunday morning may make him a more loving and generous man than an hour in church (unless he has a bad round!). I have to respect his way of spending the Sabbath. For him it's restful, and if it will make him a more life-giving man, then so be it.

What most concerns Jesus is how we treat other people, especially those less fortunate than ourselves. That is what will determine our entry into heaven -- not church attendance. So if your child or grandchild is charitable, kind, patient, willing to assist neighbors and friends, willing to help the poor, then fear not. I really believe the child will be OK.

Remember the old saying: "Outside the Church there is no salvation"? Vatican II put that to rest. There's plenty of salvation outside the Catholic Church. All people of good will who sincerely try to do the work of God and make the world a better place are achieving their salvation, and that includes the members of your family. Even at Mass we acknowledge that fact. The Fourth Eucharistic Prayer says: "Remember all who seek you with a sincere heart… remember all the dead whose faith is known to you alone." The Third Eucharistic Prayer says the same thing: "Welcome into your kingdom… all who have left this world in your friendship." And it also helps to remember a statement by St. Augustine: "God has many whom the Church does not have; and the Church has many whom God does not have."

Now this question might be arising: If there are many roads to heaven, why bother with the Catholic Church? And my answer would be this.

Even though Vatican II said that there are many ways to God, it also said that the fullness of salvation is achieved through the Catholic Church.

Maybe I can explain by using an example. Let's say you have to build a dwelling place. If all you have is a hammer and a hand saw and a piece of string, you can build the house… but it's gonna be mighty complicated and take a very long time. There will be lots of trial and error. But if you have power tools and all the latest equipment, plus blueprints, a readily-available energy source, and a lot of helping hands, the house will be built much more easily and quickly. I like to say that full participation in the life of the Catholic Church gives us all the tools we need to efficiently and safely build a dwelling place, and it gives us many helping hands in the form of our parish community.

But not everyone wants to build the house that way. If your adult child wants to use the hammer and hand saw and string, we have to respect that decision. If they don't want to build a house at all, because of laziness or just plain not caring, then we also have to respect that decision. Sure it hurts; it hurts deeply. You wonder where you failed, what went wrong, why they rejected the Church.

But are they rejecting the way of Jesus? That's an important question to ask. Is the Lord's way strictly centered around going to Church on weekends, or is it a way of life to be lived day in and day out? Furthermore, it's been my experience that most young adults will stop going to church once they leave home (I did it when in the seminary. There was a period when weekday Mass was an utter turn-off to me). It's part of the growing up process. They want to establish their own values, to discover alternate ways of expressing and deepening their relationship to God. As a parent, you planted the seed. You did all you could to instill in them a love of the Catholic Church. Therefore, you're at peace before God. You can't be responsible for another adult's choices.

And you know what? The seed doesn't stop growing. One way or another most young adults will come back to the Church. I usually see it happening when the first child is born. All of a sudden the new parents realize their responsibility, and so they reach back to what is most familiar to them. And one of the things they reach for is the religious heritage they grew up with. In addition, priests today are challenging parents who bring in their children for baptism. They're asking: "Why do you want to have your child baptized if you don't participate in the life of the Church"? We ask the same thing during marriage preparation too.

Sometimes the young person won't come back to the Catholic Church, but will opt for another expression of Christianity (Baptist, Methodist, etc). None of these faith expressions has all the tools that the Catholic Church does, but that's okay. At least the house is being built! And if truth be told, other faith expressions are sometimes more attractive to a young person than the Catholic Church, because they have much more to offer young people or young families, such as group activities, support groups, fellowship activities, etc. Fundamentalist groups attract a lot of young people today because of the certainty they offer: "Do this and you will be saved." Many young adults today are longing for some certainty in a very confused world with too many options, so they naturally gravitate to a church that will simplify things. Again, not to worry. Fundamentalist churches are usually not cults. As I understand it, cult is usually anti-Christ, and most fundamentalists are anything but anti-Christ. As Jesus said in the Gospel: "Those who are not against us are with us."

So what's a parent to do? First of all, don't worry that God will blame you for your adult child's decision. He won't. Don't worry that your child will miss out on eternal life with God. If the child loves God, loves neighbor, and loves self, then all will be well. They might have to struggle a bit, but all will be well.

Second, it's alright to express your concern about your adult child's choice or lack of choice. But don't nag; don't push it. You have to remember that Faith is a gift of God, and if the gift isn't yet there, how can the person choose? In addition, every individual has a unique relationship to God, and they are obligated to do what they think will best develop that relationship. The way they choose might not be my way or yours, but we don't dare interfere too much lest we be hindering the work of the Spirit. I've found that the best way to proceed is to talk about your child's choice. Ask them with all love and openness what motivates them to pick this church. Ask them gently if their way of celebrating the Sabbath makes them more life-giving people. If they say they don't go to church, but do pray a lot, ask them about their prayer -- whether or not God hears their prayer, what they pray about, etc. The whole idea is to be helpful, not judgmental. As I said, you may not agree with their choices, but look for the points that bring you together instead of the ones which divide you. Your relationship with your child or relative is far more important than whether or not they go to Mass on Sunday.

Third, when the situation is right, talk about your own faith... what it means to you... the strength and support you receive. Tell of the support and friendships you enjoy from the people of your parish. Talk about homilies you're heard, articles you've read (or these fabulous letters from Fr. Yost!). Share your feelings about stories in the newspaper having to do with the Church. Again, you don't want to force it; timing is everything!

Fourth, pray. Pray that in all things your children will do the work of God by being life-givers to their brothers and sisters. Ask God to send them good companions, people who will support them on their faith journey. Ask God to grant them the gift of Faith, if it be his will, or to lead them back to full participation in the Catholic Church when it's time.

Finally, trust God. His ways are not our ways. In all the world's history, there have been many, many ways to God. I believe that the American Indian shaman who practices his divination on the plains of North Dakota will be just as much at home in heaven as the greatest saint who ever lived. If heaven is just for church-going Catholics, then I think it's a pretty thinly-populated place! But if it is for all people of good will, who in their own way give life to others, then it's a huge place... just like God's heart, which is almighty huge!

This is a longer letter than usual, but it's an important topic. I hope it's been helpful, laying to rest some of your fears and concerns. I know, however, that some may disagree with what's been said above. If so, let's talk about it. Sure, it would be nice to have the whole family gathered around the Lord's table on Sunday, but if it doesn't happen in this life, the chances are good it will happen in the next!

Chapter Forty-Eight

WHY BE CATHOLIC?

In the previous essay, I spoke about family members who chose not to be active Catholics. I urged folks not to worry or fret, because many roads lead to God, and because God's mercy and compassion are utterly beyond anything we can imagine. From that hope flows this question: "Well, if there are many ways to God, if one religion is as good as another, then why be Catholic"? I'd like to share some thoughts about this puzzle.

Why be Catholic? Am I a Catholic because my parents were Catholic? For many folks, that's sufficient reason. But for others it's not. We have to make a personal choice. I had difficulties with the Catholic Church when I was younger, and I have difficulties even now. There are many things about my Church that I do not like at all, and there is much that is beautiful. Choosing to be Catholic is not a once-and-for-all thing. I believe it's something that must be done time and again. Being Catholic is a vocation, just like marriage, religious life, single life. To be truly fruitful, there must be conscious, deliberate choices.

Vatican II began many decades ago. Prior to that time, Roman Catholics were a very distinctive group. External practices distinguished us, such as fasting during Lent, Friday abstinence, processions, and popular devotions. Liturgical services were in Latin, and there was a strong system of Catholic schools and social groups. We were a Church of law, and knew exactly what we had to do to get to heaven. Authority was clearly defined. Pope, bishops, and priests alone had the power of teaching, sanctifying, and healing. "Choice" was a bad word.

But the Church got turned upside down. Now choice, change, and uncertainty is the rule rather than the exception. Many say there's nothing distinctive anymore about being Catholic, and to some extent, they're right! Other Christian communities share the same Scriptures, the same faith, hope, and charity, the same gifts of the Spirit, and the same Baptism. Anyone who acknowledges the Lordship of Jesus of Nazareth, and who expresses that faith through ritual, witness, and service is a member of the Body of Christ. So why be Catholic?

There are several things which I find appealing about our Church. The most attractive quality is our catholicity (small "c"). There is room for everyone, and many truths and human values find a home in the Catholic Church. Now sure, some folks are excluded from full participation in the life of the Church, and sometimes truth and human values are not upheld with fairness and justice. Oftentimes many in the Church do not practice what they preach. But this only points out that the Church is sinful as well as holy. Jesus never guaranteed freedom from sinful behavior or attitudes. He never guaranteed that we would avoid mistakes. The only thing he promised was that the Church would never make a fatal mistake.

By and large, however, the Church has room for everyone. We all have different ideas and perceptions and backgrounds, but we're at home with one another. It's been that way from Day One. Peter and Paul had sharp differences over the early Church's missionary activity. Some of the apostles were fishermen, one was a tax collector, another was a radical revolutionary. Thomas Aquinas reformed the Church with his pen, while Catherine of Siena was reforming the Church by telling the Pope to be a man instead of an intimidated wimp. Pope Gregory the Great amassed great temporal power and even had his own standing army, while John Paul I, in an all-too-brief reign, captivated the world with his smile. Bonaventure stressed intellectual knowledge of God, while Bernard of Clairvaux was heatedly anti-intellectual. Ignatius of Loyola was an activist, John of the Cross a contemplative. The pacifist Dorothy Day could sit down and eat dinner with Cardinal Cooke, the bishop to our armed forces.

The same things happen in your parish and mine. For some, the parish provides a community, a place of support. Others see the parish as a place of prayer and worship; still others equate parish with a sacred building. We have people in our midst who push hard for social reform, and people who see the parish as an extension of the grade school, and folks who just want to be left alone. Some like change, others hate it. The parish is only a smaller version of the Church Universal. We are a Church of individuals, and despite our sometimes vociferous differences, there is unity! And to be honest, folks, the times when I'm least proud of my Catholicism are when I witness people in our Church proclaiming that their version of truth is the only correct interpretation, and condemning those who have the nerve to disagree. Such attitudes do not foster the unity of heart and mind which Jesus prayed for at the Last Supper.

As long as we're on the community aspect, there is a second special thing about the Catholic Church. We believe that our way to God is mediated by the community. In the earliest days of the Church, St. Paul constantly reminded the "lone rangers" that a purely individualistic way to God contradicts the Gospel. Belief in Christ and life in Christ come to their fullest development in the community of believers. Many Church Councils and Papal Encyclicals have reinforced that belief. Even God has to exist in a Community of Three!

While we are called to a personal relationship with God, that encounter is made possible through the community. Why? Because it is the community that gives us the symbols, the language, the forms of prayer, the opportunities to be of service, and the support we need in our weakness. To put it another way, my destiny is wrapped up with the destiny of the people I serve. If the folks in my present ministry (Holy Cross Association) weren't the kind of people they are, I wouldn't be the person and priest I am today. You and I have an investment in each other. We are interconnected!

To illustrate, look what happens when you go to Mass while on vacation. Sure, the Mass is the Mass, but it just feels different when you're at home, right? The community really affects our prayer, worship, and ability to live the Gospel. When my parish struggles because of change or divisiveness, I struggle with personal prayer, worship, and charity. When the parish "flows good," I flow. Doesn't the same thing happen to you? When folks go "Church-shopping," most of the time they're looking for a certain kind of community that's in tune with their values and needs. This is what I mean by saying that the community affects our way to God.

The Sacraments are a third reason I love the Catholic Church. Although all Christian churches have sacraments, Catholics have a somewhat different understanding. Most of our Christian friends will say that the sacraments foster a special relationship to God. The Catholic Church says this too, but we go one step further and say that the sacraments also foster a special relationship with the community. Go back to what I said about the vacation Mass, and you'll see how this makes sense. The idea of community is so important that the Church forbids the celebration of any sacrament unless a community is present. Even Reconciliation, that most private of sacraments, has a communal dimension. The recommended way of celebrating that sacrament is by having a communal penance service. But even if you're alone with Father Joe in the reconciliation room, the community is present in the person of the priest. Listen to the words of the sacraments you receive or witness. See how often the plural pronouns are used. Hear how frequently the Church community is mentioned.

The sacraments are precious because they touch and sanctify every aspect of human life, from birth to death. Every culture in human history has celebrated the turning points of life. They do so with ritual in the presence of the clan or tribe or community. After all, who wants to mark those turning points alone? We Catholics are no different than the rest of humankind when it comes to gathering for the special events. The sacraments are a verification that God is present when we gather. They transform the human ritual into an encounter with the divine.

When I preside at the Eucharist, the part I most enjoy and cherish is distributing the Body of Christ. One-by-one, I encounter the Church in all its beauty and fullness. I see the story of salvation writ in eyes, faces, hands. It never fails to be a "Wow" experience! This is where it all comes together for me: a community that is sacramental and catholic.

Chapter Forty-Nine

TO BE A HUMAN BEING

Several years ago, before computers became so widespread, there was a different rhythm to the production of these reflections. Because more time was needed to process things, I had to get myself in the Christmas spirit in mid-September, for example. The newsletter had to be at the printers by early October, and then it was mailed about three weeks before Advent.

Admittedly it's becoming easier as the years go by, since Christmas goods are in the stores earlier and earlier with each passing year. It's downright bizarre sometimes! But every so often the Holy Spirit steps in with some good insights.

I remember one example from several years ago. I was working in the rectory garage, wondering what kind of glad tidings I could share with folks in the Christmas newsletter. The glimmer of an idea came when I took a break from planing and smoothing some oak strips we were using in the renovation of the church where I help out. Looking down at my feet, seeing myself ankle-deep in wood shavings, feeling the smoothness of the strips of wood and remembering how rough they were, thinking how great it feels to be doing this after a day in an office, all these thoughts ran through my mind, and I marveled: "How good it is"!

You yourself must have had that kind of thought at times when you were working on a project. You look at what you've accomplished and think: "This is good, really good, really satisfying." It's a great feeling, isn't it? And then I remembered how those words were uttered at the dawn of creation. Another craftsman was at work, and after each day's activity was finished, God looked at what he had made and said: "It is good." And then came the sixth day. God looked around at the beauty he had created and saw that something was missing. So he created man and woman. And then he said: "This is *very* good." Everything else was just plain old "good"—man and woman were *very good!* Just like we take great pride in our projects and crafts, so God takes enormous pride in his masterpiece, man and woman, you and me. He's bustin' his buttons over us. He thinks we're absolutely fabulous!

Do you know how we always ask children what they want to be when they grow up? They give all kinds of answers. If you were to imagine God as a child, and you were to ask him what he wanted to be when he grew up, I know what he'd answer. Without doubt, he would say: "I want to be a human being"! As far as God is concerned, there's nothing more fabulous than a man or a woman – nothing! And so from Day One, God knew that the time would come when he would follow through on his secret dream. He would become a human being! You know the rest of the story. The time came. Mary cooperated with the Spirit, and God at last fulfilled his dream. He became one of us, bone of our bone, flesh of our flesh.

I'm sure there were times when Jesus wondered if he had done the right thing, just as there are times when we wonder if it's worth it. But at the very end, he refused to change his mind. It was good to be human— to experience love, pain, joy, sorrow, friendship, parties, meals, walks in the evening, fishing on the lake, cooking breakfast, hugging and touching. It was good to forgive and to heal, to teach and to learn, to be insistent on values and to change one's mind. It felt good to scratch that mosquito bite, to soak sore feet in cool water, to give a stupendous yawn or make a mighty stretch. Jesus laughed at his stomach rumbles, probably said a few bad words when he stubbed his toe against a rock or struck his finger with a hammer. He enjoyed being in the limelight, and enjoyed the time alone for some peace and quiet. It was so good to be human.

Even death did not dim God's ardor and enthusiasm. Despite the worse possible pain that could be inflicted on him, Jesus still thought it was fabulous to be human... and so he rose from the dead and ascended *body and soul* into heaven. He just didn't want to let go of the experience. He called his mother Mary home with him, *body and soul.* He promises us that we will be with him, *body and soul.* He enjoyed being human so much that he wants to do it for all eternity, and he wants to do it with us, with you and me!

It's hard to believe, isn't it? But it's true. We are God's delight! There are two things we celebrate at Christmas. One is, of course, the entry of God into human history through his birth as a human being. But we also celebrate ourselves. God has embraced us totally, completely, without reservation or conditions. *The Good News of Christmas is that we have a God who freely chose to live the life we live.* The beauty of Christmas is the fact that it gives you and me reason to walk tall, to walk proudly and confidently on this earth. God glories in us. This is the real tidings of joy announced by the angels!

So this Christmas, use your imagination and wrap yourself up in imaginary gift wrapping, the brighter the better! Or, for real, take one of those great big bows that has that sticky piece of cardboard on the bottom, and stick it to your forehead! And then say: "Here I am, Lord. You gave yourself to me. You said that you delight in me. So here I am, with all my goodness and all my warts, with my joys and with my sadness, with things I do like about me and things I do not"! And I believe God will react just like any wide-eyed child when they see the tree and the gifts on Christmas morning! Listen to the Sunday Advent Scriptures. They tell what God thinks of us. If you have trouble believing in your goodness and beauty, pray for the grace of belief. If you have no trouble believing in your goodness, touch the lives of others with your warmth. Then, for all of us, Christmas will truly be a day of rejoicing everyday, and for the fullness of the Lord's coming we will all be waiting with joyful hope.

About the Author

Reverend Herb Yost has years of experience as a parish priest and, since 1985, he has written the highly regarded spirtual reflections *Cross Links* as part of his work raising funds for the ministries of the Congregation of Holy Cross. Readers, colleagues and friends have urged him for years to write a book and this is the happy result.

Fr. Yost lives and works at Fatima House on the campus of the University of Notre Dame.

Corby Books...Check Us Out...
corbypublishing.com

Corby is a new, innovative publisher with a
diverse and interesting line of books.

FOR THE DEDICATED NOTRE DAME CLAN, we offer CELEBRAT-
ING NOTRE DAME, a lavish coffee-table photographic view of the campus,
by Matt Cashore, with text by Kerry Temple. A close look at life on campus
is the subject of KNOWN BY NAME: *Inside The Halls of Notre Dame*, by Fr.
James King, Rector of Sorin Hall. And THE HEART OF NOTRE DAME:
Spiritual Reflections for Students, Parents, Alumni and Friends by Nicholas
Ayo, CSC A biography of one of the great scholars in Notre Dame history is
WHEN FAITH AND REASON MEET: *The Legacy of John Zahm*, CSC by
David B. Burrell, CSC.

FOR THE FAMILY, we have CREATING HAPPY MEMORIES: *101
Ways to Start and Strengthen Family Traditions*, by Pam Ogren, and ST. NICH-
OLAS IN AMERICA: *Christmas as Holy Day and Holiday*, by Fr. Nicholas
Ayo. Business executives will benefit from BUSINESS WISE GUIDE: *80
Powerful Insights You Can't Learn in Business School*, by Mark O. Hubbard and
STOKE THE FIRE WITHIN: *A Guide to Igniting Your Life* by motivational
speaker Charlie Adams. Don't miss FRUGAL COOL: *How to Get Rich With-
out Making Very Much Money*, by Prof. John Gaski. A wonderful read is THE
IRISH WAY OF LIFE by John Shaughnessy. And Don't miss CREATIVE
AGING by Joan Zald.

OTHER NEW TITLES include the bestselling I HAD LUNCH WITH
GOD: *Biblical Inspirations for Tough Times* by Dr. Kathy Sullivan, NON-
PROFIT GOVERNANCE: *The Who What and How of Nonprofit Boardship*
by Thomas Harvey and John Tropman, MAY I HAVE YOUR ATTENTION
PLEASE: *Wit and Wisdom from the Notre Dame Pressbox*, by Mike Collins
and Sgt. Tim McCarthy, THE FORGOTTEN FOUR: *Notre Dame's Great-
est Backfield and the 1953 Undefeated Season*, by Donald Hubbard and Mark
Hubbard, THE GEESMAN GAME by Wes Doi and Chris Geesman.